Life, Accident & Health Study Book - TX

v. July, 7th, 2022

www.TSINational.com

This book is copyrighted and is NOT allowed for reprint, duplication, re-sale, digitization, replication or sharing; each book is printed for one person to utilize for studying. This book is NOT authorized to be used for any other purpose than studying for ONE state exam, or to keep for reference use after a state exam has been passed. We appreciate you abiding by these rules.
WE WILL PURSUE CIVIL & POSSIBLE CRIMINAL JUDGEMENTS AGAINST ANY VIOLATORS.

I. INTRODUCTION

We here at TSI Training want to welcome you into the insurance industry and hope you have a pleasant, lengthy and lucrative career. We have developed these materials from your point of view, brand new to the industry and eager to learn. You will find the contents easy to understand and full of information with real life examples to include context. Some of the material will involve memorization of definitions, other material you will need to know the full ins and outs of the concept. To not overload your brain with useless information, we have tried to be brief on the memorization concepts; the more in-depth materials may span multiple paragraphs for just one or two concepts. All of the concepts in this book are potential test questions; do not skip over any section, know them all in full.

Remember, **you can do this, you WILL pass.**

HOW TO STUDY:

Your test should be scheduled for 4-7 days after the 2-Day class; you may schedule your exam at www.PearsonVue.com

1. Attend live classroom class if available
2. Read each chapter of the book and while reading, associate the concepts to your real life
3. Complete each end of chapter test (answers are just before the glossary, page 170ish)
4. Take the Practice Exams online and score an 85% or higher
5. Write down the topics you had difficulty answering
6. Read the book/notes on that topic and watch the videos online
7. Pass your test!

➢ Taking the Online Practice Tests is the **best** method of preparing for your state exam. We have created flash cards, notes and games for you; those should be supplemental to the Practice Exams.

ONLINE STUDY SIGN UP:

Website: www.TSINational.com

Contact Support@TSINational.com

if you already have an account but cannot login.

Online Study Program includes:

- ➢ Practice and Expert Tests
- ➢ All PowerPoint's from class
- ➢ Phone & Tablet friendly studying
- ➢ 3 page Cheat Sheet

- ➢ Interactive Studying Program
- ➢ Full length videos of classes and topics
- ➢ 19 pages of notes, highlighted and bolded
- ➢ Much more…go login!

EXAM TIPS:

- Arrive to the testing center early, it can take up to 30 minutes to check in and you want to be relaxed.
- Watch the cheat sheet video in your car.
- **Read each question and answer three times.**
- Look for the keywords of NOT, EXCEPT, most likely, best describes, etc.
- **Trust Your Gut!** Unless you are obviously wrong, always go with your first instinct choice.
- Read each answer and think of what answer the test wants you to pick.
- Take a quick 5 minute break at the halfway mark (75 questions), go get some water or use the bathroom.
- If the question is too easy, that really is the correct answer. There are difficult questions, but there are also extremely easy questions on your test, don't syke yourself out.

"Without constant practice, the officers will be nervous and undecided when mustering for battle; without constant practice, the general will be wavering and irresolute when the crisis is at hand."
— The Art of War

The best tip we can give is to be well prepared before entering; take the practice tests **every day** up until your state exam.

Life, Accident & Health Producer – TXLAH05				
Sections:	**Number of Questions: 150**	**Passing Score: 70%**	**Time Limit: 2 ½ hours**	
General	115	70% (88 scored correct)	150 minutes	
State Specific	35			
Bonus:	20 General, 5 State		Total: 150 questions	
Test Contents:			**Number of Questions**	
Types of Life Policies	(Chapters 10)		15	10%
Policies, Riders, Provisions, Options and Exclusions	(Chapters 4 & 12)		15	10%
Completing the Application, Underwriting & Delivery	(Chapters 2 & 9)		15	10%
Taxes, Retirement and Other Concepts	(Chapter 12)		7	6%
Health Policies	(Chapters 3, 5 & 6)		10	7%
Health Provisions, Clauses and Riders	(Chapter 4)		15	10%
Social Insurance	(Chapter 8)		5	4%
Other Insurance Concepts	(Chapters 1 & 13)		25	16%
Field Underwriting Concepts	(Chapters 2 & 9)		12	8%
Common to Life and Health Insurance	(Chapters 1, 7 & 13)		10	6%
Life Only	(Chapter 9 & 11)		8	5%
Accident and Health Only	(Chapters 2 & 4)		8	5%
Health Maintenance Organizations	(Chapter 6)		5	3%

Your test will comprise of 150 total questions, but only 125 of them are scored. There will be 25 "bonus" questions that do not count towards or against your score. You will not know which ones are "bonus"; but typically they are the harder questions.

I. INTRODUCTION	2
HOW TO STUDY:	2
ONLINE STUDY SIGN UP:	2
CHAPTER I: GENERAL INSURANCE	- 9 -
B. TYPES OF INSURERS:	- 12 -
D. LAW/RULE OF AGENCY	- 17 -
E. CONTRACTS	- 18 -
F. FEDERAL REGULATION	- 20 -
PRACTICE QUESTIONS GENERAL INSURANCE	- 24 -
CHAPTER II: HEALTH INSURANCE BASICS	- 28 -
A. HEALTH INSURANCE BASICS: DEFINITIONS OF PERILS	- 28 -
B. LIMITED POLICIES	- 29 -
C. COMMON EXCLUSIONS (THINGS NOT COVERED)	- 31 -
D. MARKETING REQUIREMENTS:	- 32 -
E. UNDERWRITING	- 33 -
F. POLICY REPLACEMENT	- 34 -
G. SPECIALIZED RISK	- 34 -
PRACTICE QUESTIONS FOR HEALTH INSURANCE BASICS	- 35 -
CHAPTER 3: DENTAL INSURANCE	- 37 -
PRACTICE QUESTIONS: DENTAL INSURANCE	- 39 -
CHAPTER 4: HEALTH INSURANCE PROVISIONS	- 41 -
A. UNIFORM REQUIRED PROVISIONS	- 41 -
B. UNIFORM OPTIONAL PROVISIONS	- 44 -
7. INTOXICANTS AND NARCOTICS	- 45 -
C. OTHER PROVISIONS	- 45 -
PRACTICE QUESTIONS: HEALTH INSURANCE PROVISIONS	- 49 -
CHAPTER 5: DISABILITY INCOME INSURANCE	- 51 -
A. INDIVIDUAL DISABILITY POLICIES	- 51 -
4. COORDINATION OF BENEFITS	- 52 -
B. QUALIFYING FOR DISABILITY BENEFITS	- 55 -
4. SOCIAL SECURITY DISABILITY	- 57 -
PRACTICE QUESTIONS: DISABILITY INCOME INSURANCE	- 58 -
CHAPTER 6: HEALTH (MEDICAL) PLANS	- 60 -
A. MEDICAL PLAN CONCEPTS	- 60 -
B. HEALTH MAINTENANCE ORGANIZATIONS (HMO's)	- 61 -

C. PREFERRED PROVIDER ORGANIZATION (PPO) .... - 62 -
D. POINT OF SERVICE (POS) .... - 63 -
E. MAJOR MEDICAL CONCEPT .... - 63 -
F. MANAGED CARE AND UTILIZATION MANAGEMENT .... - 64 -
G. CONSUMER DRIVEN HEALTH PLANS (CDHP) .... - 65 -
H. TRICARE – MILITARY PERSONNEL .... - 66 -
I. INDEMNITY PLANS .... - 66 -

PRACTICE QUESTIONS: MEDICAL PLANS .... - 67 -

CHAPTER 7: GROUP INSURANCE .... - 69 -
7. GROUP LIFE INSURANCE .... - 73 -
8. NEWBORN CHILDREN ON GROUP AND INDIVIDUAL INSURANCE .... - 73 -
9. CONTRIBUTORY vs. NONCONTRIBUTORY .... - 74 -

PRACTICE QUESTIONS: GROUP INSURANCE .... - 75 -

CHAPTER 8: SOCIAL INSURANCE & SENIOR CITIZENS .... - 77 -
1. PART A: MEDICARE HOSPITAL INSURANCE .... - 78 -
2. PART B: MEDICARE PHYSCIAN SERVICES .... - 79 -
3. PART C: MEDICARE ADVANTAGE .... - 80 -
4. PART D: MEDICARE PRESCRIPTION DRUG .... - 80 -
5. PRIVATE MEDICARE SUPPLEMENT INSURANCE .... - 81 -
6. OVER 65 WORKING EMPLOYEES AND MEDICARE .... - 83 -
7. LONG TERM CARE INSURANCE (NOT MEDICARE, NOT SOCIAL/GOVT) .... - 84 -
8. OLD AGE SURVIVORS INSURANCE .... - 87 -
a. SOCIAL SECURITY BENEFITS .... - 88 -
b. SOCIAL SECURITY SURVIVOR BENEFITS .... - 88 -
c. SOCIAL SECURITY RETIREMENT BENEFITS .... - 88 -
9. MEDICAID .... - 89 -

PRACTICE QUESTIONS: SOCIAL INSURANCE .... - 90 -

CHAPTER 9: LIFE INSURANCE BASICS 94
A. WHO CAN PURCHASE INSURANCE (INSURABLE INTEREST) 94
B. REASONS TO PURCHASE LIFE INSURANCE 95
C. DETERMINING AMOUNT OF PERSONAL LIFE INSURANCE 96
D. BUSINESS USES OF LIFE INSURANCE 97
E. CATEGORIES OF LIFE INSURANCE 98
F. MARKETING PRACTICES & SALES 99
G. PREMIUMS AND INSURED CLASSIFICATION 103
H. UNDERWRITING 104

PRACTICE QUESTIONS: LIFE INSURANCE BASICS 106

CHAPTER 10: LIFE INSURANCE POLICIES 108

    A. TERM LIFE INSURANCE POLICIES 108

    B. WHOLE LIFE INSURANCE 112

    C. ADJUSTABLE LIFE 115

    D. UNIVERSAL LIFE 115

    E. SPECIALIZED POLICIES 116

    F. CREDIT LIFE 118

    D. CASH VALUE COMPONENTS IN LIFE INSURANCE 118

PRACTICE QUESTIONS: LIFE INSURANCE POLICIES 122

CHAPTER 11: LIFE PROVISIONS, NONFORFEITURE AND RIDERS 124

    A. UNIFORM POLICY PROVISIONS 124

    B. BENEFICIARIES 128

    C. LIFE INSURANCE SETTLEMENT OPTIONS 130

    D. NONFORFEITURE OPTIONS 131

    E. POLICY LOAN AND WITHDRAWAL OPTIONS 133

    F. DIVIDEND OPTIONS 134

    G. POLICY RIDERS 135

    H. ACCELERATED LIVING NEEDS BENEFIT RIDER 136

PRACTICE QUESTIONS: LIFE PROVISIONS 139

CHAPTER 12: ANNUITIES 142

    A. ANNUITY PHASES 143

    B. ANNUITY SETTLEMENT OPTIONS 143

    C. ANNUITY REFUND OPTIONS (REFUND ANNUITY) 145

    D. NEGATIVE ASPECTS OF ANNUITIES 145

    F. USES OF ANNUITIES 145

    d. SECTION 1035 EXCHANGES 150

PRACTICE QUESTIONS: ANNUITIES 151

CHAPTER 13: STATE REGULATION .... - 155 -

    A. LICENSING .... - 155 -

    B. APPOINTMENT & AGENCY PRACTICES .... - 157 -

    C. COMMISIONER AND REGULATION .... - 158 -

    D. PENALTIES AND PROCEDURES .... - 161 -

    E. INSURANCE COMMISSIONER LIMITATIONS .... - 161 -

    F. CHEMICAL DEPENDENCY .... - 162 -

    G. MANAGING GENERAL AGENT (MGA) .... - 162 -

H. LEGAL RESERVE AGENT	- 162 -
I. CERTIFIED FINANCIAL PLANNER (CFP)	- 162 -
J. CHARTERED LIFE AND HEALTH UNDERWRITERS (CLHU)	- 162 -
K. FUNERAL DIRECTORS	- 162 -
L. LIFE INSURANCE COUNSELORS	- 162 -
PRACTICE QUESTIONS: INSURANCE REGULATION	**- 163 -**
CHAPTER TEST ANSWERS	**- 167 -**

Life, Accident & Health Exam Study Book | TX

CHAPTER I: GENERAL INSURANCE

This chapter is designed to teach the basics of Insurance that apply to all lines within the insurance industry. The two main lines of Insurance are: Property & Casualty and Life & Health; P&C consists of Home, Auto and Business insurance; while Life and Health encompasses life, health and accident insurance. This book is for the exam of Life, Accident & Health insurance and there are four main parties involved:

- **Insurer:** An insurance company (Blue Cross Blue Shield, State Farm, Allstate, Safeco)
- **Insured:** The party who is covered by the policy and has insurance
- **Policyowner:** The party who purchased the policy from an insurer and pays the premiums. Only the policyowner may make changes to a policy
- **Producer:** A person who sells, solicits and markets insurance for an insurer. Also known as an insurance agent, this is most likely you
- **Underwriter:** An employee of the insurance company who checks applications, issues policies and sets premium prices.

* The policyowner may be, and typically is, the same person as the insured. A policyowner purchases insurance from an insurer, and collects premium as payment. For your state exam, many of the definitions in this chapter will be on the test, so it is important to have a firm understand of concepts such as: **Hazards, Perils, Adverse Selection, Agency Methods, Contracts and Regulation.**

I. INSURANCE DEFINITION

Insurance is the **transfer of financial risk** from an insured (person who has insurance) to an insurer (insurance company); that financial risk is then spread across a group of insureds, which the insurer pools together resources (premiums) to pay-out incurred losses. All insurance policies contain this statement: *"Whereby, for a set amount of money, one party agrees to pay the other party a set sum upon the occurrence of some covered event."*

a. RISK

Risk is the uncertainty of loss and the primary reason for insurance; there are risks in every aspect of life, however only some are insurable. The two primary types of risk are:

> **1. Pure Risk**
> A category of risk in which financial loss is the only possible outcome, there is **no chance for financial gain** in pure risk. Pure risk is related to events that are beyond the risk-taker's control and, therefore, a person cannot consciously take on pure risk. Examples: Accidents, Sickness, Fire, Disabilities etc.
>
> **2. Speculative Risk**
> A category of risk where the insured has **a chance of financial gain or financial loss,** the insured consciously takes the risks for a benefit. Examples: Gambling, Investing in markets such as Real Estate, Stocks and Commodities.

b. EXPOSURE

Exposure is a unit of measurement determining how prone a risk is to loss. **Age, Sex, Occupation, Avocation and Medical History can all be units of exposure**.

c. HAZARDS

There are 3 types of hazards from both an insured and insurers standpoint. An example of a hazard would be children's toys spread out in the path of a walking area creating a tripping hazard. Hazards do not always lead to loss, but they do **increase the chance of loss.**

- **PHYSICAL HAZARDS** are items that can be physically touched, picked up, moved, felt and are tangible. Examples: Broken steps, Trash debris or **Medical conditions**

- **MORAL HAZARDS** are when an insured is **dishonest** or has little regard toward future responsibilities. Examples: **Fraudulent claims, Lying,** Smoking and Drug addiction.

- **MORALE HAZARDS** are when an insured has an, **imprudence, indifference** or **carelessness** to loss; an example of a morale hazard would be speeding to get home to catch a tv show; morale hazards pertain to the insureds state-of-mind.

d. PERILS

The **causes of loss** listed within a policy for which the insurer will provide financial protection against. Such as Life and Health insurance protects against **Medical Expense, Death, Loss of Income** and homeowners' insurance will protect against **Fire, Wind, and Hail** etc.

e. LOSS

An insurer will pay out a claim only if it results in a financial loss to the insured. Such as rain may create hazardous road conditions, however there was no loss to the insured. Fire is a peril listed in the policy, however if the fire does not damage anything, there is no loss, thus no claim to be paid.

2. METHODS OF HANDLING RISK (RISK MANAGEMENT)

It is impossible to eliminate risk; however, these steps can help lower the probability of filing a claim:

a. AVOIDANCE

Avoidance is the act of refraining from an activity entirely, thus creating no chance for loss. This is the best risk management option, however not always practical. Example: Never driving in order to avoid having a collision claim.

b. RETENTION

Retention is when the insured retains a portion of the risk themselves, thus encouraging safe practices to lower losses. **Retention** examples:

- ✓ Higher Deductibles
- ✓ Copayments
- ✓ Self-Insurance

c. SHARING

Sharing can be utilized by splitting up a risk into many parts, thus lowering the chance of a total loss. Example: Diversifying investments into 100 stocks instead of one greatly lowers the chance of a total loss within the stock market; the risk of losing money is shared among many stocks.

d. REDUCTION

Reduction is the method of lowering the chance of a loss through maintenance of either property or body. Working out and eating healthy greatly reduces the chance of heart disease.

e. TRANSFER

Insurance is the transfer of financial risk, instead of the insured taking full responsibility for their losses; they transfer the financial risk to an insurer. Transfer is the most inefficient method of risk management.

* Ashley pays her premium of $100 per month to XYZ Health insurance company. When Ashley becomes ill, she visits the doctor; instead of Ashley paying the physician herself, XYZ insurance company pays out. Ashley has essentially transferred her financial risk of becoming ill to an insurer.

3. ELEMENTS OF INSURABLE (PURE) RISKS

All pure risks must meet the below guidelines in order to become insurable

- **Loss must be definite and measurable:** There must be a value placed on the insured person/item, a time frame and a place of loss.
- **Loss must NOT be catastrophic:** Insurer must have the capacity to afford the incurred claims. War, Nuclear, Flood and Hurricanes may be considered catastrophic.
- **Insurance must NOT be mandatory.** An insurer must not be forced to issue a policy without their own guidelines (underwriting)
- **Loss must be due to chance:** The loss must be unexpected and not intentionally caused.
- **Loss must be predictable to insurer:** There must be a statistical basis through the Law of Large Numbers to predict future losses using **actuarial justification.**

4. ADVERSE SELECTION

Many people who are adverse risks (high risks) seek insurance due to the fact they will likely incur more losses. Insurers will cover certain adverse risks, however, to off-set the increased chance of loss, the insurer can protect itself by:

- **Increased Premiums (Rated-Up)**
- **Probationary Periods or Limitation to certain plans**
- **Decline to cover the risk entirely**

An underwriter is an employee of the insurer who checks applications, sets premium prices and finally issues the policy. Underwriters & Producers both protect the insurer from Adverse Selection.

5. LAW OF LARGE NUMBERS

Actuaries must predict future claims in order to set accurate pricing structures; this is not done by magic, but through **statistics** using large data samples of previous losses via the law of large numbers. Life insurance in particular uses two main methods to predict life and health insurance claims:

> - **Mortality Tables**: Predicting Life expectancy of different types of people
> - **Morbidity Tables:** The sickness of individuals and at what age they become sick.

The larger the group, the better the rates because losses can be predicted more accurately.

6. REINSURANCE

Think of reinsurance as "insurance for insurance companies"; most insurers purchase insurance from other insurers to protect themselves from **catastrophic losses** normally through **reinsurance treaties.** The primary insurer who purchased the policy is called a **ceding** company.

* Adams Insurance Company is required by state law to have a minimum of 1.5 million dollars in policy reserves. Due to the law of large numbers, Adams Ins. Co. knows they will likely not incur total losses throughout the entire year, so Adams is able to insure 10 million worth of risk; however, Adams does purchase an 8.5 million reinsurance policy in case they incur more losses than they have in policy reserves. This protects Adams Insurance Company from catastrophic losses in the future.

7. DIVIDENDS

A dividend is considered a return of excess premium, also known as a "refund" of premium. If the insurer has a good year and earned profit, it does not need all of the money it collected. The dividend would be paid to either stockholders or policyholders on a **NON-guaranteed** basis and will also be tax-free since it is considered a refund. It is illegal misrepresentation to imply dividends are guaranteed.

B. TYPES OF INSURERS:
1. STOCK – NON-PARTICIPATING

Stock insurers are owned by **stockholders**, and dividends (profit) are paid to **stockholders.** The stockholders invest money into the insurer and when the insurer gains a profit, the stockholders are rewarded. If a stock insurer is on the stock market, it would be known as a public stock company; companies not listed on the stock market are considered private insurers.

* Porky's, a stock insurance company, only sells insurance in Florida, but is looking to expand into Georgia. There are substantial costs to expanding and Porky's does not want to raise prices on his policyholders; instead, Porky's sells stock to outside investors for the purpose of raising capital. When Porky's expands into Georgia and profits rise, the stockholders will receive a dividend check, but the Florida and Georgia policyholders/insureds will not.

2. MUTUAL – PARTICIPATING

Mutual insurers are managed by a board of trustees and are owned by **policyholders**; thus, the insureds DO participate in the profits of the company. Mutual companies have no capital stock and pay **dividends to policyholders** since the policyholders are participating in profits. Additionally, the dividends are considered tax-free because in participating companies, the dividends are considered a **return of excess premium** also known as a refund. A stock company can become a mutual company through a process called "Mutualization"

* Blackfoot, a mutual insurance company, wants to attract more customers and decides to launch a massive marketing campaign. Blackfoot raises prices on its policyholders to afford the new marketing effort; however, when more customers purchase insurance, Blackfoot starts to earn a profit. Blackfoot rewards its policyholders with a tax-free dividend check, essentially refunding some of their premium back to them. This is because the policyholders own the company and participate in profits.

- ✓ A stock insurer may charge $100 for a policy, and if the insurer generates massive profits, only the stockholders of the company will profit. Whereas, if a mutual insurer charged the same $100 for a policy and also earned a profit, the mutual insurer rewards its policyholders with a dividend check of say $10. Essentially making the mutual policy only $90, since the policyholders participate in profits.

3. FRATERNAL BENEFIT SOCIETIES

An organization which only sells insurance to **members of their organization**, these are commonly churches, charities, nonprofits and other clubs. These insurers generally receive less regulation as their primary purpose is other than insurance. Example: Fraternal order of Police.

4. RECIPROCAL

An **attorney-in-fact** creates and operates a reciprocal insurer which is comprised of individuals, corporations and other members named **subscribers.** Reciprocal insurers are able to insurer specialized risks since they tend to be **unincorporated** and can operate across state lines. Remaining unincorporated increases liability to each member of the reciprocal exchange.

5. LLOYD'S ASSOCIATIONS

There are many higher risks that standard insurers will not cover; the last option for these high risks tends to be Lloyd's associations, which instead of being one insurer, it is an **unincorporated group** which comprises of many **individual underwriters** and insurers who all **share** in each risk they insure. Since it is not a regular corporation, the insureds covered by the Lloyd's association would have little recourse if one of the underwriters failed to pay the claim, thus purchasing insurance through a Lloyds is high risk to the clients as well. *America does not allow Lloyds of London or American Lloyds,* **only Lloyd's associations are allowed within the USA.**

6. RISK RETENTION & PURCHASING GROUPS

Large corporations who are within **similar lines of business** (Lawyer and Lawyer, or Retailer and Retailer etc.) can come together and create a group to insure each other for **liability insurance.**

Instead of purchasing insurance from a standard insurer, they form their own group and spread their liability risks within the group. This lowers overhead costs from having separate insurers.

7. SELF-INSURERS

Large corporations can also self-insure, by setting aside their own funds into a separate account and paying claims out of their own account. Self-Insurers utilize the **retention** form of risk management, by retaining most of the risk themselves. These types of corporations tend to purchase insurance from a standard insurer overtop of a **stop-loss** amount to limit their own losses in the event of a catastrophe.

h. SURPLUS LINES

Surplus lines markets are for **higher risk** customers that cannot purchase insurance in a standard market. These insurers are **non-admitted** meaning that they are not recognized by the state insurance department, and usually require that the client be declined by two or more insurers prior to seeking insurance in the surplus lines market.

C. FEDERAL & STATE ORGANIZATION STRUCTURES

1. SOCIAL INSURANCE (GOVERNMENT) VS. PRIVATE INSURANCE

Social Insurance programs are government insurance funded by taxes (such as FICA – Federal Insurance Contribution Act) and provide programs such as Medicare, Medicaid, Social Security, Flood and Terrorism Insurance. Government and Private insurance may insure the same perils, such as health insurance or property insurance, but the **primary difference** is that government insurance is funded by **taxes**; whereas, private insurance is funded through premiums.

2. DEPT. OF INSURANCE & COMMISSIONER

Insurance is generally regulated by *each state* through a Department of Insurance, which is headed by one person named the **Commissioner of Insurance**. The Commissioner is appointed by the Governor and the Commissioners duties comprise of:

- Advising on **state** insurance laws
- Creating rules & procedures
- Educating the public on insurance matters

The commissioner has many roles to fulfill, primarily coordinating with the governor and the Department of Insurance to make insurance matters run smoothly within the state.

The state commissioner is also a member of the **National Association of Insurance Commissioners (NAIC).** The NAIC is not a government entity, but rather a private association comprised of all state insurance commissioners, and as a private association, the NAIC has **NO legal power.** They typically hold annual meetings to discuss insurance across the entire country and to keep up with any political/technological changes to the insurance industry. Even though insurance is regulated by each state and regulation varies from state to state, the NAIC creates certain **uniformity across state lines.** Due to the NAIC, purchasing a policy from New York would be very similar to a policy in Texas because of the uniformity in rules and procedures in each state.

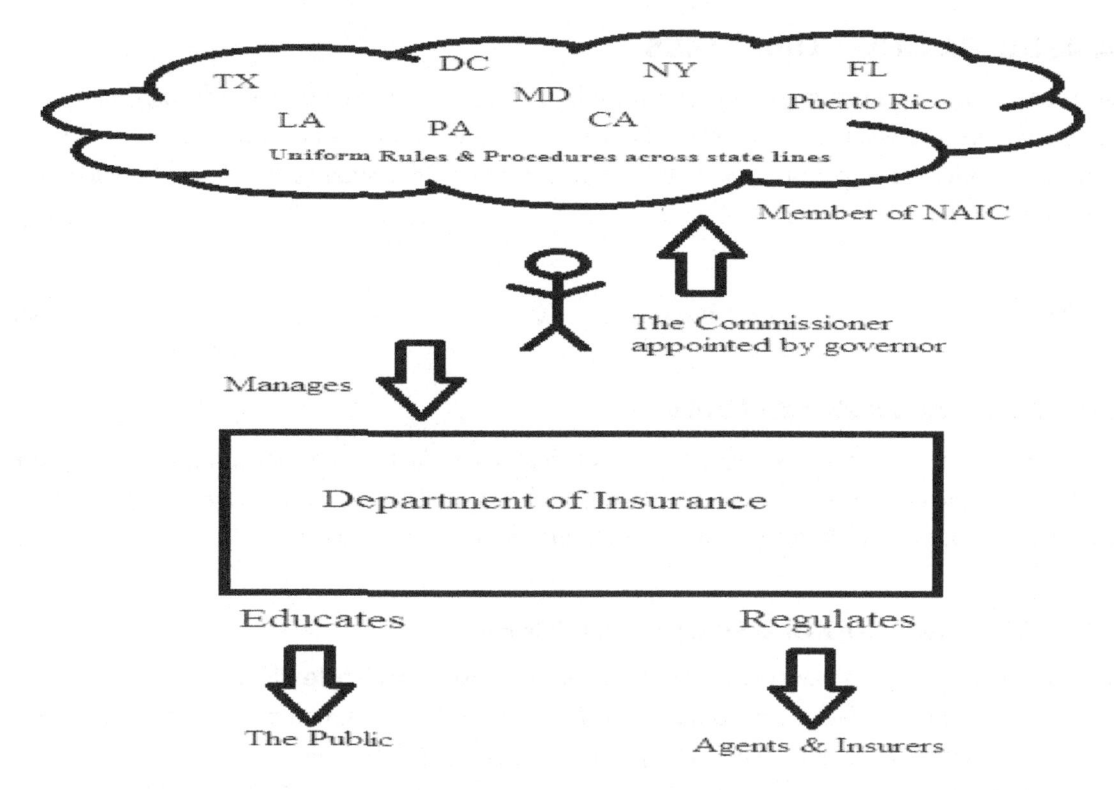

3. ADMITTED (Authorized) VS. NON-ADMITTED (Unauthorized) Insurers

The commissioner of insurance inspects insurance companies and decides whether or not they are able to transact insurance within the state:

- ❖ **Authorized:** An admitted insurer who has received a Certificate of Authority to transact insurance within the state. These companies are typically safe and the Department of Insurance provides certain protections for consumers insured by them.
- ❖ **Unauthorized:** A non-admitted insurer who did not pass the commissioners standards and has NOT received a Certificate of Authority to transact insurance. A **producer** may be held **liable** if they represent a non-admitted insurance company.

✓ A **Certificate of Authority** is the document the commissioner issues to admitted insurers to **transact insurance** which allows them to collect premiums and issue policies.

4. WHERE INSURERS ARE INCORPORATED AND CHARTERED

- ❖ **Domestic Insurers:** Incorporated within the same state they are headquartered in. **IE:** Incorporated and chartered in Texas and also headquartered within Texas.
- ❖ **Foreign Insurers:** Incorporated in *another state or U.S. Subsidiary*. **IE:** Incorporated in Iowa but headquartered in Texas. Guam, Puerto Rico, Wash. D.C. are all foreign to Texas.
- ❖ **Alien Insurers:** Incorporated in *another country* entirely. **IE:** France, Mexico, Cuba

5. FINANCIAL RATING COMPANIES

Individuals receive their credit ratings through 3 main bureaus (Transunion, Equifax, and Experian); however, Insurers, businesses, banks and even countries have their own credit rating agencies. These bureaus rate the financial strength of Insurers usually with letter grades such as A+, A, A-, B; below are the listed Financial Rating Companies:

- ✓ AM Best
- ✓ Standard & Poor
- ✓ Weiss
- ✓ Fitch
- ✓ Moody's

6. AGENCY MARKETING SYSTEMS

A producer is an "agent" who solicits', sells, or markets insurance for an insurance company. Producers are generally not employees of the insurance company and almost all producers receive compensation on a commission basis, except managerial, which is an employee of the insurer.

a. INDEPENDENT (NON-EXCLUSIVE) PRODUCERS

Independent marketing systems have producers who may represent **multiple** different insurance companies at the same time. These are commonly referred to as "independent producers" whom sign non-exclusive contracts with each insurer. The producer represents ABC insurer, but also XYZ and QRS insurers at the same time.

b. CAPTIVE (EXCLUSIVE) PRODUCERS

Captive marketing systems have producers who represent **only one or a group** of insurers and may not represent other insurers at the same time. The producer may only represent ABC insurer and its subsidiaries, but no other insurers.

c. GENERAL AGENT

General agents are responsible for training other agents and usually are responsible for thousands of agents at a time. The general agent receives compensation as **commission, but is also reimbursed for office expenses.** They usually receive a small portion of commission of each agent underneath them; however, they front the costs of marketing materials until the insurer reimburses them.

d. MANAGERIAL AGENT

Managerial agents are **employees** of the insurer and receive compensation as **salary and bonuses.** Managerial agents usually manage multiple states or a region and their job is to ensure that sales goals are met within that region. They manage the other agency systems.

d. DIRECT RESPONSE AND MASS MARKETING

Some insurers market directly to the public through **vending machines, telemarketing, television ads and phone solicitation**. These insurers do not utilize agency systems and usually develop a call center to handle sales.

7. INSURANCE GUARANTY ASSOCIATIONS

Most states have a guaranty fund which protects consumers in the event an insurer becomes **insolvent** or bankrupt. All admitted insurers pay assessments into the association, and if one of them fails to meet financial obligations, the fund will **pay claims and return unearned premium** to the consumers of that failed insurer. The association is *funded by members* (insurers) and is a **Non-Profit, Private** (not on stock market), **Stock** corporation. It is illegal for an agent to discuss this fund with potential clients, as the association has limited funds within it, so the insured may have a false sense of security knowing about the association.

D. LAW/RULE OF AGENCY

Producers, commonly referred to as agents; sell, solicit and market insurance for insurers.

1. INSURER AS THE PRINCIPAL

Insurers are commonly known as principals, and **must be represented by an agent.** Even if there is a direct response system, there is always an agent of record representing the insurer.

2. PRODUCER REPRESENTS INSURER

The producer if acting ethically will **always represent the insurer** during an insurance contract; producers enter into contracts to work with insurers, known as an **appointment**. The producer always has to keep the client's best interest in mind, but when in the end the producer represents the insurer due to the contract, they signed in order to represent the insurer.

3. AUTHORITY AND POWERS OF PRODUCERS

When the producer enters into a contract with the insurer and becomes appointed, the producer gains inherent authority. These authorities allow the producer to do their job.

1. **Express Authority:** A **written** contract with the insurer that outlines that the producer represents the insurer and what commissions will be paid.

2. **Implied Authority:** Non-Material (not written) items that an agent may assume in order to complete day-to-day activities. Such as making sales calls and printing business cards.

3. **Apparent Authority:** The appearance of authority through either: Training, Rate-books or Signage. This is authority that the customer thinks the agent has by the way the agent speaks, but the agent may or may not actually have that authority. Such as, the agent can quote policies under implied authority, but to a customer it may appear as if the agent set the rate, when in reality an underwriter determines the rates, the customer will pay.

4. ETHICAL RESPONSIBILITY OF THE PRODUCER

A producer must follow a code of ethics when dealing insurance; even though the producers first and foremost responsibility is to the **insurer**, the producer must always keep the client's best interest in mind. It is the **producers' job** to determine which products are **suitable** for clients and must not sell the client a product that would not be beneficial to them.

E. CONTRACTS
1. ELEMENTS OF LEGAL CONTRACTS

All insurance policies are legally binding contracts; all legal contracts must abide by four principles:

- ✓ Offer and Acceptance
- ✓ Consideration
- ✓ Competent Parties
- ✓ Legal Purpose

a. OFFER AND ACCEPTANCE

In order to have a legal contract, one party must make an offer and one party must accept the offer. When an applicant fills out an application and submits their initial premium, they are offering themselves to the insurer. The insurer then has the right to accept the offer by issuing the policy. There is no acceptance unless the initial premium is paid. No Negotiation is required for a contract.

b. CONSIDERATION (MONIES EXCHANGED)

Consideration is the monetary values exchanged within insurance. The insureds **premium and premium payment mode** –frequency of payment-- are found in the consideration clause and the insurers **promise to pay** in the event of a claim are also found in the consideration clause.

c. COMPETENT PARTIES

All parties must be of age (18), Sober and Mentally Sane in order to purchase. Most parties are considered automatically competent unless they can prove they were incompetent at the time.

d. LEGAL PURPOSE

The contract must be of legal essence, and obtained legally or there is no contract. Such as there must be an insurable interest in order to purchase, or the contract would not be legal.

2. CHARACTERISTICS OF AN INSURANCE CONTRACT
a. CONTRACT OF ADHESION – NON-NEGOTIABLE

The insurer is the party who originally wrote the insurance contract and created the verbiage within the contract. Since there was no negotiation, this contract is known as a **"take it or leave it"** contract. Since the insurer wrote the contract, if the contract is *ambiguous (unclear/vague)* and adversely affects an insured, should the insured sue due to the ambiguity, *the insured would likely win the lawsuit.*

b. ALEATORY CONTRACT – UNEQUAL CONTRACT

Aleatory contracts are **unequal** exchanges of value; usually when the insureds premium is low, but receives high number of benefits. IE: Term life costs $10/month but pays out $500,000 in benefits, which is an unequal amount exchanged.

c. PERSONAL CONTRACT

In order to transfer ownership of a policy, the insured must have *written permission* from an insurer. This is due to the personal nature of insurance.

d. UNILATERAL CONTRACT – ONE PARTY OBLIGATED BY LAW

When only one party is bound by law to uphold their part of the contract, this is considered a **one-sided** or unilateral contract. The insurer is regulated by laws to ensure payment of claims; however, a policyowner is not bound by law to make premium payments.

e. CONDITIONAL CONTRACT

Each party must meet certain conditions such as paying premiums in order to keep the contract in force. **IE:** A small employer must remain small to keep insurance; 2-50 employees, otherwise the policy would cancel.

3. LEGAL INTERPRETATIONS AFFECTING CONTRACTS

a. REASONABLE EXPECTATIONS

If an insured could reasonably expect coverage due to insurers marketing practices, then generally the insurer would have to pay the claim, even if the policy specifically excluded that loss. **IE:** Marketing towards Senior Citizens, except excluding everybody over age 50. The insured could have reasonably expected coverage; thus, the courts would rule in their favor.

b. INDEMNITY

The insurer is only obligated to reimburse an insured for the actual amount of loss to return them to the same financial position prior to loss. There is no profiting from insurance. **IE:** A dent in a car will be fixed rather than purchasing the insured a brand-new vehicle.

c. UTMOST GOOD FAITH

All insurance contracts are written with the assumption that both parties are truthful and must trust each other to be honest. ***All contracts are written in the utmost good faith.***

d. REPRESENTATIONS

Statements made on applications are considered representations; these are presumed to be true to the best of one's knowledge, and are treated as true statements even if they may be false. **IE:** If an insured was asked, when was the last time they were at the doctor and they respond "April"; however, they forgot in reality it was May, we still treat that as a representation since they thought it was true at the time.

e. MISREPRESENTATIONS

Statements that are knowingly untrue are considered misrepresentations. In Life, Accident and Health, these statements may void a policy if discovered within the first 2 years of a policies inception. **IE:** If an insured intentionally lies on an application or an insurer puts out a deceiving marketing piece, those are misrepresentations. An agent misleading an insured about dividend guarantees or expected outcomes are all methods of misrepresentation as well.

f. WARRANTY

Warranties are **absolutely literal** true statements backed with a guarantee; not generally used for applications. The entire contract written by the insurer is filled with warranties, the insurer states they will cover certain losses, and guarantees that claims will be paid.

g. CONCEALMENT

Omitting or withholding information from an underwriter on an **application**. Applications have limited numbers of questions on them and cannot cover every possible scenario, thus it is understood the applicant should be forthright and upcoming with any extra information. If they hide or omit a material fact during the application process, that would be considered concealment.

h. FRAUD – Material Misrepresentation

Intentional and knowingly deceiving a person for **financial gain** would be considered fraud. Stealing, Embezzling, False Financial reports are all considered Fraud.

i. WAIVER AND ESTOPPEL

    1. WAIVER the intentional giving up of a right within a contract.

    2. ESTOPPEL prevents an insurer from asserting the right that was previously waived.

Waiver and Estoppel is normally found when an insured pays their premiums late on a reoccurring basis and the insurer still accepts the funds. Since the insurer waived the premium due date, any claims that occur within this gap, the insurer may be required to pay to pay the claim.

F. FEDERAL REGULATION

All federal regulation is enacted by **Congress** and applies to all insurance on a **federal level**.

1. FAIR CREDIT REPORTING ACT (FCRA)

FCRA was implemented to provide consumers protection and ensure accuracy for what is obtained within their credit report. FCRA was affected on April 25th, 1971 and is very important for insurance because credit reports are an integral part of underwriting. If there is incorrect information the credit bureaus must **establish a method of correcting** the information, and any corrected information must sent to all other creditors of the past 2 years. There are two main reports used in insurance.

1. **Consumer Report:** A soft-pull of credit to check debts and balances. This does not affect an insureds credit score with the <u>**credit rating agencies.**</u>
2. **Investigative Consumer Report:** A 3rd party company is hired to investigate a person's Hobbies, Habits, Reputation and Employment status through **Physical Inspections.**

As a producer, any time a consumer report is ordered we must notify the insured using a Disclosure Notification Authorization, which is used to inform the insured of their privacy rights; the insured does not need to sign any document, only receive it at the time of **application** or within 3 days, a verbal notification sometimes suffices. Should the reports adversely affect insureds rates; the insured must receive a detailed letter explaining why within **5 days.** If an agent violates this process a maximum fine of **$2,500** may be imposed under federal law.

3. EMPLOYEE RETIREMENT INCOME SECURITY ACT (1974) (ERISA)

ERISA provides protections against a pension manager misusing their **fiduciary capacity** and creates reporting standards for retirement plans. Employers are NOT required to make contributions.

2. COURT CASES OF STATE VS. GOVERNMENT REGULATION

1. **Paul v. Virginia (1868):** Insurance is not considered interstate commerce.
2. **US v. Southeastern Underwriters Assn. (1944):** Insurance is interstate commerce.
3. **McCarran-Ferguson Act (1945):** Insurance is no longer interstate commerce, and it is *"in the public interest"* to be regulated on a state level.
4. **Intervention by FTC (Federal Trade Commission) (1958):** Upheld McCarran Act.
5. **Securities Exchange Commission (1959):** Variable products can be federal regulated.
6. **National Federation of Independent Business vs. Sebelius (2012):** Insurance is still a state regulated product, but the federal government may impose taxes on the product.

3. FINANCIAL SERVICES MODERNIZATION ACT (1999) Gramm-Leach-Bliley

The Financial Services Modernization Act (also known as the federal Gramm-Leach-Bliley Act of 1999 or "GLB") was passed by Congress in 1999, repealing the Glass-Steagall Act of 1933. Prior to this ruling, financial institutions, insurance companies, commercial banks, investment banks, and retail brokerages were prohibited from entering each other's line of business. The Act dissolved the prohibition. The Act also requires privacy protection of personal financial information. Personal health information that is collected in conjunction with selling or providing a financial service (including insurance) is considered as financial information.

4. CONSOLIDATED OMNIBUS BUDGET RECONCILIATION ACT (COBRA)

The Consolidated Omnibus Budget Reconciliation Act (COBRA) gives workers and their families who lose their health benefits the right to choose to continue group health benefits provided by their group health plan for limited periods of time under certain circumstances such as voluntary or involuntary job loss, reduction in the hours worked, transition between jobs, death, divorce, and other life events. Qualified individuals may be required to pay the entire premium for coverage up to **102 percent** of the cost to the plan. A person may continue coverage up to **18 months** in most circumstances, unless death of a participant, divorce, or disability of the worker occurs, upon which they may continue coverage up to 36 months.

COBRA generally requires that group health plans sponsored by employers with **20 or more** employees in the prior year offer employees and their families the opportunity for a temporary extension of health coverage (called continuation coverage) in certain instances where coverage under the plan would otherwise end. COBRA coverage may only be cancelled if the employee fails to pay the premiums, files fraudulent claims or if the **employer no longer offers group health insurance**.

- ❖ **Contributory:** When an employer and employee are sharing in premiums for group insurance. Such as, 75% employer, 25% employee; these plans require 75% participation rate of the group.
- ❖ **Noncontributory:** When only the employer is paying the premiums, 100% employer, 0% employee. If a plan is non-contributory, there MUST be 100% of all employees participating in the insurance and there will be **no medical underwriting.**
- ❖ **Fully Contributory:** When only the employee is paying the premiums, 0% employer 100% employee.

- ✓ The easiest way to remember this concept is if you read it as "employee" noncontributory or "employee" fully contributory. That would mean the employee either did not contribute or fully paid the premiums. Having 100% participation on noncontributory plans helps lower the risk of **Adverse Selection.**

* Jedidah's employer is offering a group disability insurance plan on a noncontributory basis. Jedidah was initially upset because she thought she would have to pay 100% of the premiums. After speaking with Joe, she became very happy to find out noncontributory meant the employer paid all the premiums, all of her dependents were eligible AND she did not have to go through medical underwriting.

5. USA PATRIOT ACT (October 26th, 2001)

The *Uniting and Strengthening America by Providing Appropriate Tools Required to Intercept and Obstruct Terrorism Act of* 2001 was designed to provide the federal and state governments more power and resources to protect against future terroristic attacks after September 11th, 2001. For insurance, the law has regulation in regards to money laundering through life insurance.

6. PATIENT PROTECTION & AFFORDABLE CARE ACT (PPACA, ACA)

Patient Protection & Affordable Care Act (also known as Obamacare) was enacted in 2010, with legislation being phased in through 2020. Essentially an overhaul of the health insurance industry, which made all comprehensive health insurance policies, **guaranteed issue**, meaning no person cannot be turned down or excluded due to pre-existing conditions. PPACA also created a sliding scale tax subsidy program for citizens earning between 100% of the Federal Poverty Limit (2014: $11,500 on individual, $24,000 for a family of 4) and 400% of the Federal Poverty Limit ($44,000 individual, $100,000 family of 4). If a persons' income is falls between these limits, they may qualify for lower premiums. If you need health insurance, you may enroll on www.Healthcare.gov until March 31st without any medical underwriting. Based on your income, you may qualify for lower premiums (or none at all). PPACA is primarily designed for people **without access to employer sponsored health insurance**, such as unemployed people or small business owners.

Maximum out of pocket costs include **deductibles, coinsurance and copays** and the premiums for plans are based off of **per person** who may receive a subsidy based off of **income** and paid **per person.**

6. HEALTH INSURANCE PORTABILITY & ACCOUNTABILITY ACT (HIPAA)

Enacted on August 21, 1996; it enables an insured to switch health plans without needing to satisfy a new pre-existing conditions exclusion period, as long as a person has maintained insurance, without a lapse greater than **63 days**, HIPAA also created the **credible coverage** concept; if a person has had insurance for **18 months**, pre-existing's are completely waived under a newly obtained health plan, any amount less than 18 months will apply to reduce the new plans exclusionary period. HIPAA limits pre-existing conditions to **1 year** for group plans, and **2 years** for individual insurance. HIPAA mandates that all group insurance be **guaranteed issue** and require little to no medical underwriting, and also removed pregnancy as a pre-existing condition.

* Teri had individual insurance for 8 months before obtaining a new job that offers group health insurance. Upon enrollment in the new guaranteed issue group plan, Teri shows that she had credible coverage as individual insurance, reducing her group pre-existing condition exclusions to 4 months instead of 12. When Teri leaves her job, she does not want to have a lapse of insurance greater than 63 days, or she may need to satisfy the pre-existing's exclusion all over again.

Life, Accident & Health Exam Study Book | TX

PRACTICE QUESTIONS GENERAL INSURANCE

1. Which of the following best describes a Pure Risk?
   a. A risk taken with no chance for financial gain
   b. A risk taken with a chance of financial gain
   c. A risk taken with an uncertain chance of financial gain
   d. A risk taken with a chance of financial gain or loss

2. An unincorporated insurance company which pays dividends to policyholders is best described as:
   a. A Participating Stock Insurer
   b. A Nonparticipating Stock Insurer
   c. A Participating Mutual Insurer
   d. A Nonparticipating Mutual Insurer

3. X enters into a contract of adhesion with ABC insurer to provide health insurance. When X tries to file a claim, the insurer denies coverage citing an ambiguous definition listed in the policy. Should X sue the insurer for coverage, which of the following would most likely occur?
   a. X would win
   b. ABC insurer would win
   c. A mistrial declared
   d. No lawsuit would occur

4. Congress enacted legislation in 1971 which provides consumer protection for credit usages; which of the following is the name of this Act?
   a. Credit Privacy Act of 1971
   b. Consumer Reporting Act of 1971
   c. Fair Consumer Protection Act of 1971
   d. Fair Credit Reporting Act of 1971

5. Which type of authority must be obtained in writing?
   a. Implied
   b. Apparent
   c. Express
   d. Unilateral

6. All of the following are elements of a pure risk EXCEPT:
   a. The loss must have a definite time place and value
   b. Insurance can be mandatory
   c. The loss must not be catastrophic
   d. The loss must be due to chance

7. M has a term life insurance policy with a face amount of $100,000, for which she pays $10 a month for; which of the following would best describe her policy?
   a. Aleatory contract
   b. Unilateral contract
   c. Adhesion contract
   d. Express contract

8. T represents ABC insurer who has been having financial difficulties; during a sales meeting, a potential insured questions T about ABC insurers' solvency. In response, T states that the insurer is a member of the Insurance Guaranty Association, so even if ABC becomes insolvent, the policy holders are protected. T the producers' statement is illegal for which reason?

   a. ABC insurer is not a member of the Guaranty Association
   b. Policyholders must have the policy for one year to receive protection
   c. The insured may have a false sense of security
   d. Nothing was illegal about this practice

9. If a producer is acting ethically, they are representing whom?
   a. Only the insurer
   b. The insurer while keeping the insureds best interest in mind
   c. Only the insured
   d. The insured while keeping the insurers best interest in mind

10. All of the following are NOT financial rating companies EXCEPT:
    a. NAIC
    b. FITCH
    c. NASD
    d. SEC

11. The monetary value exchanged in a contract is best described as:
    a. Consideration
    b. Implied Authority
    c. Offer and Acceptance
    d. Express Authority

12. Which of the following statements is TRUE about an admitted insurer?
    a. TDI has granted a certificate of admittance to the insurer
    b. A certificate of authorization has been granted
    c. The commissioner has granted the insurer a certificate of acceptance
    d. The insurer received a certificate of authority

13. The maximum time a person may continue coverage under the Consolidated Omnibus Budget Reconciliation Act (COBRA)?
a. 18 months
b. 6 months
c. 12 months
d. 24 months

14. Under the uniform rules and procedures set forth by the NAIC, all insurance contracts must include a provision requiring statements made on an application to be described as:
a. Warranties
b. Express statements
c. Representations
d. Waivers and Estoppels

15. All of the following are methods an underwriter may utilize to protect against Adverse Selection EXCEPT:
a. Increasing premiums
b. Declination
c. Issuing conditional coverage through probationary periods
d. Not requiring medical underwriting

16. The theoretical law stating an agent represents a principle is known as:
a. The law of large numbers
b. The law of agency
c. The law of authority
d. The law of contracts

17. Which of the following would constitute the offer in an insurance contract?
a. The applicant completing an application and submitting to the insurer
b. The insurer accepting a prepaid risk
c. The underwriter setting a premium and issuing the policy
d. The producer quoting a price to the potential applicant

18. How long does an insurer have to notify an insured if a consumer report adversely affects their premium rate?
a. 3 days
b. 5 days
c. 10 days
d. 30 days

19. H owns an insurance agency that specializes in providing training and marketing materials for hundreds of agents. Each time the agent sells a policy, H earns a small commission and is able to submit a reimbursement form for certain expenses incurred. Which type of marketing distribution system does H have?
 a. Managerial Agency
 b. General Agency
 c. Direct Agency
 d. Exclusive Agency

20. What is the primary difference between Social (Government) insurance and Private insurance?
 a. Private insurance covers risks the government does not
 b. Social insurance covers the needy whereas private insurance does not
 c. Government insurance is funded by taxes and private insurance is paid through premiums
 d. Private insurance has lower administrative costs than social insurance

21. An insurer incorporated in Guam which primarily sells insurance in Louisiana would be known as which type of insurer?
 a. Foreign
 b. Domestic
 c. Alien
 d. Unauthorized

22. Which of the following best describes a unilateral contract?
 a. A contract of unequal amounts
 b. A contract where the law requires no negotiation for the contract to be valid
 c. A contract where only one part is obligated by law to maintain their portion of the contract
 d. A contract of adhesion where the insured may take it or leave it depending on state laws

23. All insurance contracts must be made in:
 a. An aleatory manner
 b. The utmost good faith
 c. No ambiguous statements
 d. The concept of indemnity

24. A stock insurer pays (nonguaranteed) dividends to whom?
 a. Policyholders
 b. Insureds
 c. Officers
 d. Stockholders

CHAPTER II: HEALTH INSURANCE BASICS

This chapter will primarily focus on the **perils** covered under health insurance and two main distinctions of **comprehensive** and **limited** health plans. Not all insurers offer the same type of health insurance plans and there are distinct differences of insurers, and what they will offer. There will be different uses for health insurance, some are for businesses and some are for individuals.

Next, we will cover the application, collection and disclosure procedures of the producer and then the underwriting which is completed by the insurer. An underwriter will be a person who works for an insurance company to check applications, check medical reports, classify risks and issue policies.

Try to remember in this chapter that insurance is used to replace financial loss, the health products sold will not keep the insured healthy, but the insurance will be there to cover expenses incurred.

A. HEALTH INSURANCE BASICS: DEFINITIONS OF PERILS

There are two forms of perils covered through health insurance, accident and sickness; which are covered in the majority of comprehensive health plans.

1. ACCIDENT

There are three definitions of an accident:
1. **Accident**: Unforeseen and unexpected/unintended event.
2. **Accidental Bodily Injury**: Only the injury is result of an accident
3. **Accidental Means**: Cause and Injury both need to be accidental

Most health insurance policies utilize the definition of Accidental Bodily Injury; where the insured will only have to prove the injury was the result of an accident. Often times when a person is engaged in hazardous hobbies, the insurer may opt to utilize Accidental Means, which is more limiting in coverage.

* Karen enjoys engaging in mountain biking on the weekend and is shopping for a health policy to fit her needs. Her agent explains that mountain biking is an active choice, may need to pay extra for her policy to cover her hobbies and should search for a policy with the Accidental Bodily Injury definition; meaning when injured, she would only have to prove the injury was accidental and not intentional.

If Karen had chosen a policy using the Accidental Means definition; should she be injured mountain biking, the claim would have been denied. This is because the cause (mountain biking) was NOT an accident, and the Accidental Means definition requires the cause and injury to both be accidental.

2. SICKNESS

A sickness is an illness that occurs within the body and manifests over time. The flu, cancer, heart disease and diabetes are all considered sicknesses and outlined through an insurer's Morbidity Table.

3. COMPREHENSIVE VS. LIMITED PLANS

Comprehensive plans are what most people consider "health insurance", these are written as **HMO's, PPO's** and **POS** plans; generally insuring everything including accidents and sicknesses with certain exclusions.

Limited Plans also known as "supplemental", insure specific perils and do not require exclusions. Limited plans must state "This is a limited policy" on the front page. Dental, Vision, Prescription Drugs, Critical Illness, Accident Only policies, etc. are all limited insurance policies

B. LIMITED POLICIES
1. ACCIDENT ONLY & ACCIDENTAL DEATH & DISMEMBERMENT

Accident only insurance indemnifies against bodily injury, death, disability, or in some cases hospital and medical care resulting from an **accident, NOT sickness**. IE: An accidental death policy with a $20,000 death benefit would pay $20,000 if death occurred by plane crash, but zero if the death occurred by cancer. Accident polices may also pay **double or triple indemnity** (2x or 3x the benefit) if it's listed within the policy.

a. ACCIDENTAL DEATH AND DISMEMBERMENT (AD&D)

AD&D policies are limited forms of life insurance which also include dismemberment (loss of limb or eyesight) benefits. These policies only pay out if the below are due to an **accident**:

- **Principal Amount:** The full amount of the policy payable in certain events.
    a. Death or full insanity
    b. Loss of two or more limbs (hands, feet, legs, arms)
    c. Loss of eyesight
- **Capital Sum:** A percentage of the principal sum, only payable in the event one limb is lost. Fingers and toes are not considered limbs, zero would be paid for the loss of a finger.

* Connor has a $100,000 principle sum for his accidental death & dismemberment policy. Connor was involved in a motorcycle accident and loses 2 toes, a hand and is also deaf from his injuries. Connor's policy will pay zero for the loss of toes and deafness, but will pay a percentage of the $100,000 for the loss of his hand.

2. TRAVEL INSURANCE

Covers the insured while traveling to other countries, can cover costs such as medical evacuation or higher medical costs. The insured must be a **fare paying passenger on a common carrier** (airplane, cruise etc.) to be covered while going to another country.

3. DREAD DISEASE (CRITICAL ILLNESS) POLICIES

This limited policy will provide coverage for certain costs arising from specified illnesses such as **cancer, heart disease and diabetes**. Most comprehensive plans (HMO, PPO, POS) will insure these diseases as well, but the critical illness policy may provide the insured a higher level of care.

4. HOSPITAL INDEMNITY

Hospital indemnity plans pay a set amount – per day, per week, per month, or per visit – if the insured is confined in a hospital. This policy pays directly to the insured, not the hospital, and the insured can use the benefits for however they wish. The policy is used to offset the time lost to the insured because of hospital **admittance**, and typically the insureds apply the payments toward their major medical health insurance deductibles but they are not required to. Sometimes hospital indemnity polices have an **elimination period**, which is a waiting period before benefits begin.

* Chris has a hospital indemnity plan paying $200 per day he is admitted to the hospital. Chris was admitted to the hospital on Monday and released on Friday (5 days) while incurring $50/day in expenses from the hospital. Chris's hospital indemnity policy paid $1,000 directly to him, if he wishes to use it toward his medical cost of care he may, but he decided to purchase a new TV instead because his major medical insurance will pay the hospital for the cost of care.

5. CREDIT DISABILITY

Disability insurance to pay off loan balances in the event a debtor becomes disabled; the benefits would be paid to the creditor.

6. PRESCRIPTION DRUGS INSURANCE

Usually attached to comprehensive insurance, prescription drugs allow the insured to pay a **co-payment** for drugs and the insurer pays the remainder. Prescription drugs can be ordered in 30-, 60- and 90-day supplies; the insured can usually purchase the 90 supplies online at discount. Over-the-counter; experimental; and illegal drugs are not covered by Prescription drug insurance.

7. VISION INSURANCE

Covers eye glasses, contacts, frames, annual checkups and in some circumstances, even **hearing aids**. Vision insurance does **NOT** cover laser eye surgery currently.

8. BLANKET INSURANCE (TEAMS, PASSENGERS, OTHER)

Blanket policies can be written to cover medical expense, accidental death, vision insurance and more; these blanket policies cover everybody without knowing their names and do not need to list them on the policy that are engaged in an activity, such as sports teams, day cares, common carriers (airplanes).

* Harbers Lacrosse team requires all members to have medical insurance prior to joining the team. Out of the 20 team members, only 8 children had medical insurance through their parents. Coach Harber purchased a 12-person Blanket Medical policy covering the sport of lacrosse and then charged each parent $50 to allow their children on the team, which covered the costs of the health plan. The insurer did not need to know the names of the children, only the number of people.

9. DENTAL INSURANCE

Dental insurance provides for **two free checkups** a year, **one free x-ray** every two years and one free denture every **5 years.** The next chapter has more information on dental insurance

10. BASIC MEDICAL EXPENSE POLICIES

In an a-la-carte fashion, a person may purchase basic policies, picking and choosing which plans they would like. These plans may supplement comprehensive care insurance:

1. **Basic Hospital:** Covers room and board for hospital stays
2. **Basic Surgery:** Covers surgeon services and **anesthesiologists'** costs
3. **Basic Physicians:** Covers regular office visits and non-surgical physician costs in a hospital setting
4. **Basic Nurses:** Private duty nursing care
5. **Convalescent Care:** Skilled nursing facility expenses

These plans are lower cost than comprehensive care policies and are provided on a first dollar basis, meaning the insurer will pay first when a claim arises **up to the amount listed in the policy.**

C. COMMON EXCLUSIONS (THINGS NOT COVERED)

Exclusions are items listed which are NOT covered under the policy; some items may have time limits, such as 2-year exclusion, or some items may be excluded forever. The insurer typically attaches an exclusion form stating which are not covered in any circumstance (such as committing a **felony**).

1. PRE-EXISTING CONDITIONS

Pre-existing conditions are a condition an insured has sought medical treatment for within 6 months prior to the inception of a policy. Pre-existing's are excluded for **1 year** on group policies and **2 years** on individual insurance. These laws were updated in 2014; please see Patient Protection and Affordable Care Act (PPACA) for more details.

2. SELF-INFLICTED INJURIES

Injuries an insured inflicts intentionally are excluded under health insurance policies. Negligence is covered; as negligence is defined: "failure to act as a reasonable prudent person would have"; negligence is not an intentional injury, but failing to act properly. The exclusion of self-inflicted injuries protects the insurer from higher claims and encouraging people to harm themselves'. For life insurance policies, suicide is only excluded within the first 2 years of a policy after issuance.

3. WAR

Private insurance does not cover military personnel because it is catastrophic, they receive **Tri-Care**.

4. ELECTIVE COSMETIC SURGERY & EXPERIMENTAL

Elective Surgeries such as: facelifts, tummy tucks, Botox, are exclude; however, if the surgery is needed due to a **birth defect** (cleft lip, and others) or result of an injury (face burned in fire), those would be covered due to the rule of indemnity. **Experimental** procedures are also NOT covered.

5. OTHER INSURANCE EXCLUSIONS

Benefits covered by Workers Compensation, Auto policies, Government programs etc. would be excluded by private insurers. The **Coordination of Benefits clause** (shown later) will decide how each plan reacts; this is to prevent insureds from profiting off multiple insurance policies.

D. MARKETING REQUIREMENTS:
1. ADVERTISING

The **insurer** is ultimately responsible for all advertising, even if an outside firm is hired to produce that advertisement. The insurer is obligated to review all advertisements and ensure all advertisements and Sales Presentations are **truthful, clear, and accurate.**

2. OUTLINE OF COVERAGE

The Outline of Coverage is required only with **health insurance** policies which provides for full and fair disclosure, acts as simply as it sounds, as an outline of coverage. This document must be given at either the **time of application** for Medicare Supplement & Long-Term Care policies.

3. FIELD UNDERWRITING

The **producer** is known as the **field underwriter**, acting as the eyes and ears of the insurer on the frontline. As a field underwriter the producer may see things that cannot be found just through an application; the producers' job is to document this information and **help lower adverse selection.**

4. INFORMATION DISCLOSURE

Information obtained through field underwriting may only be given to outside parties, such as insurance officials; law enforcement; claims underwriters; lienholders; mortgagees or other authority figures who may have an interest in the insured. Any other disclosures must receive **written authorization** from the insured; confidential information **may NOT be used for marketing purposes.**

5. THE APPLICATION

The application (app) form used by the insurer must be approved by the **commissioner**, prior to being used in in the field by the producer. It is the **producers'** job to ask the questions and complete the application in **black ink** without using white out. Mistakes are often made, which the producer may use "scratch-out and initial", where the producer will put **one line** through a mistake, fill in the correct answer and have the **insured initial** the correction. However, best practice would always be to get a new application, but changes to the app may still be made.

> ➢ **Part 1 (General Information):** Consists of the applicants' name, address, coverage information, sex, marital status, credit and other information.
> ➢ **Part 2 (Medical Information):** Height, Weight, Medical History and Ancestry (Family history) will be included here.
> ➢ **Part 3 (Agent/Producers Report):** The agent will list their thoughts about the insured, including any adverse information seen as a field underwriter. The producers report will also list whether or not this is a replacement policy and the applicants' income.

The producer, insured and policyowner all must sign Part 1 and Part 2 of the application; **beneficiaries do not need to sign the application.** The insured will receive a copy of Part 1 and Part 2, which will become part of the **entire contract.** However, the producers report does **NOT** become part of the contract, the insured will not receive a copy of Part 3.

Applications should always be completed in person and delivered in person, to ensure the agent may answer any questions the applicant has. However, most agents' mistakes occur at the time of application or delivery; luckily agents are required to have **Errors and Omissions (E&O) insurance**, to protect them against any negligent mistakes; E&O is insurance for insurance agents.

E. UNDERWRITING

Underwriting is process of checking applications and utilizing **classification of risks,** and is performed by an employee of the insurer known as an underwriter. The underwriter works very closely with the producer and the two share information freely to ensure the timely issuance of policies, but only the **underwriter sets premium prices and issues policies.**

MEDICAL UNDERWRITING:

The first step in the underwriting process is to ensure the application is completed fully and to ensure the applicant and insured have an insurable interest in each other. Upon reviewing the medical history on the application, the underwriter may request the **producer** obtain an **Attending Physicians Statement**, which will have the applicants' physician provide a detailed report on any current medical conditions.

The underwriter may also pull the insureds medical records from the **Medical Information Bureau (MIB),** which is a *non-profit* organization that shares claims and application information. 98% of all health insurers and 80% of all life insurers are members of the MIB; each time a person applies for insurance, their application is stored at the MIB for up to 7 years. The *underwriter, producer* and *insured* are all able to see MIB report to ensure its accuracy; there is a **method** to fix any incorrect information in the MIB report and the underwriter cannot decline a risk solely on the report, information must be verified. The MIB does not actually have health insurance information, it only has the **application information** and the MIB reports are **NEVER** shared with the Department of Insurance.

Many insurance applications also require a medical exam, HIV testing and lab reports, which primarily consist of blood and urine and must be consented by the insured. The exams are paid for by the *insurer* and may only be performed by a doctor, nurse or paramedic; the agent does not perform the medical exam. If HIV or AIDS are found, the insurer must notify the applicant within 15 days, the insurer must notify the state's Department of Health and the medical exams are **not forwarded to the MIB.**

Even though the underwriter has many tools to at their disposal, there are quite a few factors that are deemed as **Unfair Discrimination**, such as: *marital status, race, national original, sexual preference, number of children, domestic violence* and other non-factors.

CLASSIFICATIONS OF RISKS (RISK CLASSIFICATION)

After the underwriter has reviewed all pertinent information, they must begin to classify the risk to determine premium prices. There are four main classifications of risks.

- **Preferred Risks** will receive a discount on their premiums, typically this is a risk that is in the correct height and weight proportions with little to no medical problems and is a non-smoker.
- **Standard Risks** are representative of the average person; the standard risk is the insurers' *base rate* and is not rated-up or rated down.
- **Substandard Risks** typically have medical issues and receive a *rated-up* (increased) premium.
- **Declined Risks** will not receive an insurance policy; there are many instances of being declined, such as no insurable interest, extremely high medical issues, too old or too young.

F. POLICY REPLACEMENT

Frequently when an insured is obtaining a new insurance policy, they may be doing so to replace an existing one. It is very important for the agent to determine whether or not it is a replacement policy and if replacing the policy, the agent should always **place the new policy in force, then cancel the existing policy ensuring it is done on the same day.** Policy replacement is also strictly and heavily regulated to ensure that the customer is making the replacement in their best interest, and it is the **agents' job** to determine whether or not the replacement is suitable for the potential insured

Many factors need to be assessed before making the replacement; **primarily pre-existing conditions**, as the new policy may not cover everything the old policy did; also, there may be certain probationary periods (30, 60, 90 days) for sicknesses where the coverage will only cover accidents.

Premiums will also likely change when performing a replacement of a policy due to new underwriting considerations.

G. SPECIALIZED RISK

A specialized risk policy insures extreme or high-risk situations or items for people who would normally be excluded. Pilots, Actors, Football & Sports Athletes, Models, Singers etc. may receive a specialized risk policy to provide protection for their field.

Pilots typically receive an exclusion called the **Aviation Exclusion**, which allows a policy to be issued with the same premiums, but excludes any death/injury due to piloting an aircraft.

Life, Accident & Health Exam Study Book | TX

PRACTICE QUESTIONS FOR HEALTH INSURANCE BASICS

1. K has a hospital indemnity policy paying $7,000 per week of hospitalization. K is hospitalized for a $2,500 surgery on Monday, upon which her surgeon clears her for release on Saturday. When K is released, how much will her policy pay?
   a. $7,000
   b. $4,500
   c. $2,500
   d. $0

2. Prescription Drugs will NOT cover which of the following?
   a. Cancer treatment drugs
   b. Chronic Illness drugs
   c. Experimental Drugs
   d. Allergy Drugs

3. Which of the following would be covered under a basic hospital & surgery policy?
   a. Annual checkups and blood-work
   b. Outpatient rehabilitation after a lung transplant
   c. Anesthesiologist costs for an appendectomy
   d. In-patient IV fluids for dehydration

4. A hospital indemnity policy may be purchased on all-of-the following basis EXCEPT:
   a. Per year
   b. Per month
   c. Per day
   d. Per week

5. A blanket insurance policy may be best described as:
   a. A comprehensive health insurance policy covering all needs
   b. A limited health insurance policy covering people engaged in a specific activity
   c. An integrated health insurance policy combining nursing and surgical care
   d. A combination plan providing blanket social health care needs funded through taxes

6. G has a health insurance policy scheduled to renew on Friday at a higher rate. G contacts an agent who decides to replace his current policy with a lower cost one. On what day should G's agent place his new policy in force?
   a. Friday
   b. Thursday
   c. Saturday
   d. Never, the new policy is worse than the old

7. An accidental death & dismemberment policy will pay the principal sum for all of the following, EXCEPT:
a. Death
b. Deafness
c. Loss of eyesight
d. Loss of an arm and a leg

8. An outline of coverage would be given for which of the following policies, and when?
a. Medicare Supplement, at the time of application
b. Whole life, at the time of application
c. Long Term Care, at the time of delivery
d. Adjustable life, at the time of delivery

9. The process of underwriting where risks are placed into categories for rating purposes is known as?
a. Underwriting Review
b. Premium Risk Rating
c. Classification of Risks
d. Medical Information Bureau

10. Accidental Bodily Injury is best described as:
a. An unforeseen and unintended incident
b. When only the injury is unforeseen and unintended
c. When only the cause is unforeseen and unintended
d. When the cause and injury are both accidental

CHAPTER 3: DENTAL INSURANCE

In the previous chapter we learned that HMOs are limited networks and PPOs provide the insured to choose any provider they wish; dental insurance may also be written as HMO and DPO (Dental Provider Organization) networks, but dental insurance is still a limited line of insurance which only pertains to the treatment of teeth. The premiums for dental insurance vary from $15-$50 per month, with the lower plans having further limitations on care than the more expensive policies.

Included with the dental policy will be a **Benefit Schedule,** which will outline how much the policy will cover for a specific procedure. The Benefit Schedule prices are designed around the **Usual, Customary & Reasonable** costs that the providers are charging in the geographical area of the insured. This allows a person to know how much each procedure will cost prior to care; but sometimes a **Pre-Determination of Benefits** may be required prior to treatment if the procedure is more in-depth. These two documents allow the insured and provider to accurately judge costs before endeavoring into a procedure.

1. LEVELS OF CARE

Dental insurance provides for 3 classes of care:

1. **Preventative Care (Class 1):** Care is provided with no deductible or coinsurance and provides for these services:
    a. **Annual Checkups:** Two scheduled doctor visits each year for free.
    b. **X-Rays:** One bitewing x-ray every two years as preventative care.
    c. **Fluoride Treatments:** As preventative maintenance to build up enamel

2. **Basic Services (Class 2):** There is a 20% coinsurance requirement for basic services under dental.
    a. **Restorative Care:** Dental work to restore the teeth, such as fillings
    b. **Oral Surgery:** Oral Surgery is included under **basic** services providing for wisdom teeth removal and dental implants
    c. **Periodontics:** Diseases affecting the teeth and gum, such as gingivitis

3. **Major Services (Class 3):** These services are considered major because there are added costs to create the hardware involved in treating the problem. There is a 50% coinsurance for major services because of the increased cost of the hardware.
    a. **Prosthodontics:** The addition of synthetic teeth, such as Dentures and Bridgework to simulate the use of normal teeth. One denture may be provided for every **5 years.**
    b. **Orthodontics:** Aligning of the teeth using hardware such as braces, retainers, and other devices
    c. **Endodontics:** The treatment of dental pulp (root canals) using inlayed **crowns.**

2. DEDUCTIBLES & COINSURANCE

Dental plans vary by deductibles and coinsurance, primarily whether it is based off an existing group (employer sponsored) plan or purchased as a stand-alone individual plan.

- **Stand-Alone Plans:** The dental plan is completely separate from any other insurance, and the dental plan will have its own specific deductibles and coinsurance.
- **Integrated Plans:** Deductibles and coinsurance are tied to a comprehensive health plan; where there is only one deductible and coinsurance for comprehensive health and dental.

Along with integrated and stand-alone; dental insurance is also either Scheduled or Non-Scheduled:

- **Scheduled:** There is a set price for each procedure the insured will pay, which is outlined in the Benefit Schedule. Most likely Scheduled plans have NO deductibles and NO coinsurance because there is a set price they pay per service.
- **Non-Scheduled:** Services are subjected to Deductibles and Coinsurance, and the policy may have a maximum yearly limit. The insured has more choice of providers, but may use up their limit quickly if it is too low.

* Blue works for an employer that offers him an integrated non-scheduled dental and medical insurance plan. His overall deductible is $500 and coinsurance of 80/20 with a stop-loss of $1,000. One day Blue is lighting his fireplace and burns his hand, to the tune of a $400 medical bill. Later in the year, Blue visits the dentist and incurs an extra $500 in costs. Since Blue has an integrated plan, he only has $100 left of his deductible and pays coinsurance of 20% on the remaining $400 of his dental claim; putting his out-of-pocket costs at the dentist at only $180. Blue is thankful he has an integrated dental plan

3. EXCLUSIONS

Dental insurance is considered a limited plan and any level of care not listed in the policy would be excluded, which includes cosmetic dental work

4. DENTAL INDEMNITY

A type of dental plan where the insured may visit ANY dentist they wish, but will have to pay out of pocket for services. After services are rendered, the insured submits a bill to the insurer and is reimbursed for the costs.

PRACTICE QUESTIONS: DENTAL INSURANCE

1. Which of the following is a form of medical health insurance covering the treatment and care of gum disease?
   a. Endodontics
   b. Orthodontics
   c. Periodontics
   d. Oral surgery

2. What is the term that means the replacement of missing teeth with artificial devices, like dentures?
   a. Restorative
   b. Orthodontics
   c. Endodontics
   d. Prosthodontics

3. What level of care is diagnostic and preventive?
   a. Level 1
   b. Level 2
   c. Level 3
   d. Level 4

4. What plan is when benefits are paid on a reasonable and customary basis, and are subject to deductibles and coinsurance?
   a. Scheduled
   b. Primary
   c. Non-scheduled
   d. Secondary

5. Fillings, oral surgery and Periodontics are what type of services?
   a. Major
   b. Basic
   c. Regular
   d. Minor

6. The treatment of the dental pulp within the natural teeth, like a root canal is called:
   a. Endodontics
   b. Orthodontics
   c. Oral surgery
   d. Prosthodontics

7. What type of plan pays benefits from a list of procedures up to an amount shown in a schedule?
   a. Scheduled
   b. Non-scheduled
   c. Serviced
   d. Non-serviced

8. Fillings and crowns are examples of what type of care?
   a. Routine
   b. Diagnostic
   c. Restorative
   d. Preventive

9. The treatment of teeth using braces or appliances is called:
   a. Routine
   b. Orthodontics
   c. Preventive Services
   d. Periodontics

10. Periodic teeth cleaning are which type of treatment?
    a. Restorative
    b. Prosthodontics
    c. Diagnostic and Preventive
    d. Orthodontics

CHAPTER 4: HEALTH INSURANCE PROVISIONS

This chapter is designed to show the show uniform provisions that can be found in almost all health insurance policies. These provisions are usually found after the first two pages of the policy which includes many definitions and also outlines the claims process, coordination of benefits and also how the policy will renew. It will be important in this chapter to remember the exact names of the provisions and also be able to match up a definition to the correct name of the provision.

A. UNIFORM REQUIRED PROVISIONS

These provisions were determined by the NAIC to be uniform across state lines.

1. ENTIRE CONTRACT

The entire contract comprises of the **policy and a copy of the application**; these two items encompass all conditions, benefits, exclusions and consideration on both parties' behalf. Only an **executive officer** of the **insurer** may make changes to the contract, but any changes must be in the benefit of the insured and also have the insureds written consent.

2. TIME LIMIT ON CERTAIN DEFENSES

The Time Limit on Certain Defenses clause sets a two-year time limit from the **issue date** of a policy that an insurer may deny claims or void a policy due to pre-existing conditions. If an insured does not list a pre-existing condition on an application and it is not discovered within the first 2 years of the policy, the insurer **must pay the claim**. Should an insurer discover an intentional and **material misrepresentation** on an application within 2 years of policy inception, the insurer will deny the claim, void the policy and refund premium to the policyowner.

* Amy was just diagnosed with Hepatitis C, but does not have insurance. Upon leaving the physicians' office, she heads down the street to an insurance agency and applies for health insurance. On Amy's application she does not state she has any illnesses and during underwriting nothing is found because she was just diagnosed, so the policy is issued. As long as Amy keeps the policy for exactly two years, Hepatitis C will be covered; but if she files a claim within the first two years, the insurer would discover the misrepresentation on the application and void the policy.

3. GRACE PERIOD

The grace period helps **prevent the unintentional lapse** of a policy by giving an insured extra time to make their premium payment after the due date. The insured is still covered during the grace period and if there are any claims, the claim benefit will be **reduced by any unpaid premium**. The grace period for policies paid on a weekly basis is 7 days, monthly basis 10 days and **annual, semi-annual, and quarterly have a 31-day period.**

* Radu has an accidental death policy due on January 1st of every year; unfortunately, this year Radu is on a cruise and forgets to pay his premium. On January 15th, Radu falls overboard on the cruise and dies from the accident. The insurer pays his death benefit, but will reduce it by 15 days' worth of premiums.

4. REINSTATEMENT – 45 Days

If a policy has lapsed due to nonpayment, the insured will have **45 days** to reinstate the policy. The insured will have to pay the back premiums to reinstate, but the policy will go back to its original status. **Accidents** will be **covered immediately;** Sickness will have a **10-day** waiting period. Sometimes the insurer requests new medical underwriting during reinstatement to prove insurability.

* Jake has a Major Medical HMO that lapsed on May 28th due to non-payment. On June 5th, Jake enters his agent's office and reinstates the policy by submitting his past premiums. On June 8th, when Jake submits a claim for the flu, it is declined due to the 10-day sickness waiting period; had it been an accident, the claim would have been paid.

5. NOTICE OF CLAIM – 20 Days

After an accident or sickness, if the insured intends to file a claim on their policy, they will have **20 days,** or within a reasonable time, to notify the insurer of the incident. Normally the physician is the one to make notice, however it is the insureds responsibility. Notification to an insurer can be done by phone, e-mail, mail and even notifying the agent will satisfy the requirement.

* Kim had a claim for an accident on December 2nd; she will have until December 22nd to notify the insurance company of that claim. If she does not notify them, the claim could possibly be declined.

6. CLAIM FORMS – 15 Days

Upon receiving notification, the insurer will have **15 days** to provide the insured with a claims form, this claims form will **act as proof of loss** that the insured will need to complete and submit to the insurer.

7. PROOF OF LOSS – 90 Days

The claims form will act as **written** proof of loss and must be submitted to an insurer within **90 days** with a maximum of up to 1 year in certain circumstances. Disability insurance policies may have to file proof of loss every 6 months. If no claims form is provided to the insured, they may submit proof of loss in any way possible as long as it is **written,** even a napkin will suffice. Claims cannot be denied if the insurer did not present the insured with a claims form. Disability policies file every 6 months.

* Adrian had a claim on January 1st and notified the insurer on the same date. The insurer had 15 days to send her the claims form, but the mail truck crashed in a Blizzard, so Adrian never received the form. Regardless of not having the claims form, Adrian will have until April 1st (90 days) to submit signed sworn written proof of loss. It would be preferred to fill out the information on a claims form, but she could write proof of loss on anything she has available.

8. TIME OF PAYMENT OF CLAIMS

After the insurer receives written proof of loss, claims are supposed to be paid **immediately**. Otherwise, claims must be paid within a **30-day** time-frame; especially disability policies. However, some states (Texas) have increased this to a 60-day time-frame to give insurers extra time.

Life, Accident & Health Exam Study Book | TX

The Time Payment of Claims clause allows an insurer to **investigate** a claim to determine its legitimacy; they may reinvestigate at a later date as well.

* Lisa died on November 1st due to a suspicious death. The insurer was supposed to pay immediately, but her insurer will have 60 days to investigate and either decide to pay the claim or deny it by January 1st. If the insurer delays the ruling past January 1st that would be Unfair Claims Settlement practices.

9. PHYSICAL EXAMINATION AND AUTOPSY

Most insurers will require the applicant to go through a physical examination, including blood-work, prior to issuing the policy. After the policy is issued, if the applicant dies, the insurer (in most states) may perform an autopsy **as often as reasonably necessary** unless prohibited by state law. The **insurer** will pay for exams and autopsies at **their own expense**

10. PAYMENT OF CLAIMS – Who gets paid the claim

This clause designates to whom the insurer will pay claims to; in most Medical Expense policies, the benefits are paid directly to the physician or hospital. However, in Accident, Disability and Indemnity policies, the benefits normally are paid to the insured. If the insured is deceased, the benefits will go to the next beneficiary (usually family/relatives) and if the beneficiary predeceases the insured or **no beneficiary** is listed, the payments will go to the **estate**. Many states also include a **facility of payments clause** which provides for **$3,000** in emergency payments.

11. LEGAL ACTIONS

The policyowner cannot sue an insurer within the first 60 days of a claim, after the 60 days the policyowner has up to **3 years** to bring a suit; this is due to the **statute of limitations.**

* Ronin had a claim on April 20th 2014 and his insurer denied the claim immediately. He cannot bring a lawsuit until June 20th due to the Legal Actions clause and will only have until April 20th 2017 to file.

12. CHANGE OF BENEFICIARY

The **policyowner** uses a change of beneficiary form to change the beneficiary on a Life/Accident policy.

13. CANCELLATION OF POLICY

The insured may cancel their policy at any point due to the unilateral nature of insurance; if the insured initiates the cancellation, they may be subject to a cancellation fee, and this is known as **short-rate** cancellation. In certain circumstances, the insurer may cancel a policy (normally non-payment of premium); if the insurer terminates the policy, they must give the policyowner at least **10 days'** notice and the policy will cancel on a **pro-rata**, sometimes known as pro-rated, basis.

* Karen has a $1000/year disability policy that she has paid up for the entire year on January 1st. Halfway through the year on July 1st, Karen decides she no longer needs the policy and decides to cancel. Her insurer will refund her $500; however, since Karen initiated the cancellation, the insurer charges a short-rate cancellation fee of $100, making her total refund only $400. If the insurer had cancelled the policy instead of Karen, it would be done as "pro-rata" which has no fee.

B. UNIFORM OPTIONAL PROVISIONS

The previous provisions were required to be listed in all health policies nationwide, the next provisions are **optional**; however, most insurers include them in their policies.

1. CHANGE OF OCCUPATION

The occupation of an insured is a very important factor in determining the price of health policies. Should an insured change to a more hazardous occupation, the benefits of the policy would be reduced on a pro-rated amount. If they change to a less hazardous occupation, premium may be reduced as well.

2. MISSTATEMENT OF AGE

Sometimes age is entered incorrectly on an application, or an insured may lie about their age to receive a lower premium for the policy. If the age on the policy is incorrect, the benefits will still be paid, however they will be adjusted to that of the correct age.

* Fred, age 55, applies for life insurance but misstates his age on his application as 45 to receive a lower rate. Using the age 45, he is able to purchase $100,000 of insurance at a rate of $100/month. Upon Fred's death, the insurer will receive the death certificate, discover the misstatement and adjust his benefits to that of the correct age. At the correct age of 55, the $100 would have only purchased $50,000 in insurance which is all his family would receive.

3. COORDINATION OF BENEFITS – PRIMARY AND EXCESS

The COB clause will determine which insurer is to pay a claim in the event there are multiple policies, normally in a husband-and-wife situation where they each have separate plans but list the other as a dependent, essentially having two policies on each. This clause will determine which plan is **primary** and which plan is **excess**. In the event both parents add the child as a dependent, the **birthday rule** is used for the child; stating whichever parents' birthday comes first in the year is primary. Note, it is not the age of the parent but the birthday that matters. If a person has **Workers Compensation**, all claims must be filed with Workers Comp as primary. Private insurance will DENY all claims until WC has paid out its benefits first. This clause **prevents insureds** from collecting under multiple insurance policies and protects the insurers.

* Trey, born May 22nd; and Elsa, born December 11th, have a child named Bethany listed as a dependent on both of their health insurance policies. When Bethany goes to the doctor, the parents present both insurance cards for payment. When the claim is processed, Trey's policy will be primary because his birthday is first in the year; anything that Treys' policy does not cover, Elsa's plan will cover as excess.

4. INSURANCE WITH OTHER INSURERS

If an insured has multiple policies with other insurers; the policies work on a **pro-rata** expense incurred basis. This prevents double payment of claims and protects the **insurer.**

5. RELATIONSHIP OF EARNINGS TO INSURANCE

A provision used for **disability** insurance only; stating that when a disability claim is paid the insured may only receive benefits relating to their past **2 years** of income, even if the insured purchased the policy at a higher income.

* Kim purchased a policy 5 years ago when they were earning $100k/year, but when the economy went down, Kim's pay was reduced to $60k/year for the past 2 years. Since her pay was only $60k for the previous two years, 60k is the amount of benefits Kim would receive.

6. UNPAID PREMIUM

If there is any outstanding premium owed, the insurer will reduce the claims by the amount due.

* If John had an accidental death policy with a death benefit of $10,000, which cost him $100 per year, due on May 1st. If John forgets to pay his bill and dies on May 15th, the insurer would still pay the claim because John is in the Grace period; however, the beneficiary would receive $10,000 minus any unpaid premium.

7. INTOXICANTS AND NARCOTICS

An optional provision that states the policy is not liable for losses that occur as a result of the policyholder being intoxicated or taking a narcotic without a physician's supervision.

C. OTHER PROVISIONS
1. FREE LOOK PERIOD (REMORSE CLAUSE)

When a policy is **delivered** to an insured and is found on the **front page** of the policy., they will have **10 days** to return the policy to the insurer and receive a full refund for all of their premiums. This allows the insured to look over the policy and determine if it is suitable for them. The free look period is **30 days** for Medicare Supplement and Long-Term Care policies, and the time of delivery usually occurs when a **delivery receipt** is signed.

* Mary purchased a new health insurance policy on February 10th, the insurer mailed it to Mary's agent on February 22nd and the agent then delivered the policy to Mary on March 2nd. If Mary returns the policy on or before March 12th, she will receive all of her money back.

2. INSURING CLAUSE

Sometimes referred to as the summary or "heart of the policy" the insuring clause will list the **perils** covered, **exclusions**, benefits, person covered and how long coverage is provided for. The insuring clause simply outlines the Who, What, Where, When and Why of the policy. The insuring clause is a very important part of the policy.

3. CONSIDERATION CLAUSE

As learned earlier, the consideration clause is the exchange of monetary value; this is where the insured can find the "promise to pay" and also the premium **payment mode,** which refers to how often the insured will pay their premium (Monthly, Annually, Weekly etc.) and how much premium will be due.

4. RENEWABILITY CLAUSES

Most health insurance policies are written for **1-year periods** then renew into a new term. The below renewability options will describe how different policies renew; more specifically, if the insurer is allowed to increase premiums, or if the insurer has the right to cancel the policy at the end of the term.

✓ These renewability options will be on your test, please understand the differences.

Renewability Options	
Noncancellable:	Insurer may not cancel unless due to nonpayment, and premiums remain the same to age 65 allowing for it to be purchased with a **lump sum.**
Guaranteed Renewable:	Medicare Supplement and Long-Term Care insurance; insurer must renew the policy, but premiums will change each year on a class basis.
Conditional Renewable:	Insurer cannot cancel the policy unless the insured fails to meet the conditions in the policy, such as a small employer with 2-50 employees.
Optional Renewable:	**Specified dates** are listed in the policy when the insurer has the option to increase premiums or cancel the policy.
Cancellable:	Insurer may cancel at any time, as well as the insured; most commonly used for interim coverage during probationary periods.

a. NON-CANCELABLE POLICIES

Disability insurance is generally written as a non-cancelable policy, which states that the insurer **cannot change the premium** and the **insurer also cannot cancel the policy.** These policies generally last until age 65, or longer if the insured can prove they still have full-time employment. Since the premiums remain the same during this policy, the insured is able to pay off the entire policy in full if they are requesting coverage until a specific age such as, 65.

b. GUARANTEED RENEWABLE

Medicare Supplement, Long Term Care and most health insurance policies (See: PPACA), are written with the guaranteed renewability option. The **insurer cannot cancel the policy** and the **premiums may change**; however, the premiums will not change for "individuals", the insurer may only raise rates on a **class basis**. These policies must at least renew until age 50, and if issued past age 54, the policies must renew for at least 5 years.

* Tracy has an individual Long Term Care plan which she has been paying $150 per month for the last 11 months. When the policy renewed, her new premium was raised to $200 per month. Even though Tracy did not have a claim, the insurer can raise rates on any class of people (such as preferred); however, the insurer cannot cancel this policy unless Tracy does not pay her bill.

c. CONDITIONALLY RENEWABLE

Small employer (2-50 employees) plans are written on the conditional renewability option. Under conditional renewability, the insured needs to meet certain conditions in order to renew; such as staying below 50 employees, or they would no longer be considered a small employer.

d. OPTIONALLY RENEWABLE

The insurer and the insured may cancel this type of policy at any time; however, the insurer may only cancel policies on **specified contract dates**, such as premium due dates and anniversary dates. The insurer also has the right to increase premiums on those dates; this renewability option is best described as "The insurer has the option" to renew or increase premiums. All individual health insurance policies were optionally renewable until 2011, when PPACA was enacted; now all individual health policies are guaranteed renewable

* Jesus has an optional renewable policy with a specified date of January 1st. For the past 5 years, Jesus's insurer allowed the policy to renew, but also increased premiums by 4%. On the 6th year, Jesus was in the hospital for multiple cancer surgeries and chemotherapy; upon the next January 1st, the insurer decided to cancel Jesus's health policy.

e. CANCELLABLE, NON-RENEWABLE, PERIOD OF TIME, INTERIM– SHORT TERM

Cancellable policies are usually short-term, interim, coverage that can be purchased while an insured is waiting for their **probationary period** to pass at a new employer. The **insured cannot renew** the policy and the insurer may cancel this policy **at any time**; however, 30 **days' notice** must be given if the insurer decides to cancel this policy.

* John worked at ABC warehouse for 5 years and was covered by his group health plan for 4 of those years. John found a better job at XYZ warehouse and starts on Monday; unfortunately, John's benefits at XYZ would not begin until his 90-day probationary period is satisfied. John can purchase a cancelable/nonrenewable policy to cover the gap of 90 days for interim coverage.

> ✓ The **insured** may cancel any policy at any time, but the above renewability options state whether the insurer has the right to cancel a policy for anything other than fraud or non-payment of premiums.

5. INTEREST ON DELAYED CLAIMS

If a claim is not paid within 15 days after receiving proof of loss, the insurer must pay interest to the insured for any delays. The insurer will go by the current interest rate, typically based off T-bills.

6. MILITARY SUSPENSE

Many health policies will be suspended while an insured is actively serving in the military. Premiums are typically reduced to below $10 and the policy may be resumed when the insured leaves active military service.

7. CONFORMITY OF STATE STATUTES

An optional provision that allows the policy to automatically update for state laws.

8. ILLEGAL OCCUPATION

The insurer will pay zero benefits for an insured engaged in commitment of a **felony**. If the insured is trying to stop, or prevent a crime, then the claim may be paid; but not if the insured is the actual offender.

PRACTICE QUESTIONS: HEALTH INSURANCE PROVISIONS

1. Which renewability option is able to be purchased with a single lump sum payment for the longest period of time?
   a. Guaranteed Renewable
   b. Noncancellable
   c. Optional Renewable
   d. Conditional Renewable

2. All of the following are reasons the Legal Actions clause is limited to 3 years, EXCEPT:
   a. Statute of limitations
   b. Prevent catastrophic lawsuits
   c. Broaden an insurer's exposure to loss
   d. Prevent nuisance lawsuits

3. An insured has how long to submit proof of loss, and upon which form would it be completed?
   a. 15 days, claims form
   b. 20 days, proof of loss form
   c. 60 days, proof of loss form
   d. 90 days, claims form

4. Which of the following clauses dictates an insurer has 60 days to decide whether or not to remit payment of a claim?
   a. Payment of Claims
   b. Time Limit on Certain Defenses
   c. Coordination of Benefits
   d. Time Payment of Claims

5. M has a bad back; when applying for disability insurance, M does not disclose her pre-existing condition. The policy is issued, and four years M files a claim due to her bad back; under the Time Limit of Certain defenses clause, which of the following would most likely occur?
   a. The claim is denied
   b. The claim is denied and premiums refunded
   c. The claim is paid fully
   d. The claim is paid at reduced benefits

6. What is the purpose of the Coordination of Benefits clause?
   a. To determine which physician will be paid in the event of a claim
   b. To determine which policy will pay in the event of a claim
   c. To determine which insured will be paid in the event of a claim
   d. To determine the amount of time an insurer has to pay a claim

7. Which of the following portions of the policy will list the covered perils?
a. Payment of Claims
b. Consideration Clause
c. Insuring Clause
d. Notice of Claims

8. The insurance with other insurers, and insurance with this insurer clauses, protect which party in an insurance contract?
a. The insured
b. The insurer
c. The insurer and the insured
d. The producer

9. V has a comprehensive health insurance policy that lapsed on February 1st. When V went into her health insurance agent's office on May 1st to pay her policy and file a claim for the flu; how would the insurer most likely handle this claim?
a. Pay the claim
b. Pay the claim but request the insured submit proof of loss
c. Accept the premium, but deny the claim due to the 10-day sickness waiting period
d. Deny the claim and ask for a new application due to being past the reinstatement period.

10. Where can the insured find the birthday rule in their policy?
a. Coordination of Benefits Clause
b. Insuring Clause
c. Renewability Clause
d. Payment of Claims Clause

10. Where can the insured find the exclusions in their policy?
a. Coordination of Benefits Clause
b. Insuring Clause
c. Renewability Clause
d. Payment of Claims Clause

CHAPTER 5: DISABILITY INCOME INSURANCE

It is estimated that one out of three people in the United States will become disabled for at least 6 months in their lifetime. Disability insurance is a health insurance policy that is used to replace **lost income** in the event that an injury or sickness adversely affects the insured's ability to perform their job. Disability policies can be very expensive depending on the level of income; naturally an insurer provides many options that an insured may choose from to personalize the policy for themselves and their circumstances.

A. INDIVIDUAL DISABILITY POLICIES

Individual policies are paid for by the insured themselves with after tax dollars that are **not tax-deductible**; this allows for disability benefits to be received tax-free. Benefits are typically 60% of a person's salary.

1. TIME PAYMENT OF CLAIMS FOR DISABILITY AND BENEFIT PERIOD

At the time of purchase, the insured chooses a benefit period, which is how long they will receive income; **short term** disability will provide benefits for **0-2 years**, **long term** disability provides benefits **for 2 or more years**, usually until **age 65**. As long as the insured is not retired, they will receive benefits with a qualifying disability, even if the insured is temporarily unemployed. Once the insured qualifies as disabled, the insurer will be required by law to pay disability claims on a **monthly (30 day) basis** and the benefits will be **tax-free** for individual disability policies.

2. ELIMINATION (WAITING) PERIOD

Disability insurance policies have an elimination period, working very similar to a deductible, but measured in **days**. Elimination periods are an amount of time the insured must be disabled before benefits begin and the insured will **never be paid during the elimination period.** Elimination periods are a method of adverse selection, helping to prevent fraud. The policyowner may choose the length of the elimination period, the longer the elimination period, the lower the premiums.

*John purchased a disability policy with a 7-day elimination period for accidents and 30-day elimination period for sickness. If John is involved in a car accident that renders him disabled for 15 days; John would only receive 8 days' worth of income payments. The first 7 days he received nothing due to his elimination period for accidents.

3. INJURY AND SICKNESS

Disability policies may cover accidents and sicknesses. Accident claims tend to have higher benefits paid than sickness claims. There are three main definitions for accidents:

1. **Accident:** Unforeseen and unintended incident.
2. **Accidental Bodily Injury:** Only injury must be proved to be unforeseen and unintended.
3. **Accidental Bodily Means:** Must prove the cause and injury are both accidental.

Accidental Bodily Injury is the standard for most disability policies and provides a better benefit. If the insured has a pre-existing condition, the insurer typically adds an **Impairment Rider** to exclude that specific condition or body part. No claims would be paid if that body part was the disabling factor.

* Paul is riding on a bus, which has just stopped to let him off. Paul decides to leap off the bus, however in doing so, he breaks his ankle. In this scenario, Accidental Bodily Injury would pay the claim because the leap (cause) was not an accident, but only the injury (ankle) was accidental. If the insurer had used Accidental Means, the claim would have been denied because the cause (leaping) was not an accident.

a. RECURRENT DISABILITIES

When added in disability policies, this provision allows the insured to only go through one medical exam for **chronic injuries/illnesses.** The insured can move fluidly between disability income and returning to work without having to return to the doctor each time and re-qualifying each time. This is sometimes known as the "return-to-work" clause and helps the insurer minimize payments by allowing the insured to try their best to return to work. Chronic illnesses reoccur within a 12-month period.

* Heidi was bending down at work when she injured her neck; she visited the doctor who qualified her as disabled. Heidi receives income payments for 6 months while her neck heals and returns to work on the 7th month. Two weeks later she is bending down again at work and her neck injury reoccurs; in this scenario with recurrent disability, Heidi would not need to return to the doctor and prove she's disabled again, the neck injury would be considered chronic and she would be entitled to benefits.

b. WAIVER OF PREMIUM

As long as the insured is permanently disabled the insured will no longer have to pay premiums. There is usually a **6 month** waiting period before this provision kicks in but they are reimbursed for that time.

c. PARTIAL/RESIDUAL DISABILITY

Encouraging insureds to return back to work is one of the insurers' primary duties after a claim. If an insured is unable to return to work full-time, however they are able to work part-time, the insured may be eligible for **partial/residual** disability benefits; which will provide for the income difference between **full-time and part-time** disability.

* Patty was picking up a box and injures her back, rendering her disabled. To help with pain she has physical therapy 3x per week and is unable to work 40 hours, but can work 28 hours part-time. The Partial/Residual disability provision will pay her for the lost 12 hours of income each week.

4. COORDINATION OF BENEFITS

A person may be entitled to multiple disability insurance benefits, such as Workers Compensation and Social Security Disability. Workers' compensation will always be primary if the person is injured at work, then Social Security Disability is factored in; and finally, private disability insurance will act as **excess** insurance. This reduces the chance an insured is likely to be overpaid for a claim by coordinating with other types of insurance.

a. SOCIAL INSURANCE SUPPLEMENT (SIS)

A rider that may pay the insured benefits while they are waiting for Social Security disability benefits to be paid. S.S.D. has a 5-month waiting period, with benefits being paid on the 6th month, so this rider would pay 6 months income until the insured can receive S.S.D. benefits.

b. OCCUPATIONAL AND NON-OCCUPATIONAL COVERAGE

The applicant will have the choice of which setting they would like to be covered in:

- **Occupational** provides coverage for injuries/illnesses occurring on the job and off the job.
- **Non-Occupational** provides coverage only for illnesses occurring off the job. This definition is best suited for somebody already covered by Workers Compensation.

The occupational definition would require more premiums from the insured, and since Workers Compensation covers on-the-job injuries, there would no need for coverage at work from a disability policy.

5. RIDERS FOR INCREASING BENEFITS

A rider is an extra attachment onto a policy that may change the way the policy works, usually providing a better benefit for the insured. Riders cost money and each works independently from the next.

a. COST OF LIVING ADJUSTMENT (COLA) RIDER

COLA will increase the disability benefits each year at the rate of **inflation**. Inflation is considered the **devaluing of money** which is predicted through the Consumer Price Index (CPI).

* Craig purchased a disability policy with benefits of $100 per month with a COLA rider attached to the policy. Next year inflation is calculated at 4%, so Craig's benefits will be increased to $104 per month, keeping his income competitive with the cost of living increases each year.

b. FUTURE INCREASE OPTION – GUARANTEED INSURAIBILITY

Insuring a younger applicant can be rather difficult when estimating the amount of benefits that will be needed. This rider will allow the insured to begin with a lower benefit amount, however they will have the option to increase benefits **every 3 years,** usually up to age 40, or in certain **life events** (such as marriage, children and home purchases). When the insured increases their benefits, they will **not have to prove insurability again** but they will have to pay **increased premium**.

* Tyson purchased a disability policy at age 24 with benefits a benefit amount of $1,000 per month and the guaranteed insurability rider. Tyson gets married at age 30 and shortly after contracts diabetes; which he then realizes $1,000 per month will not be enough to cover his income and provide his spouse with an adequate quality of life in the event he becomes disabled. Tyson contacts his insurer, utilizes his guaranteed insurability rider, increasing his benefits to $3,000 per month and he does not need to go through a medical exam. His premium increases, but he will pay the standard rate instead of the substandard rate due to diabetes.

c. ANNUAL RENEWABLE TERM RIDER
The Annually Renewable Term Rider attaches a term life insurance policy to the disability policy; which will pay a death benefit in the event an insured dies while the policy is in force.

d. RELATIONSHIP OF EARNINGS TO INSURANCE
States the insureds past 2 years of income will determine their benefits paid out by the policy. Even if the insureds income was higher at the time of purchase, benefits would be reduced to the current income and any overpaid premiums will be returned to them.

* George was a pro football player earning $450,000 per year. George understood his career was extremely hazardous and decided to purchase a disability policy to protect him. George retired from football and took a job in customer service for 5 years earning $60,000 per year. If George becomes disabled, he would receive payments based off $60,000 per year and any overpayment of premium would be refunded to him.

e. CHANGE OF OCCUPATION
The occupation of an insured is a very important factor in determining the price of a disability policy. Should an insured change to a more hazardous occupation, the benefits of the policy would be reduced on a pro-rated amount. If the insured changes to a less hazardous occupation, premium may be reduced.

6. EXTRA DISABILITY BENEFITS
a. REHABILITATION
Disability policies typically offer rehabilitation benefits, such as physical and speech therapy, to try to foster a quicker recovery time and reduce the chance of long-term disabilities.

b. VOCATIONAL TRAINING
Vocational training may be paid by the insurer to re-train the disabled individual into a new job. This is to encourage a disabled person to re-enter the workforce.

c. MEDICAL COSTS
Medical costs may also be refunded to an insured if the costs are associated with repairing an aspect of the disability. Typically, these costs are reimbursed directly to the insured instead of paid to the physician.

7. REFUND PROVISIONS
Disability policies must offer some form of refund options to the insured; many are optional. Should a person pay up a disability policy in full, then die early, the premiums will be refunded to their estate.

* Cole purchased a disability policy at age 30, paying it up to age 65 with a single lump sum payment of $30,000. Unfortunately, Cole dies at age 30; the insurer will refund the unearned premium. Essentially, the insurer only earned 1 year of premium, so Cole's estate will receive 34 years of premium back.

a. RETURN OF PREMIUM

An optional rider that will return 80-100% of all premiums to the policyowner if they keep the policy in force; this rider does cost extra money, but it is an added benefit to the customer.

b. CASH SURRENDER VALUE

Cash Surrender Value must also be offered, which returns premiums to the insured should they cancel the policy early.

8. EXCLUSIONS

Exclusions are excluded for life on disability policies, any disability arising from these acts would be denied by the insurer. Acts of War, Suicide, Self-Inflicted Injuries, Living Overseas and military service are common exclusions.

B. QUALIFYING FOR DISABILITY BENEFITS

In order to qualify for disability benefits, the insured must qualify; and the most **important factor** is **loss of income** arising out of the disability. A physician will perform a medical exam and ask questions to determine whether or not a person qualifies, but specifically whether or not they are able to work. Most disability policies require the insured to stay confined in a home or under a physician's care.

1. OWN OCCUPATION vs. ANY OCCUPATION

A very important factor of disability insurance is the type of job associated with the insured. The insured may choose one of these two disability definitions:

1. **Own Occupation:** A person would be automatically disabled if they were unable to perform their own job, even if they have skills to perform other jobs. This allows **highly skilled** workers to qualify for benefits easier, because they cannot perform their specific job. However, after being unable to perform their job for 2 years, the definition automatically expands to Any Occupation.

2. **Any Occupation (Total Disability):** A person would need to prove they are unable to perform ANY job for which they are **Trained, Educated or Experienced for**. It is much harder to qualify as disabled if the person needs to prove they cannot perform any job related to their field.

3. **Presumptive Disability:** An automatic qualifier listed in most disability policies; should this event happen; the person is automatically disabled. Such as Deafness, Blindness, Loss of limb.

* Peyton is a quarterback for the Denver Broncos and is shopping for a disability policy. Since being a quarterback has a specific skill, Peyton purchases the Own Occupation disability definition within his policy. At the Superbowl, Peyton injures his throwing arm and becomes disabled. Per his disability policy, he is unable to perform his own job, and begins paying him benefits; however, after 2 years, the definition expands into Any Occupation. Since Peyton has training and experience in football and coaching, he is no longer considered disabled and takes a job coaching the Houston Texans.

Life, Accident & Health Exam Study Book | TX

1. KEY-PERSON INSURANCE

Key person insurance is when the business, (the policyowner and beneficiary), purchases life or disability insurance on an employee (the insured); upon the employees' death or disability, the business would receive the benefits. This policy is used **to fund training** of a new employee or to **protect lost income** in the event of the key persons death or disability and may be any type of life insurance and may also be written as a disability insurance policy that pays a **lump sum.**

* Tammy owns a computer software firm with 20 employees and one sales manager which brings in 60% of the company's earnings. Tammy is afraid that if her sales manager dies or becomes disabled, her business will lose a lot of money and it will take a long time to train a new employee. Tammy would purchase Key Person insurance on her sales manager to protect her business.

- ✓ Key person premiums are NOT tax deductible and the benefits are received TAX FREE. The **business is the applicant,** the employee is the insured, the business receives the benefits.

2. BUY-SELL FUNDING (Buy-Out, Sell-Out)

When there are multiple owners in a corporation one of the largest concerns becomes: "Who will take over the business when an owner dies?" Proper planning can help settle the needs of not only the other owners in the corporation, but also the family members of the owners. Buy-sell agreements are contracts that may only be drafted by an **attorney**, and may be funded in four ways: cash on hand, borrowing (a loan), installment payments or typically life insurance.

The buy-sell agreements will state that when one owner dies, their family MUST sell the ownership to the other partners and the partners in the business MUST purchase ownership from the family.

1. **Cross-Purchase plans:** Each partner/owner will purchase a policy on the other owners in the amount of their interest. MOST buy-sell agreements are Cross-Purchase plans.
2. **Entity Purchase plans:** The **business itself** purchases the policies on the owners; and upon an owner's death, the business will receive the funds to purchase the shares from the family members.
3. **Stock Redemption plans:** Only used in stock corporations, the stockholders will purchase the shares of the deceased stockholder at a pre-determined price.
4. **Disability Buy-Out:** Works the same way that life insurance would, except instead of death, the policy will pay out when a partner is "economically dead". Disability buy-outs are typically written as entity purchase plans, not cross-purchase.

- ✓ Payments are all made with a lump sum to the owners and officers of the company.

3. BUSINESS OVERHEAD EXPENSE:

BOE policies are NOT used to sell the company or fund training/protect against income; BOE policies are used **to keep the business running.** This type of policy can pay for **rent, utilities**, employee salaries (not the owners) and other overhead costs. **The premiums are tax deductible and the benefits may be taxable.**

4. SOCIAL SECURITY DISABILITY

Should a worker become disabled prior to age 62, they may be eligible for Social Security Disability, which is a separate trust fund than Social Security; however, both are still funded by the FICA and SECA taxes and still rely on the **accrued credit** method to determine eligibility. After eligibility has been factored in, the insured must prove that they are indeed disabled, by using this definition:

> **S.S. Definition of Disabled:** A person either physically or mentally determined to be disabled and unable to perform substantial or gainful work for the **foreseeable (future) 12 months** or expected earlier death. The work does not have to be in their previous field.

A medical professional at a government facility will determine if the insured is disabled and upon becoming disabled there is a **five-month** waiting period before benefits can begin; the first payment will begin on the 6th month, because benefits are paid retroactively. Should the insured recover, benefits will cease, and if they become disabled again within 5 years, they will not need to satisfy the 5 period again.

Benefits are decided based off an algorithm called the **Primary Insurance Amount (PIA)**; which uses legal citizens highest 35 years of income, subtracting the lowest 5 years, and taking an average of the remaining 30 years. The worker will receive **100%** of their PIA amount, should a person die receiving SSD, their spouse or child may be entitled to only 50% of benefits.

* Cindy is age 57 and was involved in a car accident; the medical doctor determined she was disabled on January 1st and informs her she will not receive benefits for the first 5 months due to the waiting period. Cindy receives her first check on July 1st, but only for the month of June to July, she was not paid for the 5-month waiting period.

If Cindy is feeling well enough to go back to work, she may, but benefits would stop; should her injury reoccur, she may go back on disability **without** having another 5-month waiting period.

PRACTICE QUESTIONS: DISABILITY INCOME INSURANCE

1. T has a disability income policy with a 14-day elimination period for accidents and a 31-day elimination period for sickness. When T falls off a ladder, he files a claim and is disabled for 3 weeks. How long will T receive income?
a. 21 days
b. 14 days
c. 7 days
d. 0 days

2. All of the following are Business Disability policies EXCEPT:
a. Business Overhead Expense
b. Group Disability
c. Key Person Disability
d. Disability Buy-Out

3. Which of the following disability definitions would be best suited for a person with a chronic back injury?
a. Residual Disability
b. Recurrent Disability
c. Non Occupational Disability
d. Any Occupation Disability

4. How long is the waiting period for Social Security Disability?
a. 12 months
b. 6 months
c. 5 months
d. 1 month

5. All of the following are possible disability income benefits EXCEPT:
a. Workers Compensation
b. Vocational Training
c. Rehabilitation & Medical Costs
d. Speech Therapy

6. What are the tax consequences on individual disability insurance policies?
a. Non-tax deductible premiums and taxable benefits
b. Tax deductible premiums and tax free benefits
c. Tax deferred growth and taxable interest gains
d. Non-tax deductible premiums and tax free benefits

7. A person who is covered by Workers Compensation would benefit most by which disability income policy?
a. Any Occupation
b. Own Occupation
c. Occupational
d. Non Occupational

8. When is a person fully insured through Social Security Disability?
a. 40 credits
b. 6 credits
c. From birth as a citizen
d. 40 credits in the past 3 years

9. Which of the following statements is true about disability income insurance?
a. Key person insurance is used to fund the sale of a business
b. Disability income is used to offset an uncertain economy
c. Insureds must be under a physician's care while receiving benefits
d. Disability income is based off of future earnings potential

10. All of the following are presumptive disabilities EXCEPT:
a. Loss of two limbs
b. Loss of hearing
c. Loss of one eye
d. Loss of speech

CHAPTER 6: HEALTH (MEDICAL) PLANS

This chapter will discuss the three primary Comprehensive health insurance plans (HMO, PPO, POS); including: Deductibles, Coinsurance, Copayments and other aspects. Due to the 2003 tax treatment of Health Savings Accounts, Flexible Spending Accounts and Health Reimbursement accounts through Consumer Driven Health Systems, deductibles have skyrocketed in the past 10 years. These plans and components are separate from the limited health plans earlier in the book.

A. MEDICAL PLAN CONCEPTS

Medical plans are designed to cover medical expenses relating to an injury or sickness that the insured has incurred. There are multiple different types of medical plans:

1. **Comprehensive Plans:** Cover almost all expenses for accidents and illnesses, the three types of comprehensive plans are **HMO, PPO** and **POS.**
2. **Basic Plans:** Considered to be *"First Dollar Coverage"* plans which have no coinsurance or deductibles, these are lower cost but lower benefit plans.
3. **Major Medical:** Plans with **coinsurance** and **deductibles.**
4. **Managed Care:** Lowering costs of insurance through usage of prospective review and concurrent review, typically requiring pre-authorization before a surgery or entering hospice.
5. **Consumer Driven Health Plan:** Must have a high deductible health plan ($2,500+) and provides tax advantages through HSA's and HRA's.

✓ A person could have a Consumer Driven, Major Medical, Managed Care, Comprehensive HMO/PPO/POS supplemented with a Basic plan. This would be a person with a high deductible plan including coinsurance, that lowers costs through authorization forms, and provides care for accidents and sickness through an HMO and also they have a separate basic plan to cover costs the comprehensive plan did not.

Medical plans pay benefits to the physician or hospital after treating the insured; a laypersons definition of "health insurance" would be a major medical, comprehensive plan. Such as an HMO, PPO or POS plan that also includes deductibles and coinsurance.

1. COMPREHENSIVE PLANS

Comprehensive plans cover all costs related to injuries and illnesses, unless the plan specifically excludes an item. Health Maintenance Organizations **(HMO)**, Preferred Provider Organizations **(PPO)**, Point of Service **(POS)** and Exclusive Provider Organizations **(EPOs)** are all comprehensive.

* If John broke his ankle on Monday, contracted the flu on Tuesday and was diagnosed with cancer on Wednesday, his comprehensive insurance plan would help cover the costs of all 3 medical issues.

2. BENEFIT SCHEDULE

A benefit schedule will outline exactly how much to pay for specific accidents or illnesses. Certain medical plans include benefit schedules to clearly state what is covered and for exactly how much.

3. USUAL – REASONABLE – CUSTOMARY

Medical plans provide payment to physicians for **eligible costs** based on the "Usual Reasonable Customary Cost" of their geographical area. Physicians cannot charge anything they want to an insurer.

* Tony is a new surgeon performing a simple procedure on an insureds leg; most physicians are able to complete the same procedure in 3 hours and usually charge $4,000 for their services. Since Tony is a newer physician, the procedure takes him 12 hours, and he charges $12,000 for the surgery. Under the Usual, Reasonable, Customary cost basis, Tony will be paid the $4,000 like other doctors in his area.

4. ANY PROVIDER VS. LIMITED CHOICE OF PROVIDERS

The majority of health insurance plans allow the **insured** to choose which provider to receive their services from, PPO's and POS plans have "in-network" and "out-of-network" providers, and HMO's have a limited choice based on a geographic service area. Choosing an "in-network" or "in-service-area" provider will have lower out of pocket costs for the insured, whereas an out-of-network provider will have higher out of pocket costs. In order for a physician to be on the **approved list** of providers, they must only **pay a fee** and **fill out an application.**

B. HEALTH MAINTENANCE ORGANIZATIONS (HMO's)

HMOs are not considered insurance; rather they are **prepaid** health contracts for the insureds well-being. The primary focus of an HMO is to provide **preventative care** and early treatment of medical conditions. HMOs are regulated by the Department of Insurance and the Department of Health which require HMOs to have a customer call center to handle complaints under state law.

a. PHYSICIANS AND PATIENTS

Physicians of an HMO receive compensation on a **prepaid (capitation)** basis and patients are not called insureds, but rather they are known as **subscribers**. It is fair to say all subscribers are insureds, but all insureds are NOT subscribers. HMOs originally began and provided care only through **local clinics** owned by the HMO.

b. SERVICE AREA

HMOs provide most care within a service area that is based off of **geographical location**, not state lines; meaning, an HMO may provide coverage in multiple surrounding states. The HMO will provide emergency care in and out of the service area, but most services are required to be within the geographical service area. Outside of the service area claims are paid on the **usual reasonable basis.**

c. PRIMARY CARE PHYSICIAN AS GATEKEEPER

A Primary Care Physician (chosen by the subscriber) is known as the "gatekeeper" in an HMO; the gatekeeper must be seen first for all non-emergency procedures, if the gatekeeper is unable to provide adequate services, the insured will be referred to a specialist. The gatekeeper model helps lower costs by having the primary care physician consulted first for minor issues; however, this is a more limiting feature of an HMO from the subscribers' point of view. Since HMO's are prepaid plans

d. CO-PAYMENT

Co-Payments are small amounts paid to the primary care physician for each visit, normally $5-$50 dollars, not to exceed 200% of the annual premium. Having the subscriber pay a small amount to the physician helps lower nuisance claims and constrains costs.

e. PREVENTIVE CARE

HMOs are required by law to offer preventative care, which is normally paid for 100% by the insurer. Preventative care is given prior to an injury or illness and may consist of: Annual checkups, Immunizations, Nutritional Counseling, X-Rays and Mammograms (age 50+ receive annual checks).

f. HOSPITAL CARE

Hospital care must be provided for at least **90 days** in or out of the service area.

g. HMO REGULATION -- DOLLARS, NUMBERS AND DATES

1. Annual Financial Report filed on **March 1st** to the **Commissioner** and the Commissioner audits HMO's once every 3 years
2. Must have $1,500,000 minimum in claims reserves
3. All officers must have $100,000 fiduciary bond
4. Must hold open enrollment period of **31 days** every 12 months

* Danielle is shopping for a health insurance plan that will help cover costs on herself, husband and children for nearly all accidents and illnesses. Danielle does not travel often and her children are young and will likely be seeing the doctor quite often, out of pocket expenses are definitely a factor. An HMO would be best suited for Danielle since she does not travel, would like lower out of pocket costs, but still requires comprehensive insurance.

C. PREFERRED PROVIDER ORGANIZATION (PPO)

PPOs are distinctly different from an HMO, as PPOs are on a **fee for service** basis where the insurer enters into contracts with physicians, hospitals and clinics that offer **discounts** on their rates.

1. IN-NETWORK AND OUT-OF-NETWORK

The doctors who offer discounts to the insurer are known as "in-network" and will provide the insured with lower out of pocket costs; whereas an "out-of-network" doctor does not provide a discount and the insured will incur higher out of pocket costs. **There is no service area with a PPO,** the insured may obtain care anywhere in the country but will likely incur higher coinsurance & deductibles.

2. PHYSICIAN TYPES

A physician may be either **open panel**, where they take patients of multiple insurers; or **closed panel** where they are considered an **employee** of the PPO and have their patients assigned to them. There is **NO gatekeeper** with a PPO; the insured may see a specialist without a referral.

* Scott, living in Texas, has a severe medical condition that requires very specialized surgeons for treatment, which are located out of state. When choosing a health plan, Scott's agent informs him that he would rather have a PPO over an HMO, because an HMO would have limited his service area. Out of the 10 doctors in the country who can treat Scott's condition, only 3 provide discounts to his PPO. If Scott sees those physicians, his deductible is only $2,000; but should Scott want to see one not on his list, his deductible increases to $5,000, which is still better than the HMO that would have covered nothing. The PPO gives him more choices, but higher out of pocket costs.

D. POINT OF SERVICE (POS)

A Point of Service (POS) plan is a combination of the **HMO** and **PPO** comprehensive insurance plans. The insured gains the best of both plans by having prepaid coverage within the service area, but may also utilize a physician outside of the service area on a fee for service basis with higher out of pocket costs. There is **NO gatekeeper** and the insured is not required to choose a primary care physician.

E. MAJOR MEDICAL CONCEPT

Major Medical plans, which are **characterized by deductibles, coinsurance and maximum benefits,** are the standard for most health insurance plans today. The vast majority of comprehensive health insurance plans are major medical, such as: Major Medical HMO, Major Medical PPO etc.; the term Major Medical simply means the insured will incur out-of-pocket expenses. Insurance prior to 1920 was provided on a "first dollar basis" (no deductible, no coinsurance); Basic Plans were inefficient due to the fact the insureds would utilize the plan for unnecessary procedures. Insurers implemented cost-saving methods to lower unnecessary expenditures and thus, the Major Medical plan was born.

a. MAJOR MEDICAL CHARACTERISTICS

Deductibles, Coinsurance, Maximum Lifetime benefits and **catastrophic coverage**, are all characteristics of Major Medical insurance. The insured is able to choose the amount of each characteristic, which will greatly affect the premium.

b. DEDUCTIBLES

Deductibles are an insureds **annual first out of pocket** cost, meaning the insurer will not pay any benefits until the insured meets their deductible. A deductible can be as low as $100 and as high as $10,000; anything over $2,500 is considered a **High Deductible Health Plan (HDHP)**. The deductible has a large impact on the premiums in the policy, a higher deductible means lower premiums and once the insured pays their deductible, the insurer will begin paying claims. Deductibles will reset and must be met every year of the policy.

c. COINSURANCE

After the insured has met their annual deductible, they will share costs with the insurer in the form of coinsurance. Coinsurance is a percentage, typically 80%/20%, where the insured pays the lower amount. 90%/10% coinsurance would increase the premium due to the fact the insurance company will pay more for claims.

d. STOP LOSS FEATURE

The insureds **maximum out of pocket costs** each year is referred to as the stop-loss; meaning the insurer will pay 100% of the claim after the insured has met their stop-loss. The stop-loss comprises of the deductible and coinsurance, to give one limit per year.

* Eric has a Major Medical HMO plan with a deductible of $500, coinsurance of 80/20 and a stop-loss of $300. Eric is working on his roof, falls off, and breaks his ankle; his hospital charges are $1,500. Eric would first pay his annual deductible ($500), leaving $1,000 left on the claim; then pay coinsurance ($1,000 * 20% (coinsurance) = $200); with a total cost to Eric of $700. However, his stop-loss was $300 and since Eric cannot pay more than that out-of-pocket for a year, the insurer covers $1,200.

$1,500 claim
- $500 deductible
$1,000 remainder
x   20% coinsurance = $200 coinsurance costs + $500 deductible = $700 total costs without stop-loss

e. MAXIMUM LIFETIME BENEFITS

Prior to 2014 (PPACA), major medical plans had **maximum lifetime benefits** on certain injuries or illnesses (such as: cancer, spinal injuries, brain trauma). Typically, the maximum was $1,000,000, after the insurer paid the maximum, the insurer would nothing more during insureds lifetime on that injury/illness. Other injuries or illnesses will still be covered.

F. MANAGED CARE AND UTILIZATION MANAGEMENT

Today, almost all health plans are considered managed care; the term managed care means to **control costs by controlling insureds.** Basically, the insurer may deny a claim unless the physician deems it is medically necessary. This helps prevent unnecessary surgeries and prescription drugs.

1. PROSPECTIVE REVIEW (PRECERTIFICATION REVIEW)

A physician would ask the insurer for an estimate of covered costs prior to performing a non-emergency surgery. The physician would need permission before performing the surgery by **preauthorization forms.**

2. CONCURRENT REVIEW (CASE MANAGEMENT)

Concurrent Review is a process that may deter very expensive claims. Case Managers (CMs) are medical specialists within the insurance company who review cases that may potentially become large claims. These CMs work along with the patient to obtain the best care in the least expensive manner. A case manager is assigned to an ongoing claim, it is called "concurrent review." **Hospice** is a form of concurrent review, which lowers costs through pain management.

3. AMBULATORY SERVICES (OUTPATIENT SURGERIES)

Allowing the insured to go home after a surgery is much lower in costs than providing for an inpatient hospital stay, some plans will waive deductibles for ambulatory service centers as an incentive.

4. MANDATORY SECOND OPINIONS

Insurers may require a second opinion for non-life-threatening surgeries; if no second opinion is obtained, benefits may be lowered.

G. CONSUMER DRIVEN HEALTH PLANS (CDHP)

These are savings accounts are coupled with High Deductible Health Plans and designed to increase the deductibles of major medical health insurance. The concept has skyrocketed in popularity through employers when the Medicare Modernization Act of 2003 provided tax incentives for employers and employees to contribute to these plans.

a. HEALTH SAVINGS ACCOUNTS – HSA

The HSA may only be used in conjunction with a **High Deductible Health Plan (HDHP)**, and work in the same fashion as a regular saving account; meaning, they are funded by the insured, roll-over into the next year and will accrue interest. The HSA may be used for **qualified medical expenses** such as prescription drugs, doctors' visits and hospital services; but has a 10% penalty (20% under PPACA) for non-qualified medical expenses.

An employee and employer may both make contributions to an HSA up to the yearly maximum contribution amounts, but the employee has no say in how much the employer contributes. HSA's may allow for tax advantage disbursements on the following items:

- Prescription Drugs
- Physician & Specialist Visits
- Rehabilitation & Therapy
- Eyeglasses and Vision
- Mental Therapy
- Artificial Devices (Prosthetics)
- Lab work
- Allergy Testing

b. HEALTH REIMBURSEMENT ARRANGEMENT – HRA

HRA's also are used in conjunction with a **HDHP,** but are funded and **established by the employer.** The employer puts money into an account for the employee (that also rolls over into the next year); when the employee uses their health insurance, they will pay out of pocket, but then provide a receipt to the HRA administrator and be reimbursed for those costs. The employer has sole discretion over the HRA uses and receives a tax deduction for funding the account.

c. FLEXIBLE SPENDING ACCOUNT – FSA

FSA's **do not require** an HDHP to be set up, and are normally known as **"use it or lose it"** plans, due to the fact the funds do NOT roll-over into the next year. FSAs are funded with **pre-tax dollars** by the insured and are used for a wide range of qualified medical expenses, such as over the counter medicine, prescription drugs and even laser eye surgery.

* Dan has a low deductible comprehensive health plan of $100 through his employer, as well as a flexible spending account (FSA). Dan is planning his healthcare costs, and determines he needs to save about $30/month for co-pays and other expenses. Dan places $30 pre-tax dollars per month into his FSA, at the end of the year, Dan has $75 left-over in the account. Since Dan did not spend all of his money, he will lose the $75. The excess money stays with the employer and is used to pay overall premiums.

H. TRICARE – MILITARY PERSONNEL

As war and military service are excluded under most private insurance plans, the government has provided comprehensive health coverage for military personnel (Army, Navy, Air Force etc.) through TRICARE as either an HMO or PPO.

I. INDEMNITY PLANS

Indemnity insurance allows an insured to choose any physician they want and the insurer will cover those costs. Indemnity plans allow for the greatest access to physicians, but typically have high deductibles, high premiums and high maximum out of pocket cost. The insurer does not negotiate prices with the physicians, the payments are made on the usual reasonable customary cost and as a fee for service basis. If the physician charges more than the usual reasonable customary cost, the insured will have to pay the excess.

Indemnity plans were the first type of health insurance created and are not very common in todays' markets. PPO's have overtaken Indemnity plans because the PPO allows the insured to choose any physician as well, but the insurer negotiates payments with the physician. Since the PPO doctors offer discounts for services, the cost of care has been reduced to the insurer and the PPO's premiums would be much lower than an Indemnity plan.

PRACTICE QUESTIONS: MEDICAL PLANS

1. All of the following are comprehensive health plans EXCEPT:
a. HMO
b. PPO
c. POS
d. Indemnity

2. K has a major medical HMO with flat deductible of $100 and 80/20 coinsurance. K is involved in a claim incurring $1,600 in costs; what amount will K have to pay of this claim?
a. $400
b. $320
c. $300
d. $220

3. Which plan must offer preventative care by a pre-2010 law?
a. HMO
b. PPO
c. POS
d. EPO

4. Major Medical plans are characterized by which feature?
a. Managed Care Costs
b. Tax Advantaged Accounts
c. Coinsurance and Deductibles
d. Gatekeeper Concepts

5. All of the following require a High Deductible Health Plan (HDHP) except:
a. FSA
b. HRA
c. HSA
d. CDHP

6. Which best describes a physician receiving an estimate of costs prior to a surgery?
a. Concurrent Review
b. Respite Review
c. Managed Costs
d. Prospective Review

7. Which of the following is the more limiting comprehensive health plan and why?
a. PPO, it has a service area and gatekeeper
b. HMO, it has a service area and gatekeeper
c. PPO, it provides discounts for services on a prepaid basis
d. HMO, it is based off fee-for-service

8. When a nurse performs pre and post op diagnostic tests to ensure care is running smoothly, this is an example of:
a. Ambulatory Services
b. Prospective Review
c. Coordination of Benefits
d. Concurrent Review

9. When a physician can charge no more to a subscriber, other than a co-pay, this is an example of which payment basis?
a. Usual Reasonable Customary Costs
b. Prepaid Basis
c. Fee for Service Basis
d. Deductible

10. Which of the following statements is NOT true about a Health Reimbursement Account?
a. The employer makes the contributions
b. The employee may use funds towards their deductible
c. The funds do not roll-over into the next year
d. The employer has sole discretion over its use

CHAPTER 7: GROUP INSURANCE

Group health insurance is **less expensive** than individual insurance due to the lower **administrative expenses** by insuring many people but only needing one access point, typically a Human Resources Department. Over 80% of health insurance is written as a group contract, the three main groups consist of Employer Sponsored, Labor Unions and Associations. A group **cannot** be formed for the sole purpose of purchasing insurance and must have **at least two** members.

Group insurance is considered **Third Party Ownership,** because the members of the group do not actually own the policies on themselves. The actual contract is between **the employer and insurer**, the employee is just a subscriber to the plan; since group insurance is third-party ownership, the employee has limited options and input as to which plans the group sponsor chooses. Third Party Ownership is primarily used in **business and estate planning,** but even a parent purchasing insurance on their child is considered Third Party Ownership.

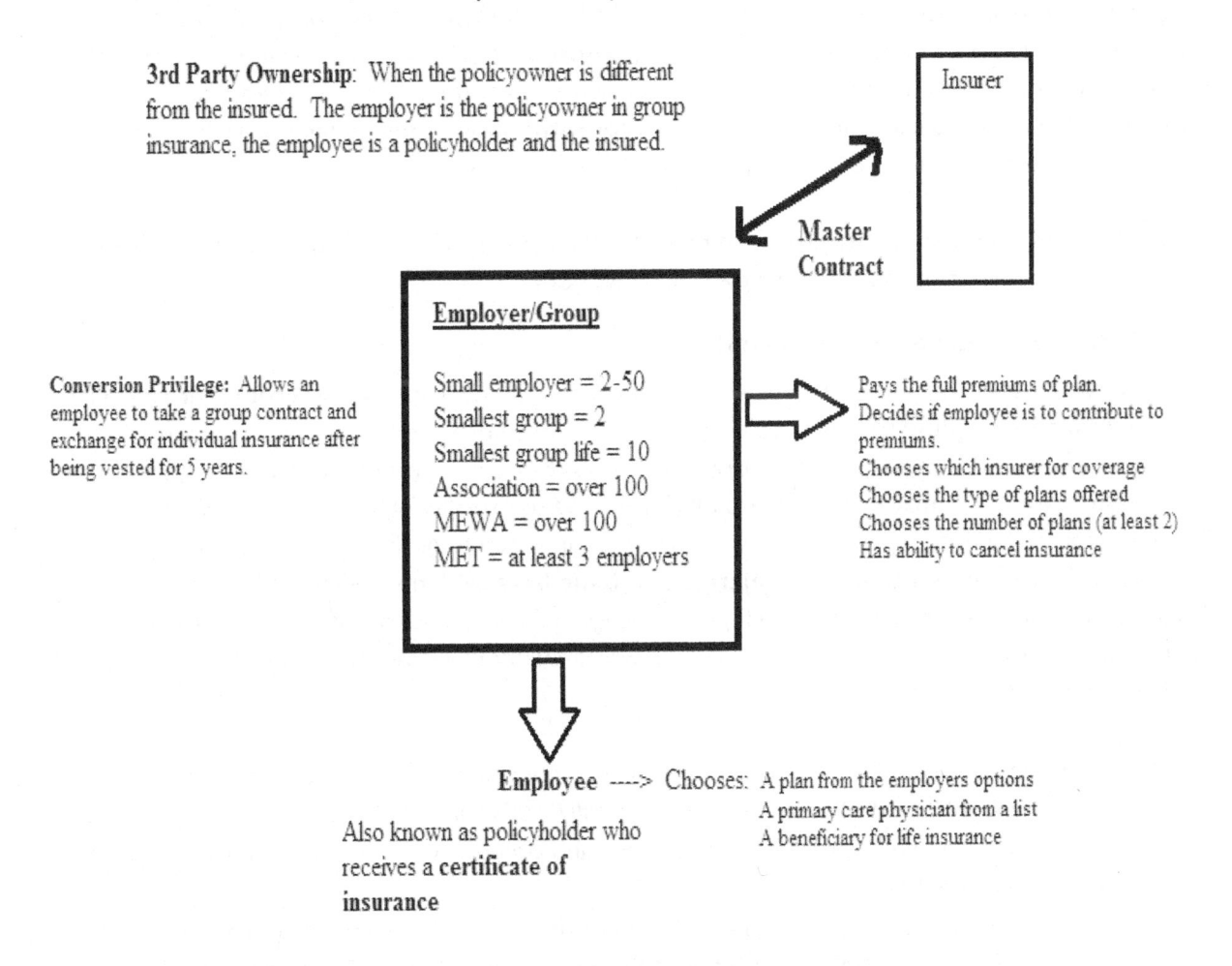

3rd Party Ownership: When the policyowner is different from the insured. The employer is the policyowner in group insurance, the employee is a policyholder and the insured.

Conversion Privilege: Allows an employee to take a group contract and exchange for individual insurance after being vested for 5 years.

Employer/Group
Small employer = 2-50
Smallest group = 2
Smallest group life = 10
Association = over 100
MEWA = over 100
MET = at least 3 employers

Master Contract → Insurer

Pays the full premiums of plan.
Decides if employee is to contribute to premiums.
Chooses which insurer for coverage
Chooses the type of plans offered
Chooses the number of plans (at least 2)
Has ability to cancel insurance

Employee ----> Chooses: A plan from the employers options
A primary care physician from a list
A beneficiary for life insurance

Also known as policyholder who receives a **certificate of insurance**

1. MASTER POLICY AND CERTIFICATE

The employer is the policyowner and chooses the insurance company to go through, which will give the employer the **master contract.** The master contract states the overall **premium, date of coverage, length of coverage, deductibles, coinsurance** and most other details of the policy.

The employee will be the policyholder and receives a **certificate of insurance,** which will act as evidence of insurance. The policyholder (also known as **subscriber**) receives very limited rights within the group contract; they can change these few things:

> - Choice between at least two different plans
> - Naming of the beneficiary in case of death
> - Choice of the date for premium withdrawal

A major difference between group and individual plans is how the insurance company determines the rates for the group plans. Group plans are based on **experience rating** where the insurer performs an annual review of the group and adjusts premium either up or down on the past years claims experience. Individual plans are written as **community rating**, where the premiums are based on the claims experience of the insurance company as a whole.

Experience rating allows lower risk groups to receive a reduction in premium and the employer has a vested interest in recruiting and maintaining a healthy workforce.

2. EMPLOYER SPONSORED PLANS

There are two distinct definitions of employer sponsored health insurance: **small employer** which has between **2 and 50 employees**, and large employer with 51+ employees. A full-time employee is one who works **over 30 hours** per week and large employers (51+ employees) must offer health insurance to all full-time workers. Small employers are NOT required to provide for group health insurance. The underwriter's job is to try to lower adverse selection in group plans; in large groups (51+ employees), the insurance is issued on a **guaranteed issue** basis, with no medical underwriting. This means that all full-time (30 hour) employees are eligible for insurance and cannot be declined or rated-up for medical conditions, the group plans are written without individual underwriting. Here is a list of common underwriting factors:

- There must be at least **two members** of the group and the employer must provide **two different choices** of plans. Typically, HMO and PPO with varying deductibles.
- Premiums will be based on the age, sex and occupation of the entire group, not on an individual basis
- The **size** of the group will greatly impact the premiums, as well as **turnover** of the group and the **financial status** of the group (being able to afford coverage).
- There must be an open enrollment period of **30 days** each year for employees who have chosen not to participate or new employees.

- Some employers may add probationary periods (30, 60 or 90 days) where the employee would not be covered to protect against adverse selection.
- Pre-Existing conditions may be excluded for a maximum of 1 year under group plans; if there is a probationary period, coverage will begin after the probationary period is satisfied. PPACA removes all pre-existing condition exclusions.
- Employers are also expected to maintain their coverage for longer than 1 year with their chosen insurance company; switching insurance companies each year would be considered a higher risk to the insurer.

Employer plans are also required to offer insurance to all eligible dependents, such as a spouse or a child. Any child **under the age of 26** is considered an eligible dependent; the child does NOT have to be in school and can even be married. Children over the age of 26 who cannot take care of themselves (such as downs syndrome or autistic) can still be eligible as a dependent on their parent's policy.

3. SELF INSURED EMPLOYER PLANS

The larger the employer, the more costly the health insurance plan, due to the sheer number of members subscribed to the plan. Employers have sought many ways to lower administrative costs, below are four common ways of self-insuring rather than utilizing an insurer:

1. **Self-Funded Plan:** The employer places funds into an account from current revenue and then pays claims from that account. This plan typically has a Third-Party Administrator to handle claims.
2. **Multiple Employer Welfare Arrangement (MEWA):** For groups with over **100 members**, the MEWA can consist of multiple employers who **pool together resources** to self-insure, these are commonly seen with payroll companies.
3. **Multiple Employer Trust (MET):** A group of **at least 3 small employers** who join together to partially self-insure as long as they are of similar business types. IE: Lawyers, Physicians etc.
4. **Labor Unions:** If a labor union is utilized, all members of the union must be included in the health plan and may also add coverage for the members' dependents. Some employees may be excluded for coverage if they are not members of the union itself.

Associations work very similar to employer sponsored plans but there does not need to be an employer-employee relationship. An association can provide insurance for professional groups, alumni organizations, fraternities and even churches. The group has to work similar to a corporation though in the fact that there are certain guidelines:

- The group must have over 100 members and be in operation for at least 2 years
- The group must have a constitution, by-laws and hold annual meetings
- The group cannot be formed for the sole purpose to purchase insurance

Meeting all of those criteria allows for an association to qualify for group insurance on the members. Since there are many employers and associations that operate across state lines, the regulatory jurisdiction will fall on **place of delivery** (state of delivery), but must still comply with state law of where the plan is sold.

5. SMALL EMPLOYERS HEALTH INSURANCE (FRANCHISE INSURANCE)

Small employers have tax advantages and other protections to ensure affordable health care is accessible to the employees. Due to the tax advantages, small employer (franchise) premiums are lower than individual insurance, but higher than a large employers' premium. Small employers have certain criteria to meet in order to receive these benefits:

1. Maintain between **2 and 50** full-time employees working at least 50% of the year.
2. Offer a minimum of **two** choices to employees for plans. Typically, a high deductible and a lower deductible plan.
3. Maintain at least **75%** participation and the employer must pay at least **75%** of premiums.
4. Have no longer than a 1-year pre-existing condition exclusion, but as of 2014 due to PPACA, there are no pre-existing exclusions.

6. CANCELLATION AND CHANGE OF COVERAGE

Under PPACA enaction, the insurers opportunity to cancel group health insurance is severely limited due to the fact that all health insurance plans are written as **guaranteed renewable,** which does not allow an insurer to cancel a plan solely due to high claims; but the most common cause of health insurance termination is **non-payment of premium.** Otherwise, the insurer may only cancel the group contract if they cancel all group plans statewide, or if the insurance commissioner deems the group plan to not be in the best interest of the insurance company. Upon those two options, the insurer must provide the insureds with a 31-day cancellation notice stating exactly why the plan has been cancelled.

Employers who switch health insurance companies frequently are deemed poor risks to the insurer; however, it is likely that an employer will change insurance companies sooner or later. Employees that are actively at work on the date of plan replacements will **carry-over** seamlessly; however, employees that are not at work on that date will continue with the old plan until they return to work. Employees who are disabled must receive **at least 90 days** of continued coverage; up until a **maximum of 18 months.**

Upon reaching age 65, the insured must be notified of their Medicare eligibility. Even though the employer notifies the employee of their Medicare eligibility, **group coverage must be continued** to employees over age 65 and group benefits may not be reduced for that employee.

Life, Accident & Health Exam Study Book | TX

7. GROUP LIFE INSURANCE

Group life insurance works very similar to group health insurance with the plans being **guaranteed issue** with no medical underwriting and the plans typically being contributory in nature (sharing in premiums). Here are some characteristics of group life insurance:

1. **Minimum Participation:** At **least 10 employees** must be included if the plan is noncontributory, 100% of employees must be added.
2. **Annually Renewable Term:** Group life is written as a 1-year term policy that will renew with possible premium increases
3. **Premiums:** Premiums are based off the average age of the group and ratio of men to women; the employer may also take a tax deduction of up to $50,000. Any amount over $50,000 will be taxed as income to the employees on a ratio basis.
4. **Conversion Privilege:** After subscribing to a group life plan for **five years** a policyholder may convert the group term policy into individual **whole** life insurance. Should a vested (5 years) employee leave their job, they will have 31 days to utilize the conversion privilege. The downside of this is that premiums will increase, and the death benefit may decrease to **$10,000**.
5. **Guaranteed Issue:** There is no medical underwriting required typically for the first 1-2x a persons' salary for death benefit.
6. **Dependents:** A spouse or unmarried child (under 19) may be added to the group plan as a dependent on the policy. Adopted, court appointed and foster children all count as dependents.
7. **Death Benefits:** Death benefits are tax-free and paid to the beneficiary named by the employee.

* Donald works for EXP Company as a data analyst and is offered a group life policy. When Donald enrolled, he did not have to take a medical exam for the first $90,000 of death benefit coverage and his employer stated they would contribute 75% towards his premiums. Five years later, Donald left his company; and on his last day he was involved in a car accident killing him. Donald's policy would pay out because he still had 31 days to use the conversion privilege. If Donald had worked for the company less than 5 years, nothing would be paid.

8. NEWBORN CHILDREN ON GROUP AND INDIVIDUAL INSURANCE

Newborn, Adopted, or legally required children are **automatically** covered on the parent or legal guardian's policy beginning **at the time of birth.** Children are considered guaranteed issue meaning there is no medical underwriting required adding the child to the parent/guardian's policy.

1. **Health Insurance:** Children are covered automatically for 31 days on their parent/guardian's policy. This applies to group and individual health insurance policies.
2. **Group Life:** Children are automatically covered for 14 days on group life insurance policies
3. **Individual Life:** The child would need to have its own policy and some insurers could require medical underwriting, but most are still guaranteed issue.

*Paul, age 6, had both parents killed in a car accident last week. The court legally appoints his grandparents to be Paul's guardians. Paul is automatically added onto his grandparent's health insurance for 31 days; to continue coverage, the grandparents would need to inform the insurer and list Paul on the policy. The same rules apply for his grandparent's group life insurance policy, but they only have 14 days to list Paul on the policy.

9. CONTRIBUTORY vs. NONCONTRIBUTORY

- ❖ **Contributory:** When an employer and employee are sharing in premiums for group insurance. Such as, 75% employer, 25% employee; these plans require 75% participation rate of the group.
- ❖ **Noncontributory:** When only the employer is paying the premiums, 100% employer, 0% employee. If a plan is non-contributory, there MUST be 100% of all employees participating in the insurance and there will be **no medical underwriting.**
- ❖ **Fully Contributory:** When only the employee is paying the premiums, 0% employer 100% employee.

✓ The easiest way to remember this concept is if you read it as "employee" noncontributory or "employee" fully contributory. That would mean the employee either did not contribute or fully paid the premiums. Having 100% participation on noncontributory plans helps lower the risk of **Adverse Selection.**

* Jedidah's employer is offering a group disability insurance plan on a noncontributory basis. Jedidah was initially upset because she thought she would have to pay 100% of the premiums. After speaking with Joe, she became very happy to find out noncontributory meant the employer paid all the premiums, all of her dependents were eligible AND she did not have to go through medical underwriting.

Life, Accident & Health Exam Study Book | TX

PRACTICE QUESTIONS: GROUP INSURANCE

1. Under group insurance, whom is the contract between?
a. Employer and Insurer
b. Employer and Employee
c. Employee and Insurer
d. Employee and Producer

2. Which of the following may an employee choose in a group contract?
a. The insurance company
b. The number of plans offered
c. Deductibles and coinsurance
d. Beneficiary Designations

3. All of the following are true about an Association EXCEPT:
a. The association cannot be formed for the purchase of insurance
b. The association must have less than 100 members
c. The association must have a constitution and by-laws
d. The association must hold annual meetings

4. What is the minimum number of choices a group contract must include for insurer health plans?
a. 10
b. 3
c. 2
d. 1

5. In a group contract, which document would the policyholder (employee) receive?
a. Certificate of Insurance
b. Master Policy
c. A Standard Policy
d. Certificate of Coverage

6. Which of the following best describes a Multiple Employer Trust (MET)?
a. A pooling together of 100 or more members to partially self-insure
b. Multiple Employers who trust each other with health information
c. At least 3 small employers who band together for health insurance
d. An association formed for the purpose of employer's health plans

7. The minimum number of members for a group health plan is:
a. 20
b. 10
c. 3
d. 2

8. Which of the following is NOT a benefit of group insurance?
a. Group premiums are lower than individual
b. Group insurance has lower administrative costs
c. Group plans have medical underwriting
d. Group plans may have tax advantages

9. A small employer is best described as:
a. 1-10 employees
b. 1-100 employees
c. 2-50 employees
d. 2-100 employees

10. When may a person utilize the conversion privilege for group life?
a. After 31 days
b. After 5 years
c. After 3 years
d. After 1 year

11. In a noncontributory long term disability plan, which of the following would most likely not be true?
a. The employee must sign up for payroll deduction
b. The benefits will tax free
c. The employer will keep the master policy
d. The employee must sign an enrollment card

CHAPTER 8: SOCIAL INSURANCE & SENIOR CITIZENS

In the United States, there are many **social insurance** programs available to its citizens, which are administered by the U.S. Federal and State governments; the majority of these programs are funded by taxes, namely the payroll taxes: Federal Income Contribution Act (FICA), Medicare tax. The four primary social insurance programs are:

1. **Medicare:** A federal health program primarily for ages **65 and older** comprising of four parts:
   - **Part A:** Hospital Services
   - **Part B:** Medical & Physician Services
   - **Part C:** Medicare Advantage (Privately Administered)
   - **Part D:** Prescription Drugs

2. **Medicaid & CHIP:** Federal and state health programs for the lower income, indigent population; primarily insuring children, the deaf and blind, and people over 65 but unable to afford care

3. **Social Security:** A federal retirement and survivorship program for ages 62+, funded by the FICA tax; *also known as Old Age Survivors Insurance.*

4. **Social Security Disability:** A federal income program for disabled individuals

Social insurance programs were created as a safety-net for the United States citizens, as such the social programs tend to provide only basic benefits and have *many gaps in their coverage.* To help cover costs the social programs do not, there have been many private insurance solutions created, such as:

> - **Medicare Supplement:** Privatized insurance (not government) that cover costs that Medicare does not. Also known as MediGap and SELECT.
> - **Long Term Care:** Providing care related to aging, such as nursing homes, adult day care, home health nurses and custodial care. LTC is private insurance, **NOT** Medicare.

* David's birthday was Tuesday, on which he celebrated his 65th birthday and his retirement from work; David is feeling very secure today knowing he has guaranteed health coverage and income, because earlier that day he enrolled for his Medicare and Social Security benefits. Knowing Social Security only provides him roughly $2,000 per month and Medicare has deductibles and gaps in coverage, David has used his 401k for extra income and also purchased a Medigap policy to cover Medicare's extra deductibles and shortcomings.

Planning for the future, David also took a distribution from his 401k for the sole purpose of purchasing a Long-Term Care policy to cover skilled nursing costs, due to the fact Medicare only provides for 100 days of coverage.

QUALIFYING FOR MEDICARE BENEFITS

Eligible individuals can enroll during their Initial Enrollment Period (IEP), or *the six-month period that starts three months before their 65th birthday*. Many will be automatically enrolled in Part A, in which case Medicare sends an initial enrollment package with general Medicare information, a questionnaire, and a red-white-and-blue Medicare card. Those who are younger than age 65 with a disability are automatically enrolled in Medicare Part A in the 25th month of their disability payments.

There are four determining factors as to whether or not a person qualifies to receive benefits; they only need one to be eligible for benefits:

1. Age 65 and older
2. Receiving Social Security Disability payments for 2+ years
3. Diagnosed with End Stage Renal Disease (ESRD, kidney failure)
4. Diagnosed with Amyotrophic Lateral Sclerosis (ALS, Lou Gehrig's disease)
5. Blindness

The vast majorities of enrollees are age 65+, however even an 18-year-old may enroll in Medicare if they have one of the other qualifying factors. If a child has one of the three factors, they would be eligible for Medicaid, since children may not be enrolled in Medicare. If a person is still working and enrolls in Medicare, their group health insurance will remain primary insurance and Medicare will be considered secondary excess coverage; in the case of ESRD, the group health plan is primary for only 18 months.

1. PART A: MEDICARE HOSPITAL INSURANCE

Medicare Part A is **the only required** portion of Medicare in order to obtain the other parts and upon attaining age 65, a citizen is automatically enrolled in Part A: Hospital Insurance for free, since it is paid fully by the payroll tax.

Medicare Part A pays some of the charges for:

> **Hospital stays.** The amount covered depends on how long you're in the hospital. In 2013, for the first 60 days, you pay a maximum of $1,184 ($28 more than in 2012) and Medicare pays the rest. After that, the longer you stay, the more you pay. You pay $296 per day for days 61 through 90. After that, you pay $592 per day until the 60 days of "lifetime benefits" run out. Then, you pay all the costs. **Medicare partially pays for up to 90 days of hospital stays.**

> **Skilled nursing facility care.** This is to allow you to recover after a stay in the hospital; Medicare does not pay for long stays in a nursing facility. Medicare pays **fully for the first 20 days**. From the 21st to 100th day, you pay a co-pay of $148 per day. After that, you pay all the costs of your stay in a skilled nursing facility. Medicare provides coverage for a **total amount of 100 days.**

- **Home health care.** If you are recovering from an illness or injury -- and your doctor says you need short-term skilled care -- Medicare Part A pays for nurses and some therapists to provide services in your home. As long as the treatment is Medicare-approved and the provider is certified by Medicare, you pay nothing -- **except for 20%** of the Medicare-approved amount for some medical equipment, such as wheelchairs and walkers.

- **Hospice care.** This covers 100% of care for people who are **terminally ill,** and death is expected within 0 – 2 years. The enrollee must choose to enter hospice, which may be done at home or at a facility; however once in hospice, the only type of care that may be given is **pain management.** The hospice personnel may not provide antibiotics, immunizations or any type of life lengthening or life-saving services.

- **Blood transfusions.** After **you pay for the first three pints**, Medicare Part A pays 80% of any additional blood you need in the hospital. In most cases, the hospital gets blood from a blood bank at no charge, and you won't have to pay for it or replace it. If the hospital has to buy blood for you, you must either pay the hospital costs for the first three units of blood you get in a calendar year or have the blood donated. Again, Medicare does **NOT** pay for the first three pints of blood.

2. PART B: MEDICARE PHYSCIAN SERVICES

Medicare Part B pays for outpatient medical care, such as doctor visits, home health services, some laboratory tests, some medications, and some medical equipment. (Hospital stays are covered under Medicare Part A.) If you qualify to get Medicare Part A, you're also qualified for Medicare Part B, however Part B is completely **voluntary** due to the fact it costs **premium each month**. Typically, $104 - $199 per month taken deducted from the persons Social Security benefit check.

There is also a yearly deductible, which increased $7 to $147.00 in 2013. After you pay $147.00 yourself, your benefits kick in. After that, **Medicare will pay 80% of the cost of most Part B services**, and you (or your Medigap policy) pay the other 20%.

Finally, it's important to know that there is a penalty for enrolling late for Part B. If you don't sign up for Medicare Part B when you first become eligible (and you don't have comparable coverage from an employer), you may be penalized **one percent for each month** you did not sign up for Part B. A person may only late enroll in Medicare Part B during the **open enrollment period** of **January 1st through March 31st.**

- **Medical and other services.** Medicare Part B pays 80% of most doctor's services, outpatient treatments, and durable medical equipment (like oxygen or wheelchairs). You pay the other 20%. Medicare also pays for 55% of most mental health care costs.
- **Laboratory and radiology services.** This includes blood tests, X-rays, and other tests.
- **Outpatient hospital services.** Medicare Part B covers some of these fees. You also have to pay a co-payment. The exact amount varies depending on the service.

- **Home health care.** Medicare Part B pays for nurses and some therapists to provide occasional or part-time services in your home. As long as the provider is certified by Medicare, you pay nothing -- except for 20% of the charges for some medical equipment, such as wheelchairs and walkers.
- **Preventive services.** Medicare Part B helps pay for a number of tests, screenings, **vaccinations**, and a one-time physical exam to help you stay healthy. Many of these services are free. As of 2013, Part B will add coverage of "alcohol misuse" screening and counseling (for people who are not considered alcoholic), obesity screening and counseling, screening for depression, sexually transmitted infections screening and counseling, and cardiovascular behavioral counseling.

Medicare Parts A & B are considered "Traditional Medicare" due to the fact they are the original Medicare programs. The two-work hand in hand together, Part A covering most hospital stays and Part B covering routine checkups and doctor visits.

3. PART C: MEDICARE ADVANTAGE

Medicare Advantage covers the same benefits as Medicare Parts A & B, except administered through private insurance companies **(PPO's and HMO's)** instead of the federal government; the Advantage insurers are required to offer the same services as "traditional Medicare", and some may even offer extras such as: prescription drugs, vision and dental care because **Medicare does not cover dental or vision.**

These extras do not come free for everybody though, the insurer may charge extra for Part C plans, averaging $33 extra per month. When a person chooses their Medicare Advantage insurer, they are then locked into that network of doctors on the HMO/PPO; they may not be able to retain their current Medicare doctor due to this fact. In order to enroll for Part C, a person must already be enrolled in Parts A and B of Medicare.

Medicare Advantage was enacted in 1996 under the Balanced Budget Act of 1997, with the thinking that private insurance companies have better infrastructure and claims processing than the federal government. Under Medicare Advantage, the government pays a set monthly fee to private insurers, *known as "capitation"* for removing people from Parts A&B and placing them on Part C. Essentially Medicare Advantage created "privatized Medicare".

Unfortunately, privatized Medicare Advantage is much less efficient than traditional Medicare.

4. PART D: MEDICARE PRESCRIPTION DRUG

Medicare Part D is a prescription drug plan for senior citizens, and was placed into law through the Medicare Modernization Act of 2003. Prescription drugs can be extremely expensive, so the government has used a little creative accounting for Medicare Part D and created the **donut hole:**

Part (D)onut Hole

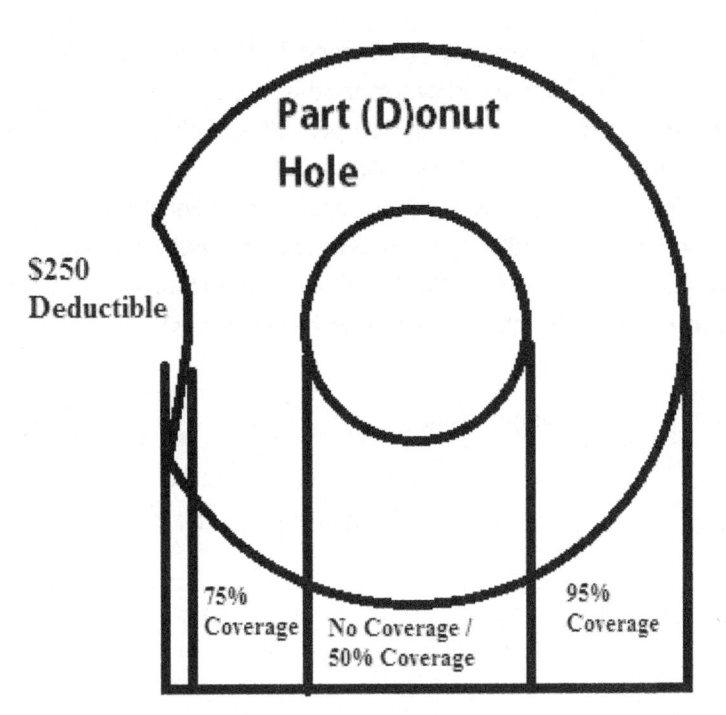

$250 Deductible

75% Coverage | No Coverage / 50% Coverage | 95% Coverage

The donut hole is where the insured must pay 100% of all prescription drugs; this was reduced to 47.5% in 2013 under PPACA and in order for a person to enroll into Part D, the person must also be enrolled in Parts A&B. By 2020, PPACA will fix and close the donut hole.

5. PRIVATE MEDICARE SUPPLEMENT INSURANCE

As you may have noticed, Medicare has many holes and gaps in coverage which may leave the enrollee with extra out of pocket costs; Medicare Supplement policies were designed by private insurers to help with these costs, typically known as Medigap & Medicare SELECT plans.

A person becomes eligible for a supplement policy without medical underwriting three months before attaining age 65 and three months after. Otherwise, if enrolling later than the open enrollment period, medical underwriting may be required and the insurer may decline to offer coverage.

There are three methods the insurer may use for rating policies
- **Attained Age:** The insureds current age at each renewal, prices typically increase each year of renewal.
- **Issue Age:** The insureds age at the time of application, prices do not increase or decrease upon renewal.
- **Community Rating:** Not dependent upon age, but all insureds within a specific area (usually county) will receive the same rate

On the next page, you will notice there are many differences in Medicare Supplement plans, so it is **the producer's responsibility** to determine which plan is suitable for the insured. To protect the senior citizen, there have been many limitations imposed on the sale of Supplement policies:

- Producers first year commissions may not exceed 200% of the renewal commission
- When replacing a Supplement policy for another Supplement policy, the new insurer must **waive all** waiting periods, exclusion periods and elimination periods that have already been satisfied under the first policy.
- The commissioner must approve all Medicare Supplement Advertisements
- Advertisements may only utilize government statistics published within the last 5 years
- Supplement plans must include a **30-Day Free Look Period** and must be written as **guaranteed renewable** (chapter 4 renewability options).

Medigap Benefits	Medigap Plans								
	A	B	C	D	F*	G	K	L	M	N
Part A hospital past 365 days	Yes	Yes	Yes	Yes	Yes	Yes	Yes	Yes	Yes	Yes
Part B coinsurance or copayment	Yes	Yes	Yes	Yes	Yes	Yes	50%	75%	Yes	Yes***
Blood (first 3 pints)	Yes	Yes	Yes	Yes	Yes	Yes	50%	75%	Yes	Yes
Part A hospice care coinsurance	Yes	Yes	Yes	Yes	Yes	Yes	50%	75%	Yes	Yes
Skilled nursing coinsurance	No	No	Yes	Yes	Yes	Yes	50%	75%	Yes	Yes
Part A deductible	No	Yes	Yes	Yes	Yes	Yes	50%	75%	50%	Yes
Part B deductible	No	No	Yes	No	Yes	No	No	No	No	No
Part B excess charges	No	No	No	No	Yes	Yes	No	No	No	No
Foreign travel exchange (up to plan limits)	No	No	Yes	Yes	Yes	Yes	No	No	Yes	Yes

Source: Medicare.Gov   N/A = not applicable

✓ It is **NOT** necessary to memorize this chart for your state exam.

Medicare Supplement policies must offer these core benefits to supplement Medicare Part A and B:

1. Copayments for hospital visits and lifetime reserve limits 60 – 150 days and extend hospital cost up to 365 days
2. The first 3 pints of blood must be covered
3. Part B's 20% coinsurance amount

ELGIBILITY FOR MEDICARE SUPPLEMENT ENROLLMENT

A person may enroll in Medicare & Supplement policies, for 3 months prior to age 65 and 3 months after attaining age 65 without any issues or medical underwriting. Senior citizens are typically enrolled in Medicare Parts A & B automatically upon attaining age 65; however, some may choose to opt-out at 65 and to enroll at a later date. If a person is a late enrollee, they may only enroll during the open enrollment period between **January 1st and March 31st**; and will also incur a 1% per month penalty added onto their premium for each month they chose not to enroll. Remember, the open enrollment period and penalties only apply if the person declined Medicare upon attaining age 65.

* Eunice has reached age 65 and received her Medicare enrollment package in the mail. Eunice decided not to enroll into Medicare Part B or Medicare Supplement because she feels healthy at the time. Eunice gets sick at age 66 and tries to enroll in Medicare, but is informed she will have to wait until January 1st, at which time she'll be 67. Eunice enrolls January 15th, 24 months after when she was originally eligible; her premiums will be 24% higher due to the penalty, and if she wants Medicare Supplement, she may have to go through medical underwriting to obtain coverage.

6. OVER 65 WORKING EMPLOYEES AND MEDICARE

Employees and their dependent spouses may find themselves still working at age 65 and still covered by group health insurance or may even be under age 65, but become disabled or diagnosed with Kidney Failure. Group health insurance and Medicare will work together in different ways

- **WORKING EMPLOYEES OVER 65:** Medicare must be offered, but group health is typically primary and Medicare is secondary insurance.
    - Companies under 20 employees: Medicare is primary
    - Companies over 20 employees: Group health is primary, Medicare is Secondary
- **DISABLED EMPLOYEES & SPOUSES UNDER 65:** Companies with over 100 employees must continue to cover disabled employees or their disabled spouses through group health; group health is primary, Medicare is secondary.
- **Employees with ESRD (Kidney Failure):** For the first 30 months, group health insurance is primary; after 30 months, Medicare becomes the primary insurance.

* Mary works full-time for XYZ Company, which has 120 employees. She has large group health plan coverage for herself and her husband. Her husband has Medicare because of a disability, so Mary's group health plan coverage pays first for Mary's husband, and Medicare pays second.

* Bill has Medicare coverage because of ESRD (kidney failure). He also has group health plan coverage through his company. Bill's group health plan coverage will pay first for the first 30 months after he becomes eligible for Medicare. After 30 months, Medicare pays first.

7. LONG TERM CARE INSURANCE (NOT MEDICARE, NOT SOCIAL/GOVT)

Long Term Care (LTC) insurance provides coverage for the costs of **aging**, such as nursing homes and is a very important part of a person's retirement planning due to the fact Medicare will not cover these costs. The majority of aging costs are related to **chronic illnesses** and LTC's objective is to provide chronically ill individuals with diagnostic, preventive, therapeutic, and rehabilitative services, and health maintenance and personal care services for at least 90 days, but full benefits must be for 12 months.

a. LONG TERM CARE BENEFITS

LTC policies are purchased either as expense incurred or indemnity, with benefits to be paid per day, week or month basis that will continue on for a set number of years; most often between $100 and $300 per day for AT LEAST **1 year (12 months)**.

Expense Incurred: The insured is only reimbursed for costs that they have paid out-of-pocket, up to an amount listed in the policy.
Indemnity: The insured will receive the full amount of benefits listed in the policy regardless of how much the cost of care is. Any amount over the cost of care received will be taxable.

* Jarrod purchased an indemnity LTC policy with a flat dollar amount of $200 per day; later on in life, Jarrod entered a nursing home which charges $150 per day to care for him. Jarrod would receive the full $200 per day, and at the end of the year file taxes on the extra $50 per day of income. If his cost of care were higher than $200/day, Jarrod would be responsible for that out-of-pocket.

b. QUALIFYING FOR BENEFITS

A person will be eligible to begin receiving their Long-Term Care benefits when they are unable to care for themselves on a **chronic** basis on one of two levels:
1. **Physical:** Unable to perform at least **two** of five Activities of Daily Living without help.
    a. **Activities of Daily Living (ADL's):** The first 5-7 things you perform when you wake up; mobility, dressing, eating, bathing, transferring, continence and personal hygiene.
2. **Cognitive:** Unable to protect their health or safety without substantial supervision and diagnosed with a condition in the past 12 months (Alzheimer's); cognitive relates to the thought processes of reasoning, intuition, or perception

There are also two types of illnesses
- **Acute Illnesses** are serious conditions that are easily treatable, such as the flu or pneumonia
- **Chronic Illnesses** happen on a reoccurring basis and for which the insured will not recover fully from; such as Arthritis or Alzheimer's

Physical or Cognitive levels must occur from a Chronic Illness, not an Acute illness.

c. LEVELS OF CARE

Long Term Care will pay for a multitude of different care levels:

1. **Skilled Nursing Care** must be prescribed by a doctor and followed through by skilled medical professionals. This level of care is the most expensive because the insured requires **24/7** around the clock care and is most often performed in a nursing home setting or hospital.

2. **Intermediate Care** is other-than 24/7 care, but is still performed by medical professionals on a daily basis under the supervision of a physician. Typically performed in a nursing home as well, but the insured is stable.

3. **Custodial Care** may be performed at home or at a nursing facility (facilitative care) and will help the insured with personal care to perform their **ADL's**. The care provider **does not need medical training** because custodial care helps only with dressing, eating, bathing etc. Custodial care may be also considered Home Health Care.

4. **Home Health Care** is performed on a **part-time basis,** at home, and may entail physical therapy or other daily activities like shopping, cooking etc.

5. **Adult Day Care** works very similar to child day care, where the participants engage in activities, exercises, education and meals. The senior would arrive at the day care while the primary caregiver goes to work, since the senior returns home each night; Adult Day Care is also considered Home Health Care and is perfect for mental illnesses such as Alzheimer's.

6. **Respite Care** is temporary relief for the caregiver that may be performed at Home or at a facility. Being a caregiver can be extremely difficult, so they may need a break for a few hours, or a weekend; Respite care could provide for a "baby sitter" type of person, or a facility for temporary care to allow for an extended weekend.

7. **Continuing Care** may be considered a "retirement community" that is typically sponsored by religious or nonprofit organizations. It allows for the senior to have more of an independent living, but still have access to care when needed.

Custodial care, Home Health Care, Adult Day Care and Respite Care can all be considered Home Health Care since they may be administered either at the home, and the senior citizen does not stay in a facility for the entire 24 hours. The level of care needed will be dependent upon the senior's chronic medical condition.

d. LONG TERM CARE PARTNERSHIPS

The majority of bankruptcies in America can be attributed to the growing costs of medical bills, and nursing homes. If a senior citizen without Long Term Care insurance required nursing care, they would likely need to sell their home to afford the costs and when all assets are expended; many seniors end up on Medicaid when they have zero assets.

Some states have long-term care insurance programs designed to help people with the financial impact of spending down to meet Medicaid eligibility standards. Under these "partnership" programs, when you buy a federally qualified partnership policy, you will receive partial protection against the normal Medicaid requirement to spend down your assets to become eligible.

e. EXCLUSIONS FOR LONG TERM CARE

Alzheimer's cannot be excluded; however, some other mental illnesses (schizophrenia etc.) may be excluded. The other normal exclusions apply such as: War, Suicide, Intentional Harm, and Felonious Acts.

f. OPTIONAL RIDERS FOR LONG TERM CARE

Many LTC policies allow insureds to purchase additional coverage in the form of riders. The riders will cost extra money, but they also include some key benefits, the riders may be:

- **Waiver of Premium:** Must be offered or included on all LTC policies, it will waive the premium once the insured begins to use the benefits. It could also waive the premium for the spouse if they both have LTC policies.
- **Return of Premium Rider:** Refunds premium to the insureds estate if the insured dies before the policy is utilized. Basically, adds a life insurance policy in the amount of premiums to the policy.
- **Paid Up Premium:** Allows the insured to pay off the policy early by paying extra premiums early on.
- **Guaranteed Insurability (Future Increase Option):** Allows the insured the option to increase benefits later on in life regardless of health status.
- **Cost of Living Adjustment:** Automatically increases benefits at the rate of inflation, this will ensure the customer always has enough coverage no matter how long they have the policy.

MEDICARE SPECIFIC DEFINITIONS:

1. **Ambulatory Service Center:** A non-overnight surgical center where the insured may walk in, receive care and walk-out. Typically seen as "urgent care" centers; ambulatory has nothing to do with ambulances.
2. **Actual Charge:** The amount a physician actually charges for a covered service.
3. **Approved Amount:** The amount Medicare pays for a specific service
4. **Excess Charge:** The amount in between the Actual Charge and Approved amount, the insured may be responsible for the excess charge

* Karen is age 65 and broke her leg while bouncing on a trampoline. Her sister rushed Karen to an ambulatory service center because it was cheaper than going to the hospital. Upon receiving care, the physician's actual charge was $600, but Medicare only approved $400 of those charges. Thus, Karen was responsible for the excess charge of $200.

Characteristics of LTC POLICIES
- Purchased with a flat dollar amount usually per day in benefits and any amount over the cost of care is taxed as earned income
- Written as **Guaranteed Renewable**
- Policy benefit periods typically 1 to 5 years, with a minimum of 1 years
- Must provide coverage for Alzheimer's, but does not need to cover alcoholism or other mental illnesses
- Free Look period must be expanded to **30 days**
- An Outline of Coverage must be given at the time of **application** to provide for full and fair disclosure

8. OLD AGE SURVIVORS INSURANCE

Social Security was passed by Congress in 1935 as a social entitle program, with the original name of "Old Age Survivors and Disability Insurance" (OASDI) and its purpose is to provide for the general welfare of U.S. citizens. Social Security is a Federal program and funded through two taxes:

> **Federal Insurance Contribution Act (FICA):** Known as the payroll tax, usually taken directly from an employee's paycheck, 7.65% is paid by the employee and the employer pays 7.65% as well, for a combined tax of 15.3%
> **Self Employed Contributions Act (SECA):** For self-employed individuals the total tax is paid of 15.3% because there is no employer contribution.

The taxes are split between Medicare and OASDI, with 6.20% (FICA) or 12.40% (SECA) going towards OASDI and 1.45% (FICA) or 2.90% (SECA) attributed to Medicare; for the total of 15.3% taxes paid.

Eligibility for benefits is contingent upon a citizen's **accrued credit**, each quarter a person pays their taxes, they gain one accrued credit. Since there are four quarters in a year, a person may only accrue four credits in any given year; upon obtaining **40 credits**, a person is considered **fully insured** and will receive full Social Security Benefits. They may also become **partially insured** if they have **6 credits** in the past 13 quarters, or 3.25 years. If a person has never worked, they would not receive Social Security due to the fact they have not paid their taxes and accrued no credit.

* Elise was a stay-at-home wife for most of her life, but prior to getting married at 29, she worked full-time from ages 18 to 28. During those 10 years she had her FICA tax taken from her check and paid into the Social Security system. When Elise arrived at age 65, she was afraid she would not receive benefits since she hasn't worked in 36 years; however, Elise is entitled to full benefits since she had worked those 10 years and acquired 40 credits.

a. SOCIAL SECURITY BENEFITS

Social Security benefits are paid out in three ways: **death, retirement and disability** benefits and these benefits may be paid to the insured, spouse or child depending on the situation.

Benefits are determined based off a person's highest 35 years of income, *weighted* for inflation, to determine the "average indexed monthly earnings" AIME. Then the AIME is plugged into a formula based off of the person's age and when they plan to retire to give a monthly figure. The amount of benefits a person receives from Social Security is called the **Primary Insurance Amount (PIA)**.

b. SOCIAL SECURITY SURVIVOR BENEFITS

If the insured dies, either the surviving spouse, dependent child or dependent parents may be eligible for death benefits. The survivor will receive a one-time lump sum payment for of $255, and then may continue receiving benefits over-time, dependent upon the survivor's age.

- Surviving Spouse:
    - Age 65 and above are entitled to full benefits
    - Age 60-64 will receive a reduced benefit
    - Spouse with dependent child under age 16 (or 22 if disabled) will receive 75% benefits, and if the child remains disabled benefits will continue indefinitely
- Surviving Child:
    - Under age 18, or 19 if in high school, or 22 if disabled, the child receives 75% benefits; unless married, then benefits cease.
- Surviving Parents:
    - One dependent parent will receive 82.5%
    - Two dependent parents receive 75% each

Widows or widowers and children, termed "survivors" by the Social Security Administration, are eligible for survivor benefits if the surviving spouse is left to care for children under the age of 16, or age 22 if the child has been continuously disabled. When the youngest child becomes of age, the benefits stop and won't resume until the surviving parent reaches age 60. The period during which the surviving spouse doesn't receive benefits from Social Security is called the blackout period.

c. SOCIAL SECURITY RETIREMENT BENEFITS

Social Security provides for retirement benefits paid on a monthly basis to the fully insured with full benefits being paid at age 66. A person may receive early retirement benefits at age 62, but benefits will be reduced forever or they may take delayed retirement benefits after age 66 to receive a higher lifetime benefit. A person receiving OASI at 62 would still receive Medicare at 65.

* Aubrey, age 62, has been working her entire life and is looking forward to retiring ASAP. She begins to draw her S.S. retirement benefits, but they are lower than she would have received if she waited until age 66. She also learns that she is ineligible for Medicare, because she is under the age 65.

9. MEDICAID

Medicaid is health insurance for the lower income **(needy)** indigent population, or easily remembered as: the people who are in financial aid. Medicaid was enacted as part of the Social Security Amendment Act of 1965 and has been expanded multiple times over the years, but it still remains as a **Federal and State** program, because it has federal minimum guidelines, but states are also allowed to expand the program themselves. Medicaid covers about 95% of all health-related costs, including dental, vision, prescriptions, and is completely free to the impoverished.

The child portion of Medicaid is called CHIP, standing for Children's Health Insurance Plan, but may go under a different name. The primary difference between actual Medicaid and CHIP are the family income limits, Medicaid eligibility is related to 100% of the poverty limit (currently $11,490 income per year) whereas CHIP eligibility is 200% of the poverty limit. CHIP typically costs a family around $50/year to insure all children and works under the same rules of Medicaid. Roughly 60% of Medicaid recipients are children, another 25% are the single parents of the children and the remaining 15% are the permanent blind or elderly over the age 65 and confined in a **skilled nursing facility**, such as a nursing home. Medicare does not cover nursing home charges, so a senior citizen without Long Term Care insurance will typically liquidate all of their assets and then finally end up on Medicaid.

PRACTICE QUESTIONS: SOCIAL INSURANCE

1. All of the following are Social (Government) Insurance EXCEPT:
   a. Long Term Care
   b. Medicare
   c. Social Security
   d. Medicaid

2. Medicare covers skilled nursing for how many days?
   a. 100
   b. 80
   c. 20
   d. 3

3. What renewability option is Medicare Supplement (MediGap and SELECT) written as?
   a. Noncancellable
   b. Guaranteed Renewable
   c. Optional Renewable
   d. Cancellable

4. Long Term Care insurance must NOT exclude which of the following?
   a. ALS
   b. Renal Failure
   c. Alzheimer's
   d. Disability

5. A person receives Old Age Survivors Insurance at age 62, when will they be eligible for Medicare?
   a. 67
   b. 65
   c. 64
   d. 62

6. Which part of Medicare has a donut hole?
   a. Part A
   b. Part B
   c. Part C
   d. Part D

7. Which of the following best describes Medicare?
a. A medical plan primarily covering the costs of aging
b. A private insurance plan for the disabled
c. Social insurance best used for the indigent population
d. A basic hospital and medical program

8. Which of the following levels of care does NOT need to be performed by a skilled person?
a. Custodial Care
b. Intermediate Care
c. Skilled Care
d. Home Health Care

9. What are the tax consequences of Long Term Care insurance?
a. Tax deductible premiums and completely tax free benefits
b. Tax deductible premiums and tax free benefits, with any excess amount over the cost of care being taxed
c. Non tax deductible premiums and completely tax free benefits
d. Non Tax deductible premiums and tax free benefits, with any excess amount over the cost of care being taxed

10. Medicaid is regulated by which entities?
a. State governments
b. Federal government
c. Federal and State governments
d. National Association of Insurance Commissioners

CHAPTER 9: LIFE INSURANCE BASICS

Life insurance serves several purposes; a sufficient amount of death benefit can provide income or funeral expenses for the insured's family, loved ones or even business partners after their demise. The death benefit can be part of their estate or it can be in place of an estate for those who have no estate to leave behind. If the policy is **permanent** insurance covering the insured to age 100, such as **whole** life, there will be a death benefit and it will also build up a separate cash value account, which can be borrowed against, or even cashed in if need be. A term life insurance policy would provide the insured with temporary coverage for a set amount of years, but only provide a death benefit without a cash value account; which will be much lower cost. Here are the parties involved in life insurance:

- **Policyowner:** Person who purchased the policy and must pay the premiums, the policyowner has all of the rights to the contract
- **Insured:** The natural person's life which the policy is contingent upon; the policy owner and the insured may be the same person or a separate person
- **Beneficiary:** Death benefits are only payable to the beneficiary; the insured **cannot** be the beneficiary. If no beneficiary is listed, the death benefit will be paid to the estate.

* Jason wanted to protect his family against the future funeral costs in the event of death. Jason decided to purchase two separate policies, one on himself and one on his wife, Rushmi; on each policy he names the other person as the beneficiary. Since Jason is the one purchasing the policies, Jason is the policyowner on both policies, but only the insured on one. In the event Jason dies, Rushmi will receive the death benefit, if Rushmi dies, Jason will get the death benefits. If both were to die at the same time, the estate will receive the death benefit.

The death benefit may be paid out in multiple ways, a great aspect of life insurance is the fact **death benefits are received tax-free** if paid in a lump sum; unless, they are paid to the estate. Not only can the beneficiary receive the benefits in a lump-sum, but they can also receive the funds over time, either annually or monthly through the use of an Annuity. Annuities are simply a cash value account that will be liquidated in a structured way; such as a $1,000,000 death benefit being paid out over 30 years.

A. WHO CAN PURCHASE INSURANCE (INSURABLE INTEREST)

You cannot just purchase insurance on any random person, there must be a reasonable financial interest between the policyowner and the insured **at the time of application**; this term is called **insurable interest**. This means that a Husband and Wife may purchase insurance on each other, even if they become divorced, the policy will remain in-force and still pay the benefits to the beneficiary.

1. **Stranger Originated Life Insurance (STOLI) (Illegal):** An agent/stranger who purchases a policy on a retired person; the agent pays the premium and then
2. **Investor Originated Life Insurance (IOLI) (Illegal):** Same as STOLI, except the policy is then sold to an investor rather than the agent keeping the policy.

STOLI AND IOLI are illegal because the primary purpose was the purchase insurance without an insurable interest and the **owner** is the one profiting.

These are the four LEGAL insurable interests:

- **Blood:** Insuring your own life, or a family member (parents, children etc.)
- **Love:** Insuring a spouses life developed through marriage
- **Business:** Business Partners, Owners, Directors and other key personnel of a company may purchase life insurance on each other. Typically: **Key Person** or **Buy-Sell** policies
- **Economic:** A financial reason existing, such as a Mortgage company/Bank on a borrower, or an auto finance company on a borrower, called **Credit Insurance**

* Paul and Kevin each own 50% in their Jet Ski business which is worth 10 million dollars. Kevin and Paul are planning for how the business will change hands in the event of one of their deaths. They each have a financial interest in the business and decide to purchase life insurance to perform a buy-out of the other person's shares. Two years later, the jet-ski business is bankrupt and both owners move on to new separate ventures, but they both continue to pay the premiums. 25 years later, Kevin dies, Paul will still receive the death benefit because they had **an insurable interest at the time of application.** It is not needed at the time of death.

VIATICAL SETTLEMENT

A viatical settlement is not illegal; it is when a person has an existing life insurance policy, which upon **terminal illness**, they sell the policy to a 3rd party known as a viatical settlement company. This allows the person to pay down medical bills, or long-term care costs in the last stages of death. The insured is known as the **viator** and the agent will represent the viator in all actions. Upon the death of the viator, the death benefit will be paid to the viatical settlement company, their family will receive nothing. Even though viatical settlements are not illegal, it would be illegal to purchase life insurance for the sole purpose of selling it later on. Viatical settlement proceeds **are taxed**.

* Tom has a $1,000,000 death benefit life policy and has just been diagnosed with Ebola and is currently in hospice. Tom performs a viatical settlement, whereby a 3rd party company pays him $500,000 upfront while he's alive, and he commits an absolute assignment over to them. Upon Tom's death, the death benefit will be paid to the viatical settlement.

B. REASONS TO PURCHASE LIFE INSURANCE

1. **Survivor Protection:** The **most important** reason for life insurance is utilized to maintain the lifestyle for the family, such as replacement of income in the event of the wage-earning spouse's death. Final Expense (Funeral) Funds, Education Funds, Emergency Funds, Monthly Income etc.

2. **Estate Creation:** An estate consists of a person's Assets, Liabilities and Taxes (Probate, Estate, Death taxes). If a person has a negative net worth upon death, if any assets are left to family/heirs, the creditors may sue the heirs for the amount willed to them. Estate creation will create an estate and allow cash to be left to the heir.

3. **Estate Conservation:** There are federal and state estate taxes ("death tax") on any amount left to an heir other than a spouse. Life insurance can be used to pay off those taxes, so the assets do not need to be sold. Assets left to a spouse are not taxed, but assets left to children are.

4. **Liquid Cash Accumulation:** Life insurance is the only form of insurance to accumulate cash (permanent policy with a cash value account) and that cash value is a liquid asset, meaning the funds are easily accessible without needing to sell stocks or a home for access to the cash value.

* Whitney and Travis own a 200-acre farm valued at $10,000,000 and would like to leave the farm to their children in the event of death. The estate tax for them would be 50%, so they purchase a policy covering both of them for $5,000,000; upon Travis's death, the farm transfers to Whitney without an estate tax, but when Whitney dies, the farm transfers to their children and the 50% tax applies. The death benefit would be paid to the estate and used to pay off the 5 million in taxes, allowing the children to keep the farm without needing to sell it to pay for the death tax i.e.: **estate conservation.**

C. DETERMINING AMOUNT OF PERSONAL LIFE INSURANCE

Once the producer has discovered the reason for the insureds purchase of the policy, the producer will need to determine the amount of insurance to purchase. If the producer were to just ask the insured "How much life insurance do you think you'll need?" that would be tantamount to guessing; thus, there are two primary mathematical methods of setting the death benefit amount.

> **Human Life Value Approach:** Developed in 1924 by Dr. Solomon Heubner, this approach takes into account **only the applicants** net worth. The HLV method includes the age, occupation, applicants' investments, applicants age to retirement and future earnings potential when placing a value on their life; while completely disregarding the applicant's family's needs, inflation, and increase in standard of living.

> **Needs Benefit Analysis (Needs Approach):** The Needs Approach was designed to replace the HLV method, as the approach takes into account the surviving family members when determining the amount of insurance needed. The spouse's income, child's education funds, Social Security, Pension plans, and all other forms of income are now included in the method. The needs approach is much more thorough than the HLV approach.

A large factor when determining the amount of insurance needed will be the Social Security benefits of the deceased. The spouse or child may be entitled to receive the insureds Social Security benefits in the event of death, but the producer must be aware of the **Social Security Blackout Period.**

D. BUSINESS USES OF LIFE INSURANCE

Now that we've explored the reasons for individuals to purchase insurance, we can expand our learning into the business purposes of life insurance. A business may act a lot like the breadwinner of a family; many people rely on the business for paychecks, not just the employees, but also the business owner's family.

- What will happen to the business if one of the owners will die and who will take ownership? What about the business owner's family?
- What will happen to the employees and the infrastructure of the business?
- What if one of the key employees dies, will the business lose money? Will the stock go down? What about training costs of the new employee to replace the deceased?

Life insurance may be used as a funding medium and business interruption protection. Let's explore the different types of policies available to protect a business.

1. KEY-PERSON INSURANCE

Key person insurance is when the business, (the policyowner and beneficiary), purchases life or disability insurance on an employee (the insured); upon the employees' death or disability, the business would receive the benefits. This policy is used **to fund training** of a new employee or to **protect lost income** in the event of the key persons death or disability and may be any type of life insurance, such as term, whole, adjustable or universal and may also be written as a disability insurance policy that pays a **lump sum.**

* Tammy owns a computer software firm with 20 employees and one sales manager which brings in 60% of the company's earnings. Tammy is afraid that if her sales manager dies or becomes disabled, her business will lose a lot of money and it will take a long time to train a new employee. Tammy would purchase Key Person insurance on her sales manager to protect her business.

- ✓ **Key person premiums are NOT tax deductible and the benefits are received TAX FREE.**

2. BUY-SELL FUNDING (Buy-Out, Sell-Out)

When there are multiple owners in a corporation one of the largest concerns becomes: "Who will take over the business when an owner dies?" Proper planning can help settle the needs of not only the other owners in the corporation, but also the family members of the owners. Buy-sell agreements are contracts that may only be drafted by an **attorney**, and may be funded in four ways: cash on hand, borrowing (a loan), installment payments or typically life insurance.

The buy-sell agreements will state that when one owner dies, their family MUST sell the ownership to the other partners and the partners in the business MUST purchase ownership from the family.

1. **Cross-Purchase plans:** Each partner/owner will purchase a policy on the other owners in the amount of their interest. MOST buy-sell agreements are Cross-Purchase plans.
2. **Stock Redemption plans:** Only used in stock corporations, the stockholders will purchase the shares of the deceased stockholder at a pre-determined price.
3. **Disability Buy-Out:** Works the same way that life insurance would, except instead of death, the policy will pay out when a partner is "economically dead". Disability buy-outs are typically written as entity purchase plans, not cross-purchase.

3. BUSINESS OVERHEAD EXPENSE:
BOE policies are used **to keep the business running.** This type of policy can pay for **rent, utilities,** employee salaries (not the owners) and other overhead costs. **The premiums are tax deductible and the benefits may be taxable.** This is explained more in the disability chapter, as BOE policies are only used in disability insurance.

* Mary, John and Patty all have equal ownership within their nail salon business. In the event one of the owners dies, the other owners are afraid of the family coming in and trying to tell them how to run their business. All 3 owners and their families meet with an attorney to enter into a cross-purchase buy-sell agreement. Mary purchases 2 policies, one on John and one on Patty; John purchases 2 policies, one on Mary and one on Patty and Patty purchases 2 as well, for a total of 6 life insurance policies; if there were four owners, then 12 total policies would be needed.

4. EXECUTIVE BONUS
Executive Bonus is an arrangement between the employer and employee, where the employer has offered to give the employee, a wage increase in the amount of the premium of a new life insurance policy on the employee. Due to the bonus arrangement, since the employer has treated the premium as a pay increase, the amount is tax deductible as a business expense to the employer and the income taxable to the employee. Executive bonus policies are typically **Split Dollar** policies where the employer and employee share (or "split the dollar") in premiums.

E. CATEGORIES OF LIFE INSURANCE
There are three categories of individual insurance, with the most common being "ordinary" insurance.

➢ **Ordinary (Traditional) Insurance:** The most common sold insurance is Ordinary Term or Ordinary Whole life. Almost all insurance sold today can be considered "ordinary".
  o **Face Value:** Death benefits must be above $1,000 or $5,000
  o **Premiums:** Paid by the individual on an annual, monthly or weekly basis to insurer

➢ **Industrial Insurance:** Sold by "Home Service" insurers, however has declined in popularity and is rarely sold today due to its small face value
  o **Face Value:** Small death benefit, under $1,000 or $5,000

- **Premiums:** Producer collects from insureds home for the insurer
- The primary purpose of industrial was funeral expenses for "blue collar workers" such as railroad employees or mining employees

> **Group Insurance:** Provided for an employee as a benefit by the employer, the employer makes most of the decisions; however, the employee may choose the beneficiary. We cover group in another chapter in the book.

An Ordinary Whole Life policy is the exact same as a Whole Life policy, the word ordinary only states the death benefit is over $1,000; so, an ordinary whole life policy would still cover the insured to age 100 and build cash value.

1. U.S. GOVERNMENT PLANS

There are two **U.S. Government Life Insurance** plans that are not available to the general public:
- Service Members Group Life Insurance (SGLI), which is term group life insurance, is issued to all members of the uniformed armed forces while the individual is on active duty. Members have the option to purchase up to $400,000 that is guaranteed. The coverage is convertible after separation from the military, into individual coverage in participating or eligible private insurance.
- Federal Employees Group Life Insurance is issued only as group term life insurance. All federal employees are automatically covered unless coverage is waived. The basic insurance cost is shared between the Federal Employee (2/3) and the Federal Government (pays 1/3).

F. MARKETING PRACTICES & SALES
1. SOLICITATION AND SALES PRESENTATIONS

Soliciting Life insurance is an agent's primary duty; but solicitation does not just entail the sales aspect, but also includes the explanation of benefits and the follow-up by an agent.

a. ILLUSTRATIONS

A policy illustration would be considered a quote-sheet used by an agent. Any time an agent quotes a life insurance policy, a printout will show the persons premiums, death benefit, cash value and other factors until age 100. This allows the customer to receive a picture of what their policy will look like in future years. Illustrations must be approved by the insurer (company) and the producer (agent) may not change them. The **illustrations** must make distinctions between guaranteed and projected amounts in a contract. The agent and the insured both must sign an illustration.

b. POLICY SUMMARY

A Policy Summary is a document that **highlights** the coverage, benefits, limitations, exclusions, costs and terms of the proposed life insurance policy. Policy Summaries are required to be delivered to applicants when the policy is delivered. It contains general information including the name of the agent, office information and name of the policy.

c. BUYERS GUIDE

A booklet that describes insurance policies and concepts, and also provides general information, approved by the Insurance Commissioner, to help an applicant make an informed decision about choosing insurance. The Buyers Guide must be provided to the applicant when the policy is delivered.

2. COST COMPARISONS

a. INTEREST-ADJUSTED NET COST METHOD

Utilizing inflation, also known as the **time value of money**; the interested-adjusted net cost method determines how much money would be saved by keeping a death benefit tied to inflation rates.

b. COMPARATIVE METHOD

Comparing the costs of whole life vs. decreasing term insurance; since, whole life builds cash value a person could forego that aspect and just purchase term. Then invest the savings in a side fund.

3. REPLACEMENT

Replacement is a new policy or annuity written to take the place of one currently in force.
The replacement policy must be in the best interest of the insured. An example of replacement is when an insured cancels a whole-life policy to purchase a term policy. Policy replacement his **heavily and strictly** regulated due to claims arising 30 and 50 years after a policy has been replaced; the insurance commissioner has set forth some simple rules:

1. The agent must ask if the new policy is replacing an old one, if so, the **Agent & Applicant** must sign a replacement form
2. The agent must fully explain the benefits and determine if any nonforfeiture cash values exist
3. The new insurer must notify the existing insurer of the policy replacement and keep documentation on hand for future inquiries
4. Replacement & Cancellation should be completed on **the exact same day** to prevent a lapse of coverage or over-insurance.

A Disclosure Authorization Form must be given to the insured at the time of application, and also updated and re-sent to the insured **once per year**. This form has been approved by **the commissioner** and states that an insurer may not share privacy information with any person not entitled to view it. The commissioner, auditors, law enforcement, underwriters and others may view private information; but it may NOT be used for marketing purposes. Most often times identifying information is removed from privacy sensitive documents.

5. FIELD UNDERWRITING

Field underwriting is the initial screening of an applicant, most often performed by the producer. **The agent is the field underwriter** and the insurer's front line of underwriting.

a. AGENTS FIELD UNDERWRITING DUTIES

- Solicitation and Marketing of potential clients
- Ask questions and complete the application
- Sign ALL documents and acquire the policyowner/insureds signatures
- If a document is unsigned, the agent is to go back and get it signed
- Collect the first installment premium
- Decide which receipt is appropriate and
- Preferably hand deliver the policy to ensure accuracy and answer questions
- Inform the underwriter of any potential adverse selection concerns

b. APPLICATIONS

The application (app) will be used by the producer in the field, to collect information for the insurer on a prospective insured. It is the **producer's** responsibility to ask the questions and **complete** the application in **black ink** without using white out. Mistakes are often made, which the producer may use the "scratch-out and initial" method to correct; where the producer will put **one line** through a mistake, fill in the correct answer and have the **insured initial** the correction. However, the best practice would always be to start over a new application. There are three parts to an application:

- **Part 1 *(General Information)*:** Consists of the applicant's name, address, coverage information, sex, credit and other information.
- **Part 2 *(Medical Information)*:** Height, Weight, Medical History and Ancestry (Family history) will be included here.
- **Part 3 *(Agent/Producer Report)*:** The agent will list their thoughts and feelings about the insured, including any adverse information seen as a field underwriter. The producers report will also list whether or not this is a replacement policy and the applicant's income. The insured will **NOT** receive a copy of part 3, as these are the actual producer's notes.

✓ The producer, insured and policyowner must sign Parts 1 & 2 of the application; however, *beneficiaries will not sign the application.*

After the application has been completed, it will need to be signed by all parties involved, including: **the policyowner, insured (if different than policyowner), and the agent.** Beneficiaries will not sign the application, as they have no legal standing in the contract; they only receive the death benefit.

The application may be backdated up to **six months** to allow the insured to be rated at a younger age; which provides a discount on future premiums. However, all backdated premiums must be paid at the time of application before coverage begins.

c. AFTER THE APPLICATION

Once the application has been signed, the producer should **always** try to collect the first installment premium. The collection of the first premium up front serves multiple purposes: For the customer, coverage *may possibly begin immediately*; for the producer, commission can be paid out quickly; and for the insurer, payment is received and may be invested earlier. Upon collection of premiums, the producer must furnish the insured with one of the three receipts:

1. **Conditional Receipts**
    a. **Insurability Conditional Receipt:** Coverage would begin immediately since premium has been paid, but it is based on the condition of passing medical underwriting. If the insured dies before the policy is approved, medical underwriting is still completed as if the person is still alive. Should the person fail medical underwriting, all premiums will be refunded and death benefit will NOT be paid.

    b. **Approval Receipt:** Rarely used due to unfavorable court rulings, but coverage would begin upon being approved by medical underwriting. Should the insured die before medical underwriting, the policy is still voided.

2. **Binding (Unconditional) Receipt:** Coverage begins at the time premiums are paid, regardless if the insured would fail medical underwriting; exclusions still apply though, such as skydiving.

It is the producers' responsibility to explain the receipt to the insured, especially the conditional receipt because the **conditional receipt coverage would begin at the time of medical exam, or application date; whichever is later,** typically medical exam because it is a later date than the application date. If the insured happens to die prior to medical exam, the application and medical underwriting would continue; in lieu of the medical exam, the insurer may complete as many autopsies as reasonably necessary, unless prohibited by state law. Upon passing medical exam, the benefits would be paid, or if there is a failed medical exam, then premiums would be refunded.

The policy will be considered "effective" when the *policy issued and premiums are paid*; the anniversary of the policy will be based upon effective date.

* Ernie completed his application and paid his premium and received a conditional receipt for a decreasing term life policy. The next day (before medical underwriting), Ernie was involved in a car accident and died. The producer would still submit the application, medical underwriting would still be completed by autopsy. If Ernie passes medical underwriting his family would receive benefits; if not, his full premium would be refunded.

d. POLICY DELIVERY AND REQUIREMENTS

Most mistakes occur at the time of application or delivery when the agent is answering questions; luckily agents are required to have **Errors and Omissions (E&O) insurance**, to protect against mistakes...

Applications should always be completed in person and delivered in person, to allow the agent to answer any questions the applicant has and help lower. A producers' duties include hand delivering the policy directly to the insured whenever possible. The purpose of this hand delivery is to **answer any questions** and provide quality customer service. Upon hand delivering of the policy, the producer and the insured both must sign a **delivery receipt.**

If the insured did not pay the first installment premium at the time of application, the agent will have to obtain the premium and a **Statement of Good Health** from the insured. Coverage will not begin until the premiums are paid and the statement is signed by the producer and insured.

e. FREE LOOK PERIOD (REMORSE CLAUSE)

The Free Look provision allows a policyowner to determine if a policy is suitable for them and when a policy is **delivered** to the policyowner, and is found on the **front page of the policy**; they will have **10 days** to return the policy to the insurer and receive a full refund for all of their premiums; this allows the policyowner to look over the policy and determine if it is suitable for them. The **time of delivery** begins either when the agent hand delivers the policy, or at the time of postmark when mailed directly to the insured; if it is mailed to the producer, which is not, considered to be delivered.

* Mary purchased a new health insurance policy on February 10th, the insurer mailed it to Mary's agent on February 22nd and the agent then delivered the policy to Mary on March 2nd. If Mary returns the policy on or before March 12th, she will receive all of her money back.

f. EFFECTIVE COVERAGE DATE

The policy becomes effective when the underwriter issues the policy and the premiums are paid. If no payment was accepted upfront by the agent, before issuance of the policy, a Statement of Good Health may be required. This document will state that the insureds health condition has not substantially changed between the time of application and the time of issuance. If a health factor has changed, the insured may have to prove medical underwriting again before the policy can be fully issued.

G. PREMIUMS AND INSURED CLASSIFICATION

Premiums for life insurance are determined by an actuary of the insurer, based a set rate of per $1,000 of coverage. An actuary is a mathematician who uses statistics and the law of large numbers to predict losses for the insurer, then utilizes three primary factors to determine premium rates:

a. Mortality:

There is an industry standard Commissioners Standard Ordinary (CSO) Mortality Table, which predicts the **expectation of life** (Average number of years left to live) and the **probability of death** (Average number of deaths per year) for a group of same aged individuals.

The CSO table created by the Commissioners uses a large number of statistics over a long period of time and is distributed to insurers. The table predicts an average 29-year-old male would likely live to age 81 and an average 29-year-old female would live to age 83. Obviously not all 29-year-old men and women will live to age 81 or 83, but the mortality table predicts the average person will live to that age.

b. Interest:
Just like a bank, the majority of an insurer's revenue is derived from interest earned on investments. When a customer pays their premium, the insurer invests the premium, typically in real estate or bonds, and generates income from those gains. The insurers invest premiums so that they can **keep premiums low.** Actuaries assume that all policies are paid in advance to predict an assumed interest rate for the year to create the Net Single Premium to pay off the policy well in advance.

- ✓ **Net Single Premium = Mortality Cost – Interest**

Meaning that the customer could pay only the mortality costs up front and receive a huge discount for paying off the policy in one lump sum this would allow the insurer to invest the premiums and earn their own interest.

c. Expenses:
Insurance companies have many expenses, including overhead costs such as: postage, commission and administrative costs. One of the insurer's largest expenses comprises in the function of **policy reserves:** A set amount the insurer must keep on hand to saving for future claims.

- ✓ **Gross Premium = Net Single Premium + Expenses**

The gross premium is what the insured typically has to pay because most policies are not purchased with one lump sum payment. Any time a customer chooses to pay over time, they have to help pay some of the expenses not earned by the insurance company through interest.

* Darryl is purchasing an ordinary whole life policy and when discussing premiums, he realizes that his policy will cost him $45,000 throughout his entire life. Darryl asks if there is a way to receive a discount and his agent informs him that if Darryl paid the net single premium of $25,000 today in full, he would save $20,000 because the insurer could invest his $25,000 and earn $20,000 of their own interest without him. Darryl did not have $25,000 so he opted to pay the **Gross Premium** over time.

H. UNDERWRITING
Underwriting is process of checking applications and utilizing **classification of risks,** and is performed by an employee of the insurer known as an underwriter. The underwriter works very closely with the producer and the two-share information freely to ensure the timely issuance of policies, but only the **underwriter sets premium prices and issues policies.**

- ✓ The underwriter, producer, and insured are typically able to view any medical document. The Department of Insurance and Commissioner would NOT see medical information.

MEDICAL UNDERWRITING:

The first step in the underwriting process is to ensure the application is completed fully and to ensure the applicant and insured have an insurable interest in each other. Upon reviewing the medical history on the application, the underwriter may request the **producer** obtain an **Attending Physicians Statement**, which will have the applicants' physician provide a detailed report on any current medical conditions.

The underwriter may also pull the insureds medical records from the **Medical Information Bureau (MIB),** which is a *non-profit* organization that shares claims and application information. 98% of all health insurers and 80% of all life insurers are members of the MIB; each time a person applies for insurance, their application is stored at the MIB for up to 7 years. The **underwriter, producer** and **insured** are all able to see MIB report to ensure its accuracy; there is a **method** to fix any **incorrect** information in the MIB report and the underwriter cannot decline a risk solely on the report, information must be verified. The MIB does not actually have health insurance information, it only has the **application information** and the MIB reports are **NEVER** shared with the Department of Insurance.

Many insurance applications also require a medical exam, HIV testing and lab reports, which primarily consist of blood and urine and must be consented by the insured. The exams are paid for by the *insurer* and may only be performed by a doctor, nurse or paramedic; the agent does not perform the medical exam. If HIV or AIDS are found, the insurer must notify the applicant within 15 days, the insurer must notify the state's Department of Health and the medical exams are **NOT** forwarded to the **Department of Insurance** and also **NOT** shared with **policyowners who are not the insured.**

Even though the underwriter has many tools to at their disposal, there are quite a few factors that are deemed as Unfair Discrimination, such as: *marital status, race, national original, sexual preference, number of children, domestic violence* and other non-factors. Underwriting criteria must be approved by the **Dept. of Insurance** and also **disclosed to the insured.**

CLASSIFICATIONS OF RISKS (RISK CLASSIFICATION)

After the underwriter has reviewed all pertinent information, they must begin to classify the risk to determine premium prices. There are four main classifications of risks.

- **Preferred Risks** will receive a discount on their premiums, typically this is a risk that is in the correct height and weight proportions with little to no medical problems and is a non-smoker.
- **Standard Risks** are representative of the average person; the standard risk is the insurers' *base rate* and is not rated-up or rated down.
- **Substandard Risks** typically have medical issues and receive a *rated-up* (increased) premium.
- **Declined Risks** will not receive an insurance policy; there are many instances of being declined, such as no insurable interest, extremely high medical issues, too old or too young.

Life, Accident & Health Exam Study Book | TX

PRACTICE QUESTIONS: LIFE INSURANCE BASICS

1. M owns a small business with twenty employees and one IT manager. M is afraid if her IT manager dies or becomes disabled that her business may lose income. Which policy would be best suited for M's concerns?
   a. Group Life & Disability Insurance
   b. Buy-Sell Life & Disability Insurance
   c. Ordinary Life & Disability Insurance
   d. Key Person Life & Disability Insurance

2. When an underwriter places applicants into categories for premium rating, this is considered:
   a. Risk Management
   b. Premium Rating
   c. Classification of Risks
   d. Underwriters Ruling

3. Who is NOT required to sign an application for life insurance?
   a. The beneficiary
   b. The insured
   c. The policyowner
   d. The agent

4. R applied for life insurance on April 15th and submitted her premium the same day. Which receipt will her free look period be contingent upon?
   a. Conditional Receipt
   b. Binding Receipt
   c. Delivery Receipt
   d. Unconditional Receipt

5. Which of the following would be a factor when an underwriter is determining premiums?
   a. Spouses occupation
   b. Sexual Preference
   c. National Origin
   d. Marital Status & Insureds occupation

6. Which receipt must an agent give to a policyowner if premium is accepted at the time of application with a medical exam to follow?
   a. Binding Receipt
   b. Conditional Receipt
   c. Unconditional Receipt
   d. Delivery Receipt

7. Why is the annual premium payment mode the least expensive method of paying premium?
   a. The insurer can pay agent commissions upfront
   b. The insured can plan their budget better
   c. TDI has less regulation for annual payments
   d. The insurer has lower administrative costs

8. Net Single premium would be best described as:
   a. Mortality Costs + Interest
   b. Mortality Costs - Interest
   c. Mortality Costs + Interest - Expenses
   d. Mortality Costs – Interest + Expenses

9. J & M own a daycare together which is worth $10,000,000. J & M purchase Buy-Sell life insurance on each other to keep the business going in the event of a partner's death. Three years later the daycare goes bankrupt, and 9 years after that J dies. Which of the following would most likely occur?
   a. No death benefit is paid
   b. Death benefit is fully paid
   c. No death benefit is paid because the business was bankrupt
   d. Partial benefits are paid

10. During an executive bonus when the employer and employee share in premium, this is known as:
    a. Viatical Settlement
    b. Industrial Insurance
    c. Split Dollar Insurance
    d. This is illegal

CHAPTER 10: LIFE INSURANCE POLICIES

In this chapter we are going to discuss multiple types of life insurance policies; all life insurance will include a death benefit, but there are some distinct aspects between the different policies. It's important to meet the customers' needs when offering a product, not all customers will have the same budget and choosing the correct product for each person will be paramount to your job. Here is a brief summary of the four main types of life policies:

Fixed Premium Polices: The premiums will remain same throughout the length of the policy even as the face value or cash value increase. There are two types of fixed premium policies:

- **Term Life:** Term is the least expensive life insurance due to the fact it is purchased for a set period of time, thus is temporary, and **does not build cash value.**

- **Whole Life:** Permanent life insurance until age 100, which will build **cash value** the longer the insured has the policy. The policy endows at age 100 and pays the insured the death benefit if still alive.

Flexible Premium Policies: Allows for the insured to have some flexibility and control, the premiums may be adjusted as well as the length of coverage

- **Adjustable Life:** A combination of Term and Whole Life; the insured may convert between the two without proving insurability (medical underwriting). The policy is considered **convertible insurance** and also builds cash value due to the whole life aspect.

- **Universal Life:** The most flexible policy, where the insured has a **target premium**, but is not required to pay that exact amount. The policy is a combination of Annually Renewable Term and a Cash Value account; the insured must be careful of the **corridor** with Variable Universal Life.

That is just a summary of the policies; now let's learn them in more depth

A. TERM LIFE INSURANCE POLICIES

Term, the lowest cost of all life insurance policies, and is considered "temporary" life insurance. Term is purchased for a specific number of years, such as 1, 5-, 10-, 20- and 30-year terms or sometimes to a specific age such as 75. At the end of the term, the policy may either cancel or renew; premiums remain fixed during the term and will not change unless the policy is renewed, upon which the premium will increase due to the insureds higher age. Since term only provides for a death benefit and has no other frills, it may be considered **pure death protection** and **will not build cash value**; which results in its low price.

Term is the most popular life policy sold due to the low cost and many uses. When reading the names of the term policies, remember that the **premiums remain the same** during the term, but the death benefits are what will be changing.

> When reading the names of the term policies, remember that the premiums remain the same during the time-period, the term policy names refer to the death benefit. You may read them as Level (Death Benefit) Term, Increasing (Death Benefit) Term or Decreasing (Death Benefit) Term

There are four primary types of term life policies, listed from most expensive to least: Level Term, Increasing Term, Decreasing Term and Annually Renewable Term.

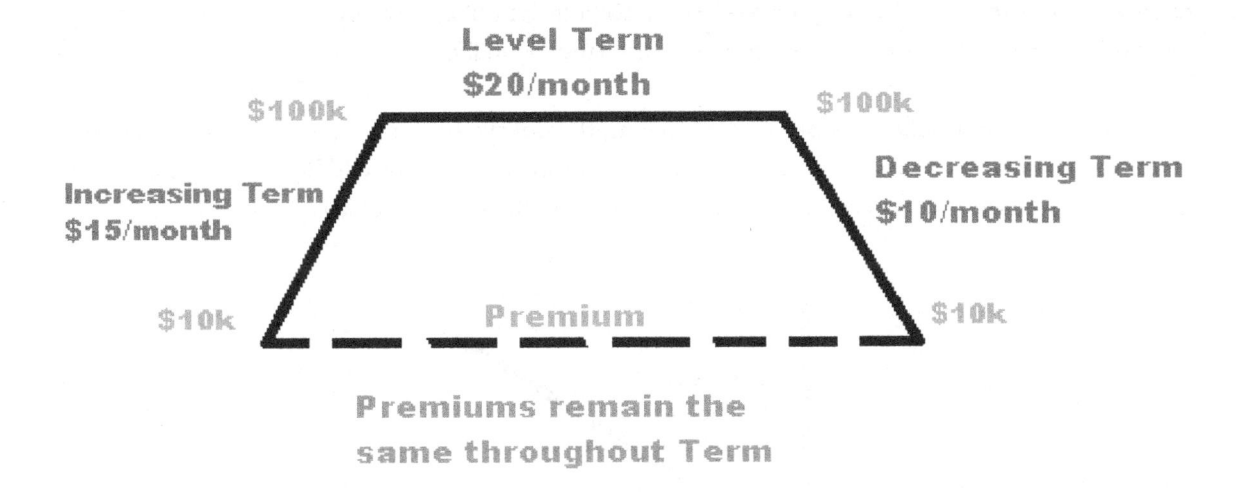

Level Term $20/month
$100k — $100k
Increasing Term $15/month
Decreasing Term $10/month
$10k — Premium — $10k
Premiums remain the same throughout Term

I. LEVEL TERM - $$$$
The most commonly purchased life policy, and the **most expensive term,** Level Terms death benefit and premiums remain the same through the length of the policy. Nothing will change, until the term either expires or the policy is cancelled. This insurance is easy to understand for a policyowner because the beneficiary will always receive the same death benefit no matter when the insured dies.

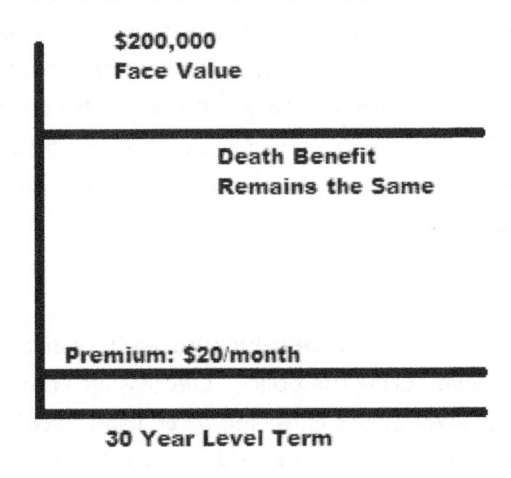

$200,000 Face Value

Death Benefit Remains the Same

Premium: $20/month

30 Year Level Term

* Shawn, age 45, is married with two kids and has a $100,000 house. Shawn would like to purchase life insurance to cover all of his bills and also have left-over money for his family should something happen to him. Shawn decides to purchase a $200,000 level 30-year term policy with a premium of $20/month, figuring that would be enough to pay off the house cover college expenses and carry his wife through retirement. Shawn is covered for the full $200,000 until age 75, which he has paid $20/month for the full thirty years. Upon attaining age 75, Shawn's policy expires and he no longer has insurance.

2. INCREASING TERM - $$$

Increasing Term policies are also purchased for a specific number of years, and the premiums are still locked in for that period, but a unique factor about increasing term is that the **death benefit will increase** over time, NOT the premiums. Increasing term policies are commonly sold to protect against **inflation and cost of living increases,** or sometimes utilized by new business, or younger people who are expecting to accumulate more wealth later on in life.

The amount the death benefit increases is not random; the policyowner may choose a specific amount of increase every year or tie the death benefit to the Consumer Price Index (CPI) ensuring the death benefit keeps pace with inflation and protects against the devaluing of the dollar.

$200,000 Face Value

Death Benefit Increases

Premium: $15/month

30 Year Increasing Term

* Gus, just recently married at age 23, realizes he needs life insurance to provide for his future children's education costs. Gus and his wife do not have many assets right now, so he to purchases a $50,000 Increasing 30-year term policy for $15/month. Education costs will continue to rise with inflation, so Gus and his agent calculated $200,000 will be enough to provide his children with adequate schooling should something happen to Gus in 30 years. Gus has saved a little bit of money on his premium by starting with a lower death benefit, as opposed to Level Term which would've been more expensive and began with the higher death benefit.

3. DECREASING TERM - $$

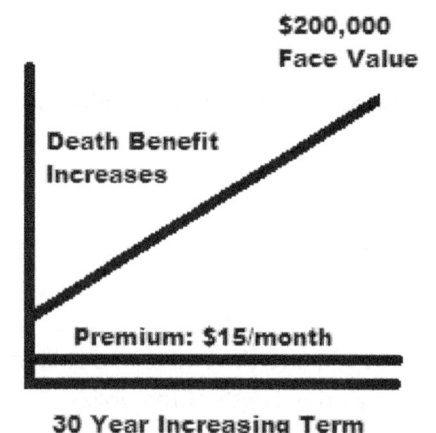

Decreasing Term policies will see the **death benefit decrease** over a period of years, but again, the premiums will still remain the same during the policy. Decreasing Term insurance is mostly used for **mortgage protection** and to cover credit lines, and to be used as collateral for loans. Since the death benefit will be decreasing as the insured gets older, the risk to the insurer is lowered and which in turn allows for the premiums to be cheaper. Decreasing terms are **NOT renewable** because at the end of the term, the death benefit is usually zero.

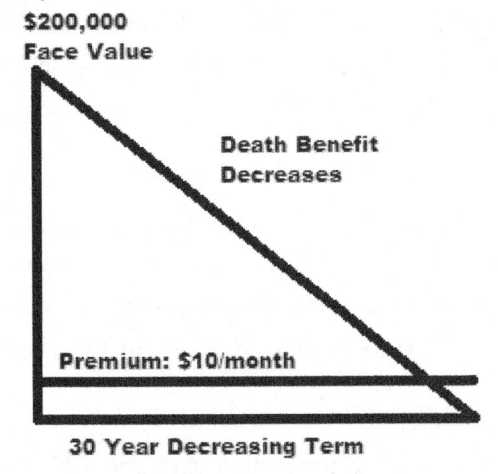

* Jules and her husband purchased a home for $200,000 and she knows her husband will be unable to pay for the mortgage should something happen to her. Jules decides to purchase a $200,000 Decreasing 30-year term policy for $10/month and she links the decrease to her amortization table on her mortgage. Should something happen to Jules, her death benefit will pay the exact amount to pay off the loan and she's saved some money on her premiums in the process.

4. ANNUALLY RENEWABLE TERM - $

Annually Renewable Term (ART) is the least expensive form of all life insurance due to the fact it is only a one-year term policy which will renew each year. Since the policy is technically good for only one year and the premiums are locked in for that one year, the **premiums will have to increase** each time the policy renews (known as a step-rate method). Luckily, each time the policy renews, the insured will NOT need to prove insurability (medical underwriting) every year, but mortality costs will only be factored in for the current year of the policy. The younger the ages of the insured, the much lower the premiums, however, the older the ages, the exponentially higher the premiums become due to the increased risk of death associated with higher **attained ages**.

Most term policies will automatically become renewable into ART upon the ending of the term. The **death benefits will still stay the same** or follow the same schedule (increasing term) that was laid out in the policy. Yet, Decreasing Term may NOT become renewable given that the death benefit will be zero at the time the term expires.

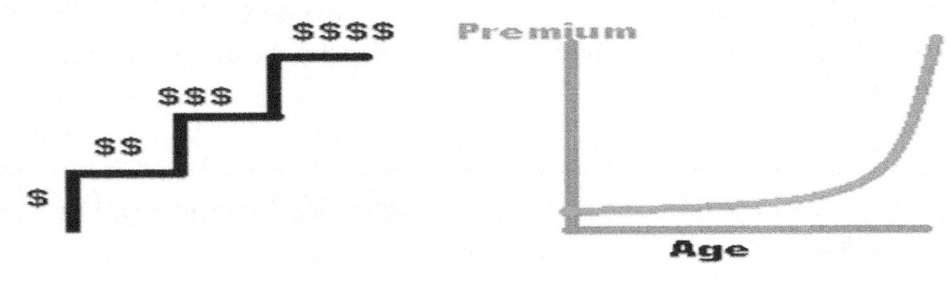

* Lassie, age 20, purchased a $200,000 30-year Level Term policy for $20/month. At age 50, Lassie's level policy may either expire or renew into ART. Should he decide to renew the policy at age 50, Lassie's premium will go from $20/month to $60/month, but he will still have the same $200,000 death benefit. When Lassie reaches age 51, his premiums will increase again from $60/month to $65/month, and keep increasing until a cut-off age listed in the policy.

5. CONVERTIBLE TERM

Many people purchase term for the benefits of having a lower premium, with the expectations to purchase permanent life insurance later on in life. Todays' term polices are all convertible, allowing the insured to exchange the term policy for a whole life policy at any time regardless of medical history. Whole life policies are allowed to be converted to Term at any time because the risk is lower.

B. WHOLE LIFE INSURANCE

Whole life insurance provides death benefit protection until **age 100**; should the insured survive to age 100, the policy will *"endow / mature"* and the face value will be paid directly to the insured without the need of death, thus providing for **permanent** protection. Whole life insurance also **builds cash value** (savings account) with each premium payment, providing a *living benefit* that the insured may tap into at any time while alive. With the combination of permanent life insurance and a cash value account, the premiums of whole life are **much higher** than the temporary protection term enjoys.

There are many different types of whole life policies, but the names are referring to the length of time that premiums are paid; meaning the policy may be paid off well before age 100, thus saving a lot of money. Whole life insurance death benefits and premiums will remain the same throughout the entirety of the policy; however, the actual premium prices may vary between the different types of whole life.

Think of it in terms of purchasing a $200,000 home:
- A 30 yr. fixed mortgage would cost $1,000/month the overall cost would be $450,000 due to interest
- A 15 yr. fixed mortgage would cost more per month, $1,500, but only $300,000 by paying it off early and saving interest
- The least expensive way to pay would be in a single cash payment of $200,000 and not needing to pay interest at all

When paying a mortgage off earlier, equity builds faster in the home. Life insurance works the same way; the sooner the policy is paid off, the more cash value the insured has. The insurance companies invest premiums and earn interest to make profits; if all of the premiums are paid early, money can be invested right away. The longer the insured takes to pay the policy off, the more expensive the overall premium.

There are four main ways to pay for whole life policies, and they all have different names; these are still all whole life, the only difference is when the policy is paid off: **Straight Life, Limited Pay, Life Paid up @ 65 and Single Premium.**

Life, Accident & Health Exam Study Book | TX

1. STRAIGHT (WHOLE) LIFE: $$$

Straight life insurance is whole life, but the premiums will be paid every year until age 100, meaning the policy is NOT paid off early. Straight life is the **most expensive overall** type of whole life because the payments are stretched for the longest period of time (age: 100). Since the policy is not paid off early, the insured will need to pay the insurance company's profit. These policies build slow cash value.

* Mandy lives paycheck to paycheck, but knows she needs some permanent life insurance for funeral expenses. She decides to purchase a $25,000 whole life policy and when choosing her premium payment options, she chooses the Straight Life option because it has the lowest monthly cost. Mandy understands that even if she's 99 years old, she will need to continue making premium payments, but she justifies this fact by the affordability of the policy into her budget.

$100,000 death benefit for all charts

Straight Life
Premium: $100/month
Age ——— 100
Annual Cost: $100/month
$1,200/year
Overall Cost: $60,000

Life Paid Up @ 65
Premium: $250/month
Age — 65 — 100
Annual Cost: $250/month
$3,000/year
Overall Cost: $45,000

Single Premium
Premium: $30,000
Age ——— 100
Annual Cost: $30,000 one-time
Overall Cost: $30,000

2. LIFE PAID UP @ 65 (WHOLE LIFE): $$

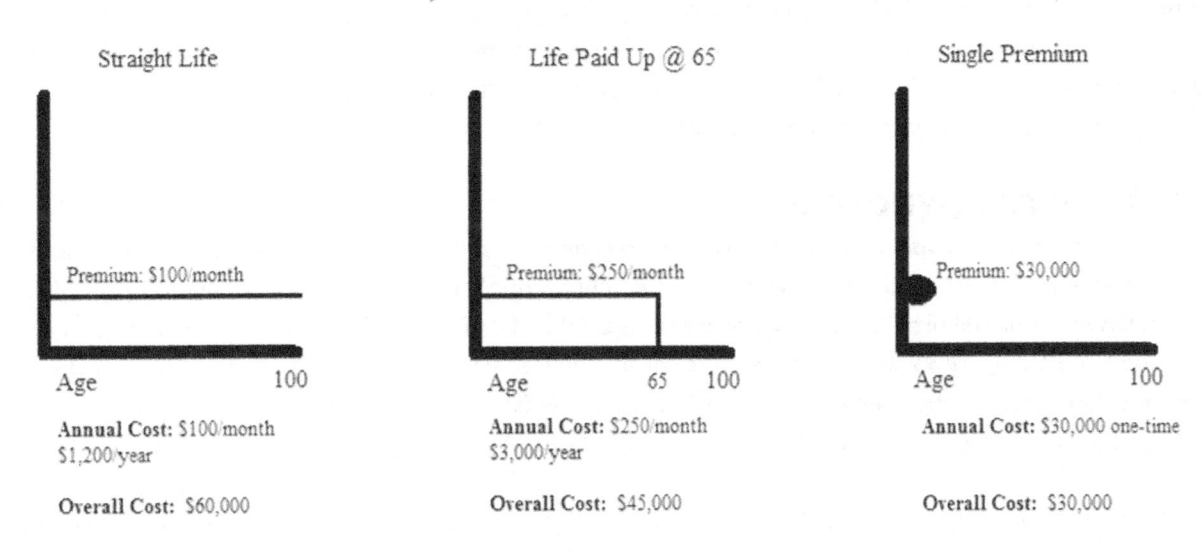

The whole life policy is paid up (paid off) at age 65, but the insured still has insurance until **age 100**, which is ideal for retirement. The benefit of paying up at age 65 is the **lower overall cost instead of straight life** because the policyowner is saving on interest. The insurer will have the entire premium earlier then age 100 and is able to invest the premiums themselves, resulting in a discount for the policyowner. However, since the premiums are paid off prior to age 100, the policyowner must make higher monthly/annually payments to finish paying earlier. The first annual cost (first year cost) will be higher on Life Paid up as opposed to Straight life which allows for more cash value than Straight Life.

* Andy, age 50, has decided to start planning for his retirement at age 65. He would like to purchase a whole life policy for the permanent protection, but knows his income will be severely limited when he retires. Andy chooses the Life Paid Up @ 65 option because he can afford a higher monthly bill while he's working and when he reaches retirement age, his policy will be paid off. Andy is happy he will effectively have life insurance from 65 to 100, but not need to make any premium payments during that time, making it easier to budget.

3. SINGLE PREMIUM (WHOLE LIFE): $

Single premium whole life is paid off in one lump sum, meaning there are no additional premiums required; the policy is paid up fully. The single premium may be relatively high, into the tens of thousands of dollars; but Single Premium Whole Life is the **LEAST expensive overall** because the insurer will have the longest amount of time to invest the premiums, which provides a large discount.

Single Premium Whole Life policies are the only type to generate cash value immediately, but may have a **surrender charge** (penalty) if the cash value is withdrawn early; the penalty is usually 10% and decreases each year as long as the funds have not been withdrawn. Single Premium builds **the most cash value.**

* North purchased a $100,000 whole life policy and chose the Single Premium option. North paid the full policy off with a $30,000 check, which immediately gave her $25,000 in cash value. She could withdraw or take a loan against the immediate cash value, but she would hit a penalty; if North dies early, the insurer will pay the death benefit and reimburse a portion of the cash value to her family, otherwise she would still be insured to age 100.

4. LIMITED PAY (WHOLE LIFE):

Any policy that is paid up prior to age 100 will be considered "Limited Pay", meaning that the premiums have been limited to before the endowment age. A 10-pay whole life policy would be a policy paid off in 10 installments, but still provides **coverage until age 100.** Life Paid up @ 65, Single Premium, 20-Pay and even Life Paid up @ 99 would still be considered "Limited Pay"; however, **Straight Life is NOT Limited Pay**, because the premiums are not limited in any fashion. Limited Pay policies build cash value quicker than straight life and life paid up @ 65 because the policy premiums are going in earlier.

* Rick, age 25, is looking for whole life insurance but is planning to retire at age 55. Rick's agent explains that most retirement policies would be Life Paid up @ 65, but since Rick is retiring early that a 30-Pay whole life would be more suitable. The policy will be paid off at 55 instead of 65, and Rick's cash value will also grow at a faster rate than paid up @ 65. This policy offers Rick faster cash value growth, lower overall costs (higher monthly bill) and the benefit of having paid off life insurance at his retirement age.

a. LESS COMMONLY SOLD WHOLE LIFE:
1. **Indeterminate Premiums:** Premiums will change up and down each year based off the insurer's investments, mortality and expenses. The insured will not know what the premiums will be until the next year when accounting is finished at the insurer.
2. **Modified Whole Life:** Lower premiums for the first 3-5 years, then increased; good for insureds with low income in financial need. Cash Value Grows Slow.
3. **Graded Whole Life:** Lower premiums for 3-10 years, then increased; used commonly with older insureds.
4. **Endowment Contract:** Any policy that endows; these contracts can endow before 100 and may have *rapid* cash value growth. The primary purpose is for cash value.
5. **Variable Life:** A FIXED premium whole life policy but the cash value is invested in stocks.

C. ADJUSTABLE LIFE

Prior to 1971, insureds only had the choice between Term Life and Whole Life, which were very limiting in nature and were not convertible, thus if a person's medical status changed for the worse, they may be unable to qualify for a new life policy. To fix this problem and fill a need, an insurer developed Adjustable Life insurance, to provide customers with more flexibility. Adjustable life insurance is **convertible** between Term and Whole life, meaning the customer may switch between Term to Whole or Whole to Term at any time WITHOUT proving insurability.

$100,000 Death Benefit
$10/month 10-year Term → $60/month Whole Life
$15/month 15-year Term ← $60/month Whole Life
$15/month 15-year Term → $80/month Whole Life

Converting allows the insured to control many factors a without needing to prove insurability, such as:

- Control premium payments by switching
- Control length of coverage by switching
- Decrease death benefit without proving insurability
- Increasing of death benefit, but will **likely need to take a medical exam**

Adjustable life insurance **may or may not build cash value**, because it may be switched to whole life at any point and begin building cash value. Should the insured decide to switch back to term, the policy will no longer build cash value, and any previous cash value is typically used to pay for the term premiums. Adjustable life builds slower cash value than whole life.

* Burton purchased an adjustable life term when he was young knowing he could convert it to permanent insurance at any time. When Burton obtains a new high paying job, he decides to switch his adjustable term for adjustable whole life, covering him until age 100; his premiums increased, but he is also building cash value. When Burton hits a mid-life crisis and loses his job, he can convert the policy back to adjustable term for lower premium payments and use the previous cash value to pay for the policy.

D. UNIVERSAL LIFE

Universal life insurance was invented around 1990 and was designed to offer the **most flexible** life insurance policy to date; basically, allowing the insured to control almost all aspects of the policy and even invest the cash value in the stock market, should the insured earn enough interest, they may not have to pay future premiums. In order to create this flexible of a product, the insurers combine **Annually Renewable Term** and a **Cash Account.**

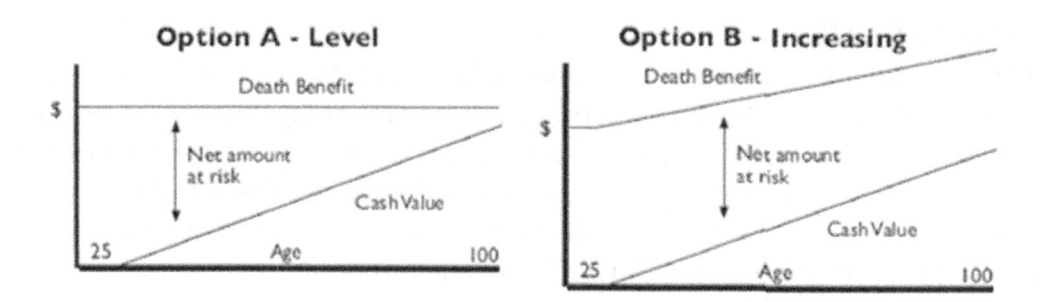

Universal Life insurance is quoted with a **target premium,** the amount of premiums needed to insure for permanent protection well past age 100. However, the insured is not required to pay the target premium since it is based on lifetime protection; the insured only needs enough cash value to cover each month Annually Renewable Term coverage. As long as the cash value account has cash, the policy remains in force, but if the cash value account **reaches zero, coverage ends.**

There are two types of Universal Life insurance; Option A (Level) and Option B (Increasing):

1. OPTION A (LEVEL) UNIVERSAL LIFE
Option A is less expensive because the death benefit comprises of insurance and the cash value account. The insureds cash value is essentially part of the death benefit, so the mortality cost of Annually Renewable Term is much lower; with the lower cost of ART and coupled with variable stock market investments, the policies cash value could grow very quickly. The IRS has established an **IRS corridor** that must be maintained should the cash value encroach on the death benefit, maintaining a pure insurance limit. If the insured passes the corridor the policy becomes a Modified Endowment Contract.

2. OPTION B (INCREASING) UNIVERSAL LIFE
Option B (Increasing) universal life has the same pure insurance amount throughout the entire policy. If the cash value grows, the death benefit increases as well to ensure that the policyowner maintains the same pure insurance amount. This option is more costly as the cash value and death benefit are two separate factors, resulting in a higher amount paid at death by the insurer.

Universal life insurance is typically written as **Variable Universal Life** or **Indexed Universal Life**, where the cash value may be invested in stocks or tied to an index such as the S&P 500. See the previous chapter for more information on Variable and Indexed products. This may result in a **vanishing premium** because the stock market earnings pay the premium of the policy.

E. SPECIALIZED POLICIES
1. FAMILY (FAMILY PROTECTION POLICY)
Insurers offer a combination of whole-life for the head of the household and convertible insurance for the spouse and children. The spouse may convert to permanent coverage up until age 65. The children are automatically covered after birth for a specific period of time, most often 30 to 31 days. Coverage

can be continued for the newborn if the parents inform the insurer of the birth within that time period. The child may convert their term insurance coverage to permanent coverage when they turn the age of 18, 21 or 24, without any evidence of insurability.

2. JOINT LIFE (FIRST-TO-DIE)

Joint life, known as "first-to-die", insures two people on one policy and pays the death benefit when the first person dies. It is **cheaper** to purchase one life insurance policy as opposed to two, so a married couple or business partners would save money using one joint life policy as opposed to two individual policies. The premiums are based upon the average age and health status of both people and policy will **cease to exist** after it has paid the death benefit upon the first person's death.

* Vegeta and Bulma are a married couple who earn roughly the same amount of income and are looking to purchase the most cost-effective life insurance to maintain quality of life should one of the spouses die. They settle on a $500,000 Term Joint Life policy, where both are insured on one policy for a lower rate. Five years later, Vegeta dies and the policy pays the benefits to Bulma; since the policy has paid out upon the first person's death, Bulma does not have insurance anymore.

3. SURVIVORSHIP (SECOND-TO-DIE)

Survivorship Life, known as "second-to-die", is the opposite of Joint Life. The policy is used to insure two or more people on one policy but will only pay its death benefits upon **the last person's death.** If the first person dies, no benefits will be paid, the death benefit will only pay out when every person insured on the policy has died. Survivorship insurance is best used for **estate planning**, such as estate conservation, and again is lower cost as opposed to buying multiple policies.

* Wendy and Marco are married and have accumulated a sizeable sum of wealth on their farm. Current IRS rules allow Wendy or Marco to transfer assets to each other upon death without paying estate taxes because they are married; however, upon both parents' death, their children will inherit the estate and be required to pay estate taxes. They decide to purchase a $10,000,000 survivorship life policy; one policy, with two insureds, and naming the children as beneficiaries. When Marco first dies, no death benefit is paid, but when Wendy dies second (both insureds are dead), the death benefit is paid to the children. The children apply the death benefit towards the taxes and will not need to sell the farm.

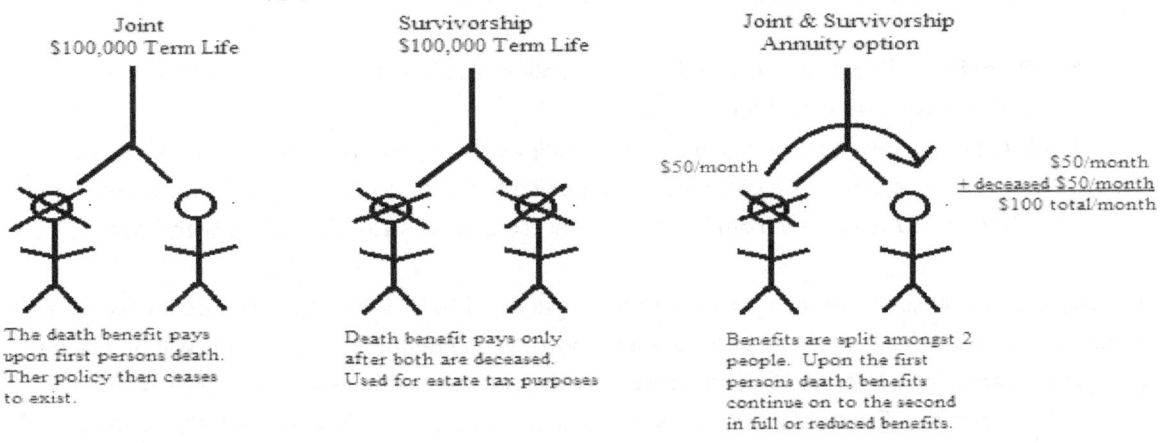

Joint
$100,000 Term Life

The death benefit pays upon first persons death. Ther policy then ceases to exist.

Survivorship
$100,000 Term Life

Death benefit pays only after both are deceased. Used for estate tax purposes

Joint & Survivorship
Annuity option

$50/month

$50/month
+ deceased $50/month
$100 total/month

Benefits are split amongst 2 people. Upon the first persons death, benefits continue on to the second in full or reduced benefits.

F. CREDIT LIFE

Credit insurance is a **decreasing term** life policy used to cover the balance of **current debts,** such as credit cards, mortgages and auto loans; usually limited to 15 year or smaller loans

1. **Creditor:** The bank or lending institution who required the loan. The creditor is the beneficiary of the policy and will receive the benefits to pay off the loan
2. **Debtor:** The policyowner & insured; the debtor must pay the premiums of the policy.

The creditor may require credit insurance to obtain the loan, but CANNOT require the policy to be purchased from them, and the benefits **CANNOT be more** than the principle credit amount. The debtor may purchase the credit policy from any insurer they choose and use it as collateral to satisfy the credit insurance requirements. If the creditor required the debtor to purchase it from them, that would be an **Unfair Trade Practice** known as **coercion.**

* Wolf is looking to purchase a new vehicle for $26,000, of which he plans to put 50% down. The XYZ auto finance company offers Wolf credit life and disability insurance to cover the remaining amount of his loan for $50 per month. Wolf feels that's a little steep, so he contacts his insurance producer to purchase a decreasing term life policy with a face amount of $13,000 for $15/month, naming the XYZ auto finance as the creditor and beneficiary of the policy. Wolf has satisfied the credit insurance requirements and obtains the loan.

D. CASH VALUE COMPONENTS IN LIFE INSURANCE

There are two main components to permanent life insurance:

- **Death Benefit:** Also known as the "face amount", is the amount of money a beneficiary will receive when the insured dies. All life insurance will include a death benefit; however, **annuities will not have a death benefit.**

- **Cash Value:** A savings account attached only to permanent life insurance and annuities. Essentially a portion of each premium payment goes into an account, and while the insured is alive, the policyowner may withdraw these funds, or even take a loan against it. Cash value consists of two components as well:

    - **Principle:** The premiums paid into the policy, just like placing $100 into the bank. The principle is always **tax free.**
    - **Interest:** Any money earned on the principle, through either investments or a set percentage listed in the contract. If you place $100 in the bank, next year you will have $102, the $2 is earned from interest. Interest is always **taxable** upon withdrawal.

For example: A whole life insurance policy with a face value of $200,000 may cost a policyowner $100 per month in premium. Each time the policyowner pays their premium, a portion of it will be placed into a cash value account. After say 5 years of paying the premiums, the insured may have $10,000 saved up in their account. Essentially this policy has $200,000 death benefit and a $10,000 living benefit.

The living benefit is built from the premiums paid into the policy and the interest earned on the principle. The sooner a policy is paid off, the **faster cash value will grow.**

Let's say out of the $10,000 cash value, $8,000 of it is principle and $2,000 is interest earned on the principle.

$8,000 principle
+ $2,000 interest
$10,000 cash value

Now what if we withdraw out of the cash value? Will there be any taxes involved? Well, the accounting method will depend on which type of policy it is:

- ✓ Whole Life, Adjustable and Universal will be taxed based on FIFO
- ✓ Annuities (Pay-in Phase) and Modified Endowment Contracts will be LIFO

❖ **First In First Out (FIFO):** Whole life and Universal life insurance utilize FIFO, where you will withdraw principle first, then withdraw interest second. Principle was First In; therefore, Principle is First Out; meaning you could withdraw $8,000 tax free because you would withdraw all principle. Upon withdrawing $8,001; the one dollar would be taxable as interest.

❖ **Last In First Out (LIFO):** Annuities during their Pay-In Phase and Modified Endowment Contracts (MECs) utilize LIFO. Interest will be withdrawn first and taxes will be paid on it; after all of the interest is withdrawn, then principle comes next. If you withdrew $8,000, you would pay taxes on $2,000 and then $6,000 would come out tax free.

❖ **Policy Loans:** Policy loans are not taxable; they are supposed to be paid back and are not considered earned income; but the insurer will charge an extra 6-8% interest for taking the loan. If the policyowner does not pay back the loan, the loan will become larger the following year because the insurer will tack the interest onto the loan. Should the policyowner die with an outstanding loan, the insurer will deduct the amount of the loan and any excess interest from the death benefit.

* Leo has a $300,000 death benefit Modified Endowment Contract with $100,000 cash value, comprising of $70,000 principle and $30,000 interest. If Leo withdraws $40,000, he would need to pay taxes on $30,000 (interest) and then the remaining $10,000 would be tax free. Since MEC's utilize LIFO, Leo pays more taxes than he would have with a regular life insurance policy. If it were just whole life, the full $40,000 would have been pulled from principle and Leo would not have paid any taxes.

* Barrack has a $25,000 death benefit Straight Life policy with $7,500 in cash value, comprising of $4,000 principle. When Barrack was golfing, he injured his rotator cuff at a cost of $6,000; he decided to use his cash value life insurance to pay for the doctors' bills. When Barrack withdrew the $6,000; the first $4,000 was tax free but he had to pay taxes on the next $2,000. That is because whole life policies are based off of FIFO, so Barrack withdrew the principle (4k) first then interest second.

a. INTEREST EARNED IN CASH VALUE ACCOUNTS

We have discussed that cash value consists of principle and interest, but we never said how much interest is earned. In life insurance, any money earned on principle is considered interest; so, in the life insurance world, if you purchased a stock at $40/share and sold it at $45/share, then you have gained $5/share in interest, we do NOT use the word capital gains in regards to life insurance taxation for this test.

The different ways a policy may earn interest:

- ❖ **Fixed Interest Rates:** The policy has fixed **contract** percentage rate that the insurer guarantees will be earned each year in the cash value account. This is typically around the 5% mark and provides for level predictable growth, best suitable for retirement planning.
    - o **General Account:** Fixed cash value products are placed into the insurer's general account. The insurer will purchase bonds, treasury bills and other low risk investments, hoping to earn more than 5% themselves, while paying the policyowner a guaranteed 5%
    - o **Inflation:** A disadvantage of Fixed products is the devaluing of money. If inflation is 3% and the account is earning 5%, then the policyowner only really earned 2%; should inflation ever go above 5%, the policyowners money would devalue faster than they were earning money.

- ❖ **Variable Interest Rates:** The cash value is invested in **stocks and investments**, which pay the policyowner the **current rate** of the investment. Variable products seek higher gains, but are riskier investments; most retirement accounts such as 401ks are variable products.
    - o **Separate Account:** Since the product is invested in the stock market, each policyowner will have their funds held in separate escrow accounts.
    - o **Inflation:** Since variable products may earn higher interest rates in the stock market, they provide some protection against inflation.
    - o **Product Regulation:** Variable products are regulated by the Securities and Exchange Commission (SEC) and the state Department of Insurance.
    - o **Producer Regulation:** Producers must obtain a life insurance license AND a securities license through either the National Association of Securities Dealers **(NASD)** or Financial Industry Regulatory Authority **(FINRA).**

- ❖ **(Equity) Indexed Interest Rates:** Cash value is tied to a stock index such as the S&P 500 or Nasdaq 100; but not actually invested in the index. The insurer keeps the money and invests it themselves, but credits the account based on the earning of the index.
    - o **Minimum Guaranteed Floor:** Indexed products cannot lose money because the insurer sets a minimum guaranteed interest rate. If the S&P 500 goes down 10%, the account will not go down because it's not invested in the S&P 500, just tied to it. The insurer sets minimum guaranteed earnings percentage usually of 0-3%.
    - o **Fixed Product:** Since indexed products are not invested in the markets, they are considered Fixed Products, but have a **fluctuating** interest rate.

- o **Index Earnings**
  - **Ratcheting Method:** Gains are credited each year.
  - **Point to Point:** Gains are added at the end of each index term (maybe longer than a year)
- o **Changing Indexes:** The policyowner may change indexes at the end of the **index term,** which is usually 1, 3, 5 or 7 years. If the Nasdaq 100 is outperforming the S&P 500, the policyowner may switch at the end of the index term,

All of these interest rates may be added to life insurance or annuities. For instance, Variable Universal Life Insurance is a policy where the cash value is invested in the stock market, but also provides for a death benefit. A Variable Annuity would also provide for stock market earnings, but not include a death benefit.

Most Whole Life and Adjustable Life policies are "traditional" fixed interest rates; but could also be variable or indexed themselves if written that way.

* John, age 60, is beginning to plan for retirement; and is not sure what type of product would be best suited for him. His agent suggests a Fixed Annuity, because the product provides for level predictable interest growth each year. Should the stock market or economy hit a recession, John will not lose any money and continue to gain the same percentage; effectively insulating him from any downturns. The only problem is the product may not earn as much as a variable or indexed product.

* Michelle, age 28, has a long time until retirement and also needs life insurance. Her producer suggests a Variable Universal Life insurance policy because should the stock market decrease, she has plenty of time to recoup losses before she retires. She also needs a death benefit to protect her children should she die early, so a Variable Universal Life policy will provide her with cash value for retirement and a death benefit to protect her family.

- ✓ Indexed and Variable products may be considered **Interest Sensitive** because the premiums could possibly be affected by how the interest rates are credited to the account. Whereas traditional fixed products, such as whole life and adjustable are NOT interest sensitive.

b. MODIFIED ENDOWMENT CONTRACT (MEC)

A MEC is not a good thing; it is when a policyowner overfunds a cash value policy more than what the IRS guidelines say it is supposed to be funded at; an example would be making extra premium payments when the customer was not required to. A MEC is typically a whole life policy that fails the **7-Pay Test**; which means if a policy is overfunded for any 7-year period of time, the policy becomes a MEC, now any withdrawals or even policy loans are taxed based off on the LIFO concept. A MEC is not a policy you purchase, it is usually whole or universal life that was over funded, sometimes by accident, but MEC's were designed by the IRS to curb tax evasion in the 1980s.

PRACTICE QUESTIONS: LIFE INSURANCE POLICIES

1. Which policy would be best suited for mortgage protection?
   a. Whole Life
   b. Annually Renewable Term
   c. Adjustable Life
   d. Decreasing Term

2. Variable Universal Life, which offers partial protection against inflation by seeking higher gains, is held in which type of account at the insurer?
   a. Fixed account
   b. General account
   c. Separate account
   d. Trust account

3. All of the following are Limited Pay life insurance EXCEPT:
   a. Straight life
   b. Limited Pay
   c. Life Paid Up @ 65
   d. Single Premium

4. Which of the following policies would be best suited for estate conservation?
   a. Survivorship life
   b. Joint life
   c. Credit life
   d. Payor life

5. Which of the following term policies cannot be renewable term?
   a. Level Term
   b. Increasing Term
   c. Decreasing Term
   d. Annual Renewable Term

6. Of the following statements, which would you consider NOT true about Adjustable life insurance?
   a. The insured may control their length of coverage and premium payments
   b. The policy builds cash value slower than whole life
   c. The insured may convert without proving insurability
   d. The insured may increase the death benefit without proving insurability

Life, Accident & Health Exam Study Book | TX

7. A producer who sells variable products will most likely be registered with which agency?
a. National Association of Insurance Commissioners
b. Securities and Exchange Commission
c. FITCH Rating agency
d. National Association of Securities Dealers

8. H has a whole life policy with $10,000 cash value, which consists of $8,000 principle. When H takes a loan against the policy for $9,000, what amount is taxable?
a. $9,000
b. $8,000
c. $2,000
d. $0

9. All of the following could be considered Interest Sensitive policies EXCEPT:
a. Adjustable Life
b. Variable Universal Life
c. Indexed Universal Life
d. Interest Sensitive Life

10. Which of the following statements is true?
a. Straight life is less expensive than Limited Pay
b. Limited Pay is less expensive than Single Premium
c. Limited Pay is less expensive than Straight Life
d. Single Premium is more expensive than Straight Life

11. J age 45 is looking for a policy that will build cash value quickly for his retirement age of 60. Which policy would build J the highest amount of cash value?
a. 15 Pay whole life
b. Life Paid up @ 65
c. Annual Renewable Term
d. Adjustable Life

12. A flexible premium policy that builds the quickest cash value while the insured is younger would be best described as:
a. Life Paid up @ 65
b. Adjustable Life
c. Universal Life
d. Straight Life

CHAPTER 11: LIFE PROVISIONS, NONFORFEITURE AND RIDERS

A. UNIFORM POLICY PROVISIONS

Provisions explain the rights and characteristics of an insurance contract, and are fairly universal from one policy to the next. Exact wording is not required, but the basic provisions apply to most life insurance policies; these provisions are uniform across states lines due to the National Association of Insurance Commissioners (NAIC)

1. OWNERSHIP (OWNERS RIGHTS) PROVISION

The policyowner is typically the person who purchases the policy and the one with all of the rights to the policy. The policyowner is responsible for **paying the premiums, naming a beneficiary, choosing the death benefit and** determining how it will be paid out. The policyowner may also take loans against cash value, withdraw cash value or even cancel the policy. Once a policy has been issued, the only changes that can be made are by the policyowner through riders, endorsements, or amendments.

The policyowner may be the insured, or may be a separate person; such as if a father purchases a life insurance policy on his child, the father would be the policyowner and the child would be the insured; the death benefit would be payable when the insured(child) died, not when the policyowner (father) dies. If the policyowner dies the policy remains in force, and could be transferred to the policyowners estate, or the person in charge of the estate (spouse) or more commonly ownership is transferred directly to the insured.

The policyowner is also a different from a policyholder, in group contracts the employer is the policyowner and the employee is the policyholder. The policyowner is the one with the actual rights in the policy.

2. ASSIGNMENT

The assignment provision allows for the **policyowner to transfer the rights of the policy**; essentially removing rights from the current policyowner and transferring those rights to a new policyowner (called the assignee). Since life insurance and annuities may have high amounts of cash value, these policies act in the same way as regular property. They may be sold to other people or companies, and even put up as collateral for the down payment on a loan. There are two types of assignments:

> **Absolute assignment:** Allows for an irrevocable, one-way, **permanent full transfer of all rights** to the policy. The current policyowner will be fully removed and a new assignee policyowner will fully take over the contract. The absolute assignment is typically used during a viatical settlement or other sale of the contract, and may be **prevented** if there is an **irrevocable beneficiary** listed in the policy.

> **Collateral assignment**: Allows for a revocable, two-way, **temporary partial transfer of rights** to the policy. A collateral assignment is most often used when securing a debt, such as a bank loan; the creditor will obtain certain rights, such as being named as a beneficiary for the amount of the loan. After the loan is paid off, the policy is transferred back to the original policyowner; if the policyowner dies before paying off the loan, the bank will receive the death benefit covering the loan and any excess will be given to the remaining beneficiaries (usually family members).

* Ronald took out a loan to open a new restaurant, for which he used his life insurance policy as a down payment. Ronald performed a collateral assignment, which named the bank as the policyowner and beneficiary until he paid off his loan; once Ronald pays off the loan, the policy would be returned to him. Unfortunately, his restaurant went bankrupt and the bank seizes his collateral; Ronald performs an absolute assignment to the bank, where they now keep the policy forever.

3. ENTIRE CONTRACT

The entire contract comprises of the **policy and a copy of the application**; these two items encompass all conditions, benefits, exclusions and consideration on both parties' behalf. Only an **executive officer** of the insurer may make **modifications** to the contract, but any changes must be in the benefit of the insured and also have the insureds written consent.

Since the entire contract consists of a copy of the policy, which means all provisions of the contract, are included in the entire contract. The consideration clause, modifications clause, incontestability clause, free look period, coverage amounts and everything else in the policy are all part of the entire contract.

A few things are not part of the entire contract, such as the policy illustration, Producers Report & Buyers Guide.

4. RIGHT TO EXAMINE (FREE LOOK) (10 DAYS)

When a policy is **delivered** to an insured and is found on **the front page of the policy;** they will have **10 days** after the time of delivery to return the policy to the insurer and receive a full refund for all of their premiums. This allows the insured to look over the policy and determine if it is suitable for them. The free look period is **30 days** for Medicare Supplement and Long-Term Care policies, and the **time of delivery** begins either when the agent hand delivers the policy, or at the time of postmark when mailed directly to the insured.

* Mary purchased a new health insurance policy on February 10th, the insurer mailed it to Mary's agent on February 22nd, the agent then delivered the policy to Mary on March 2nd and had the delivery receipt signed. If Mary returns the policy on or before March 12th, she will receive all of her money back.

5. GRACE PERIOD

When the insureds premium due date passes without payment, the policy does not automatically lapse, the insured is still covered during their grace period. The grace period helps **prevent the unintentional lapse** of a policy by giving an insured extra time to make their premium payment past the due date. The grace period varies by which premium payment mode the insured chooses:

- ❖ **Annual & Quarterly Payments:** The grace period is 31 days
- ❖ **Monthly Payments:** The grace period is 10 days
- ❖ **Weekly Payments:** Not often utilized unless through payroll deduction, the grace period is 7 days.

✓ Claims during the grace period will be **reduced by any unpaid premium**.

* Darrell has a policy he pays every year on January 1st in full. This year, Darrell has taken a cruise in Cabos and is unable to pay his premium on time. On the return trip home, Darrell slips and falls overboard, he is declared dead on January 15th. Even though Darrell did not pay his premium on time, he is covered by his 31-day grace period; his family will receive the full death benefit, but subtracted by the 15 days of premiums he did not pay.

6. REINSTATEMENT

The reinstatement provision allows the policy owner the opportunity to put a lapsed policy back into force; subject to providing evidence of continued insurability. There is often a maximum time **limit of three (3)** years after the policy lapsed. Upon reinstatement, the policy owner must pay all back premiums, plus interest and may be required to repay any outstanding loans and interest. If a policy is reinstated, a new two-year **suicide clause does not reset.**

7. CONTESTABILITY & INCONTESTABILITY CLAUSE

The Contestability clause sets a two-year time limit, from the issuance of a policy, that an insurer may deny claims or void a policy due to a **material misrepresentation** on the application. After two years have passed, from the issuance of the policy, the insurer **may not deny claims** due to a material misrepresentation, fraud, or concealment on the application; this clause protects the **beneficiary** and insured, because prior to the incontestability clause the insurer could look back as far as possible to find any medical conditions left off an application. The first 2 years are considered the Contestability clause; after 2 years have passed it is called the Incontestability clause, where the app cannot be contested.

If an insured does not list a pre-existing condition on an application and it is **not discovered** within the first two years of the policy, the insurer **must pay the claim**. If the insurer discovers the material misrepresentation within the first two years, they may void a policy, deny a claim and must return all premiums to the policyowner (which voids the contract).

* Kyle was diagnosed with AIDS due to a neglectful blood transfusion, upon leaving his physician, he goes straight to his insurance agent's office and applies for life insurance, but states he has no current or prior medical issues. The insurer fails to detect the AIDS and issues the policy; four years later, Kyle dies due to his AIDS; when the insurer performs an autopsy, they discover the material misrepresentation on the application. The insurer however would still pay this claim, because Kyle had the policy for four years, which is past the two-year contestability clause, he was now in the incontestability clause.

There are three scenarios where the incontestability clause may not apply: Impersonation, lack of insurable interest, and intent to murder.

8. MISSTATEMENT OF AGE

Sometimes age is entered incorrectly on an application, or an insured may lie about their age to receive a lower premium for the policy. If the age on the policy is lower than the actual insureds age, the death benefit will be adjusted to reflect the correct age; if the age is higher than the insureds actual age, a partial premium refund would occur.

* John, age 55, applied for life insurance, but on the application, he told his agent he was age 45, hoping to receive lower premiums; John purchased the policy with the incorrect age paying $100/month for $200,000 in coverage. Upon death, the insurer would adjust the death benefit lower to reflect his true application age of 55. If Johns policy was a term life to age 65, his policy would not provide coverage if his true age were past 65.

9. EXCLUSIONS

Exclusions are policy provisions that exclude certain types of risks. The most common clauses are aviation and hazardous occupation or hobbies. Most companies insure fare paying passengers on commercial airlines, but **will not** cover **pilots and crewmembers**. Individuals with dangerous occupations or hobbies like **sky-diving** may have the hobby excluded or pay a higher premium.

10. SUICIDE

Suicide will be covered by life insurance policies beginning exactly **two** years from policy inception **(issue date);** the insurer **may not** decline a life insurance claim due to suicide if the policy has been in force for longer than two years, this prevents an insured from purchasing insurance for the sole intent of committing suicide. If the insured commits suicide within the first 2 years of the policy, a refund of premiums will be given to the policyowner or their estate. Should a life insurance policy lapse and then become reinstated, the suicide exclusion will NOT start over.

11. WAR CLAUSE

There are two types of war clause exclusions:
- Status Clause: excludes all causes of death while the insured is serving on active duty in the military
- The Results Clause only excludes the death benefit if the insured is killed as a result of an act of war, either declared or undeclared. Riot is covered.

B. BENEFICIARIES

The beneficiary is named by the policyowner and will be the person to receive the death benefit upon the insured's death. Beneficiaries do NOT sign the application and in most life insurance cases, the beneficiary will receive the death benefits **tax free**. There are three designations of Beneficiaries:

1. **Primary Beneficiary:** The first in line to receive the death benefit when the insured dies. There may be multiple primary beneficiaries (such as 3 children, etc.) and benefits may be split among them, as long as the total percentage equals **100%**.

2. **Contingent Beneficiary:** The second in line to receive benefits, ONLY if the primary beneficiary dies before the insured. The contingent and primary will NEVER share in death benefits; think of it as a contingency (backup) plan should the primary pre-decease the insured.

3. **Tertiary Beneficiary:** Third or more in line and will only receive benefits if the primary and contingent beneficiaries are both deceased prior to the insured's death.

✓ If there are no beneficiaries alive when the insured dies, the death benefit is paid to the **insured's estate**, and will likely be taxed.

* Mitt is the insured; his partner Lou is the primary beneficiary and Kim is the contingent beneficiary. Lou died due to lung cancer in 2010 and Mitt died due to an accident. Kim would receive the benefit.

1. BENEFICIARY CLASSES & OTHER DESIGNATIONS

If there are multiple primary beneficiaries, such as 3 children where benefits are split (40%, 40%, 20% etc.), there are two designations for deciding how benefits are split should one die prior to the insured:

- ❖ **Per Stirpes:** Meaning "By the Bloodline"; states that if one of the beneficiaries predeceases the insured, their portion of benefits will still be paid to the beneficiaries' heirs; essentially continuing down the bloodline.

- ❖ **Per Capita:** Meaning "By the Head"; states that if one of the beneficiaries predeceases the insured, their portion of the benefits will go to the remaining beneficiaries.

✓ An easy way to remember the difference is, Per Capita has the word cap in it and a cap goes on your head making it "by the head". To remember Per Stirpes, the word stirpes is similar to stripes and a line is a stripe; so, Per Stirpes "by the bloodline".

* Sochi has three children (A, B & C) with the death benefit split evenly among them at 1/3 portions. Should child A pre-decease Sochi, under the per capita rule children B & C would receive child A's benefits upon Sochi's death; however, if it were designated as per stirpes, child A's family (spouse or children) would receive child A's portion of the death benefit when Sochi dies.

2. REVOCABLE vs. IRREVOCABLE BENEFICIARIES

Common knowledge dictates that the policyowner may change the beneficiary of the policy at any time, but that is not always the case. There are two designations that determine whether or not a beneficiary may be added or removed from a policy:

- **Revocable Beneficiary:** Almost all beneficiaries are revocable, meaning the policyowner may remove or change a beneficiary at will. The beneficiary has no say in the matter and thus has no vested rights in the policy.

- **Irrevocable Beneficiary:** An irrevocable beneficiary CANNOT be removed or changed by the policyowner. Once named irrevocable, the beneficiary can remove themselves by submitting a written letter to the insurer requesting the change. The irrevocable beneficiary gains vested rights in the policy and can even **prevent the sale** of a policy, by not removing themselves.

Irrevocable beneficiaries are similar to auto lienholders and mortgage companies; the financer is listed on the policy until the loan is paid off; upon which, the finance company would request itself to be removed from the policy because their interest has ceased in the insured.

3. MINORS & TRUSTS

Minors may be named as beneficiaries, but are unable to receive the benefits until a certain age (state dependent). Upon a parents' death, the minor would be cared for by a **legal guardian**, and the death benefit proceeds would be placed into a **trust** to be paid to the child upon reaching state legal age limit.

A trust would usually be established prior to death; or if no trust was created before death, the probate courts would create one. Trusts are based on confidence and rely on the promise that the funds will be distributed to the beneficiary at the correct time. The trust is operated by a trust administrator, who ensures that funds are always invested in the best interest for the beneficiary.

4. COMMON DISASTER CLAUSE

When the insured and primary beneficiary die at the same time, or due to the **same cause of loss** (such as an accident), within a reasonable amount of time (30 days), the death benefit will be paid to the next in line beneficiary. This prevents the death benefit from being paid to the primary's estate and then being taxed.

* Andrea has life insurance, naming her husband Kelvin as primary beneficiary and daughter Rachel as contingent. The entire family is involved in a car accident, killing Andrea immediately, critically injuring Kelvin and leaving Rachel untouched; Kelvin dies 15 days later in the hospital from injuries sustained in the car accident. The death benefit is paid to Rachel, even though Kelvin survived the accident. Without this clause it would have been paid to Kelvin's estate, and then taxed when transferred to Rachel.

5. SPENDTHRIFT CLAUSE

The Spendthrift Clause prevents the beneficiary from spending the benefits recklessly. It requires the benefits to be paid in fixed periods or fixed amounts; in other words, the beneficiary cannot benefit from the proceeds of the policy until the designated time in the policy. **The clause is also designed to protect the proceeds from the beneficiary's creditors** by delaying payments over time.

6. FACILITY OF PAYMENT CLAUSE

A provision, typically in industrial life insurance, that allows the **insurer** to designate to whom the death benefit will be paid to. Usually, payments are made to a relative or other person who has incurred expenses for burial of the insured; such as $3,000 could be paid directly to a funeral home.

Settlement Options	Non-Forfeiture Options	Dividend Options
• Lump Sum • Interest Only • Fixed Amount • Fixed Period • Life Income (Life Annuity)	• Reduced Paid Up • Extended Term • Cash Surrender Value	• Cash payment • Earn Interest • Paid Up Insurance • Paid Up Additions • One Year Term

C. LIFE INSURANCE SETTLEMENT OPTIONS

Settlement options are designated by the **policyowner**, and line out the method of distribution for the death benefit. Essentially, upon the insured's death, the beneficiary must "settle up" with the insurer to receive the funds.

1. **Lump Sum:** For life insurance, the beneficiary receives a one-time tax-free check from the insurer for the full amount of the death benefit.
2. **Interest Only:** A temporary option, which will conserve the face amount until a later date, but pay the beneficiary small amounts of interest over time.
3. **Fixed Amount:** The death benefit will be placed into an annuity and the beneficiary will receive a fixed amount of money each year until funds are exhausted. During this time, the benefit will grow interest, so the money lasts much longer.
4. **Fixed Period:** The death benefit will be placed into an annuity and the beneficiary will receive the funds over a period of time. This is commonly used for lottery payments and court settlements.

* Halfway through Mitch's divorce his father dies, leaving him a $100,000 death benefit in a lump sum. Since Mitch is going through a divorce and possibly bankruptcy, he does not want to share the money with his ex. Mitch chooses the interest only option instead of receiving the lump-sum. He receives a small check of $3,000 to account for the interest and a year later when his divorce is finished, he receives the full $100,000 from the insurer for the full death benefit.

* Elisia's husband died leaving her $100,000 but he chose the fixed amount settlement option to cover her mortgage of $10,000 per year. Elisia receives a check in the amount of $10,000 each year and her funds will last much longer than 10 years...actually 23.5 years. This is because the remaining money in the annuity is still earning interest, allowing for the $100,000 lasting much longer than she expected.

* Oscar has a $100,000 business loan for 10 years owed to the bank, when he dies due to a known cancer. Oscar's business partner realizes he only left him with a $60,000 death benefit, which is not enough to cover the loan. Oscar was smart and instead of leaving his business partner the money as a lump sum, he had chosen the fixed-period option. The funds will be paid out over 10 years, which during that time the money is earning interest and will be more than enough to cover the loan.

5. LIFE ANNUITY SETTLEMENT OPTION

Life Annuity (**Straight Life Annuity**) provides monthly income to the annuitant for life, even if funds are exhausted early. This option is also known as the "life income settlement" option and the insured cannot outlive these benefits; there are multiple ways to write this:

- **Pure Life:** Life income written where one person will receive benefits for life.
- **Joint Life:** Income will be split amongst two annuitants for life; when one annuitant dies, the payments will cease to all annuitants
- **Joint & Survivorship:** Income provided to two+ annuitants, when one annuitant dies, payments continue on to the survivor either with full benefits or reduced to 66 and 2/3rds of the total payment. (SEE PICTURE: AT END OF CHAPTER 10 UNDER JOINT & SURVIVORSHIP LIFE)
    - **Period Certain Option:** The period certain option may be attached to any *life annuity* and would guarantee income for a certain period of time.

* Amy was considering the purchase of a life annuity for the guaranteed $1,500/mo. income for life, but she was afraid if she died early that she may waste the principle amount of the annuity. Amy's agent notified her that she could add the period-certain option of ten years, which would reduce her monthly income from $1,500 to $1,200, but should she perish within the first 10 years; her beneficiary would consider receiving money. Thus, protecting the principle amount from the surrender to the insurer in the event she perished early.

D. NONFORFEITURE OPTIONS

The word forfeit means to give up, so logically nonforfeiture means to "not give up"; nonforfeiture is referring to the cash value in policies such as whole, adjustable and universal life. If the insured cancels (surrenders) the policy early, the insurer cannot keep the cash value; essentially, the insured cannot give up the cash value in a policy, since it is "nonforfeiture". There are three ways to utilize the cash value in a policy upon surrender:

1. **Cash Surrender Value:** Receive the cash value in a check, minus any surrender penalties.
2. **Reduced Paid Up:** Reduces the death benefit of the policy, but uses the cash value to "pay up" or "pay-off" the policy. **IE:** 100k whole life, reduced to $60k whole life, but paid off.
3. **Extended Term:** Cancels the policy, but uses the cash value to pay for a term policy of the same death benefit. **IE:** 100k whole life exchanged for 100k term, but only for 5 years.

1. CASH SURRENDER VALUE

The policyowner may want to relinquish (or give up) the value of the policy in exchange for cash. For the first *two to three years* there **may not** be a cash surrender value. However, as time passes and premiums are paid and interest is earned, the cash surrender value increases. Any outstanding loans would be deducted from the surrender value and the cash is usually paid in one lump sum. Surrendering a policy for cash, of course, terminates the policy.

* If Dee has a policy with a stated cash value of $5,000 and still owes $500 (including interest) on a previous loan from the cash value, the insurance company would give her a total of $4,500 ($5,000 minus $500) on the cash surrender value option.

Most states also permit a delayed payment provision in which the insurer can postpone payment for a period of six months; however, this provision is rarely used.

2. REDUCED PAID-UP INSURANCE

Instead of receiving the cash surrender value and cancelling the policy, the insured may want to keep the policy by utilizing the reduced paid-up option. If the insured chooses this option, the cash value of the policy will be used to pay the current policy off in full; however, since there is not enough cash value in the policy, the face amount of the policy will be reduced to match. The Reduced Paid-Up option will allow the insured to maintain **the same type of policy, (whole life).**

* Juan has a $100,000 whole life policy with $7,000 in cash value, which he has been paying $200/month for the past 10 years. Juan has lost his job and can no longer afford the monthly payment, so he utilizes the reduced paid-up option. His cash value will be used to pay off his current policy; however, $7,000 is not enough to afford $100,000 in face amount. His policies death benefit will be reduced to $45,000 but paid completely off until age 100 by using his cash value.

Juan's $100,000 whole life would be reduced to $45,000, but he will no longer have to pay premiums. The Reduced Paid-Up option provides for the **longest time period** of coverage of the three nonforfeiture options since Juan will keep his whole life, just with a lower death benefit. The policy will even **continue to grow cash value** and pay dividends.

3. EXTENDED TERM

The extended term nonforfeiture option will utilize the cash value of the policy to exchange the permanent policy for a **term policy of the same face amount.** However, since term policies are temporary, the coverage will not last until age 100 as in reduced paid up, the term period will be based on 3 primary factors:

- Cash value of the policy
- Insureds Age
- Insureds Gender

The extended term option exchanges one type of life insurance for another but at the same face amount, which will provide for **the highest death benefit** of all the nonforfeiture options, although it may only provide coverage for a short period of time. If no nonforfeiture option is selected, the insurer will **automatically choose the extended term option** and the extended term option does NOT build cash value, as the new policy is term insurance.

* Roshi is 87 and has a $250,000 whole life policy with $10,000 in cash value. He has no friends or family to take care of him and has been admitted to a nursing home due to health concerns. Once admitted to the nursing home, Roshi has stopped paying his premiums; since his policy has cash value, the insurer will not cancel the policy, but instead automatically choose the extended term option for him. His $250,000 whole life will be exchanged for a $250,000 term, but only providing him coverage for 3 years. His policy will no longer generate cash value.

E. POLICY LOAN AND WITHDRAWAL OPTIONS

Policy loans may be taken from a cash value policy such as whole life or universal life by the policyowner at any time. The loan is NOT taxable, because it is going to be repaid at a later date.

1. CASH VALUES LOANS

Loans may be taken from cash value accounts at any time, but must be repaid with interest to the insurer. If a policyowner dies with an outstanding loan, the death benefit will be reduced by the amount of the loan.

2. AUTOMATIC PREMIUM (POLICY) LOAN

This rider is normally included at no extra charge to all **cash value** policies and will help **prevent the unintentional lapse of a policy.** If the policyowner misses a premium payment, a loan will automatically be taken from the cash value to pay the missed premium. If the insured continues to miss payments, the loan will become larger and larger, when there **is no cash value left the policy will end** unless the insured begins to make premium payments again.

The insurer will also charge interest on the loan; most states have a maximum of 8% interest charged. When the insured dies without paying back the loan, the loan amount will be deducted from the death benefit; the Automatic Policy Loan effectively creates a Reduced Paid-Up life policy.

3. SURRENDER CHARGES

The surrender charge is a penalty on cash value polices for early cancellation or early withdrawal from cash value. The penalty is typically 10% in the first year and will **decrease** over time, to 0%, usually after 7-10 years. A policy that is paid for in full upfront almost always has a surrender charge.

F. DIVIDEND OPTIONS

Only participating policies pay dividends and policy dividends are **not taxable income** as they are considered a return of premiums paid. Dividends are **not guaranteed** due to the fact they are based off the **mutual (participating)** insurers profits, if the insurer does not have profits, no dividends will be issued. If the dividends are left to accumulate at interest, that **interest is taxable** and a Form 1099 is issued.

Since only **participating (mutual)** insurance companies pay dividends, the policyowners are actually investing in the insurance company each time they purchase a policy. The dividends that are paid to the policy holder will be returned to the policyholder as their "profits"; below you will find the options the policyowner can utilize with these dividends

Dividends are the policyowners share of the profits of the company and are usually paid on policy anniversary dates. There are a few different options one can choose from to disburse dividend funds.

- **Cash in Hand** - Dividends can be distributed through a tax-free company check.

- **Reduction of Premium** - Dividends can be used to pay policy premiums and lessen the policyowners out-of-pocket expenses.

- **Allow Dividends to Accumulate at Interest** - Dividends do not necessarily have to be disbursed; the funds can be left in the account to accumulate with interest and be withdrawn later. Dividends are considered a nontaxable return of premium; however, any interest that has accumulated must be declared as taxable income whether or not the funds have been withdrawn.

- **Use Dividends to Buy Paid-up Additions** - Additional life insurance can be purchased as long as it is of the same kind as the original policy. Premium rates will probably be higher since the insured will be older. This is used to **offset inflation.**

- **Use Dividends to Purchase One-Year Term Insurance** - This so-called "fifth dividend option" allows the policyowner to use the dividends to purchase one-year term insurance at net rates, usually limited to no more than the current cash value on the contract.

Why is it common to limit the amount of term insurance that can be purchased under the fifth dividend option to the current cash value of the contract?

The original purpose for developing the fifth dividend option was to allow a policyowner to fill the gap in coverage created by borrowing on life insurance contracts. Thus, the option limits the amount of term insurance available to the maximum amount that can be borrowed on the contract in order to be consistent with the purpose for which the option was developed and to protect the insurer from potential adverse mortality experience.

G. POLICY RIDERS

Riders can be used to supplement an existing life insurance policy providing increased coverage, or they can be utilized so that coverage decreases. Using riders to decrease coverage will most likely decrease premium payments. On the other hand, using riders to increase coverage will most likely increase premium payments.

Eliminating coverage that is not needed is an effective way to reduce costs; "don't pay for what you don't need."

GUARANTEED INSURABILITY RIDER	Permits insured to buy specified amounts of additional insurance at specified intervals (usually 3 years) without evidence of insurability.
WAIVER OF PREMIUM	Prevents a policy from lapsing for nonpayment of premiums while insured is disabled.
AUTOMATIC PREMIUM LOAN RIDER (ACV)	Allows cash value to pay premiums.
PAYOR PROVISION ("Death and Disability Payor Benefit")	Extends until insured child reaches a specified age. Evidence of insurability required.
ACCIDENTAL DEATH BENEFIT ("Double Indemnity")	Provides additional amount usually equal to face amount if death occurs under stated conditions.
COST OF LIVING ("COLA")	Face amount increases with CPI without evidence of insurability. Maximum percentage increase.
OTHER INSUREDS	Provides coverage for more than one family member usually as a term rider.

1. GUARANTEED INSURABILITY

This rider promotes younger people to purchase insurance by giving them the option to increase the death/disability benefit at a later date, **without having to prove insurability** again. The policyowner has the right to exercise this rider every 3 years (usually up to age 40) and upon certain life events, such as: marriage, purchasing a home, children. Yes, the premium will increase when the insured increases their benefits; however, no matter what the insureds medical status (even if terminally ill), the premiums will be charged at the standard rate. Usually, the insurer requires the insured to live for 90 days for the increase to take effect.

* Vicki is 21 years old and understands insurance is best purchased when young and healthy, so she meets with her agent. Vicki is on a tight budget and has little assets because she is still in college, so her agent sells her a $25,000 life policy with the guaranteed insurability rider. When Vicki is 30, married and has children, she utilizes her rider. Even though she's now overweight and developed diabetes, the rider allows her to increase the death benefit from $25,000 to $300,000 without a medical exam. Her premiums increase, but not as high as they would have because she is charged the standard rate instead of the substandard rate. Even if she were extremely sick, she would have still been able to increase her death benefit without medical underwriting due to the guaranteed insurability rider.

2. WAIVER OF PREMIUM

A Waiver of Premium Rider allows for the insured to waive premium payments during a period of disability. Most often, insurers impose a 6-month waiting period from the start of the disability until the first premium is waived. If the insured is still disabled after the waiting period, the insurer generally will refund the premiums from the onset of the disability. Generally, the rider expires at age 65. However, if the insured is disabled prior **to age 65**, premiums will be waived for the duration of the disability.

3. WAIVER OF COST PROVISION

A Waiver of Cost Rider provides that in the event of the disability of the insured the cost of the insurance is waived. The cost of the premium amount necessary to accumulate cash value is not waived.

4. DISABILITY INCOME BENEFIT

When selected by the policy owner, the Disability Income Benefit Rider (in the event the insured becomes disabled) will waive the policy premium payments and the insured will receive monthly disability income. The Disability Income Benefit Rider has all of the same features as the Waiver of Premium Rider with the addition of a monthly income benefit paid to the insured. The benefit is most often based on a percentage of the face amount of the policy to which it is attached.

5. PAYOR BENEFIT (JUVENILE INSURANCE)

One of the best decisions a parent can make for a child is the purchase of a life insurance policy on a young child, with the intention of assigning the policy to the child when they reach adulthood. The **parent would be the payor** of the policy until the child reaches age 18 or 21 and will need protection for the policy in case the payor perishes early or becomes disabled. This ensures the child will still have the policy if something happens to the parent.

The payor benefit rider would pay the premiums until the child reached a specified age (18 or 21), in the event the payor dies or becomes disabled. This rider can be added on parent -> child relationships and even a grandparent -> grandchild relationship.

H. ACCELERATED LIVING NEEDS BENEFIT RIDER

The accelerated benefit rider provides for a loan against the death benefit should an insured be diagnosed as **terminally ill** or confined into a **Long-Term Care** facility. Essentially, this rider accelerates the death benefit to become accessible while the insured is alive, as opposed to only when the insured dies. The loan against the death benefit still accrues interest that is owed to the insurer, but this rider is a great alternative to a Viatical settlement since the remaining death benefit is still paid to the beneficiary upon death. The insured must be under the care of a **physician** to use this rider.

* Raj has a $100,000 whole life policy and was just diagnosed with terminal cancer. Raj contacts his insurance company for an accelerated benefit loan of $45,000 against his death benefit to cover his current medical bills. Raj submits his physician's paperwork and receives the loan; understanding an 8% interest rate is accruing. When Raj dies 6 months later, his family will receive $55,000 minus any interest accrued on the loan.

I. ACCIDENTAL DEATH

The accidental death rider will provide for extra death benefits in the event the insured dies due to an accident (not illness). This rider is typically defined as **double or triple indemnity**, which would double or triple the face amount of the policy when death occurs by the accident; although the rider may also pay a flat amount instead of double or triple indemnity and the insured would have to die within 90 days of the accident occurrence (think of life support/coma).

* Laurie purchases a $10,000 whole life policy with a $10,000 accidental death rider. If Laurie dies due to cancer, her policy would only pay the first $10,000 from the whole life; but if Laurie dies due to a vehicle accident, her policy would pay $20,000. Had Laurie presented it as triple indemnity as opposed to a flat $10,000, her policy would have paid $30,000 when the accident killed her.

J. OTHER INSURED RIDERS (TERM RIDERS)

Instead of purchasing multiple policies for each family member, the breadwinner of the family may take out one large policy on themselves and subsequently add smaller term policies for family members to cover burial expenses. These smaller term policies are added as a rider, and the rider cost will be cheaper than purchasing multiple policies.

The other insured riders are typically in the form of a **spousal term, child's term or family term rider.** A spousal term rider will insure the spouse; a child's term rider will insure all children in the household and the family term rider will insure the spouse + children on the policy. The child's term is added as a decreasing term policy, with the premiums based on the average number of children in the household.

* Oscar purchases a $500,000 whole life policy on himself because he is the primary income source for his family. He wants to purchase burial expense policies on his wife and children; his agent suggests a Family Term rider would be a perfect fit. The Family Term rider will add $20,000 in death benefit for each family member, in the event one of his family dies before him, Oscar's policy still remains in force but will pay out the death benefit of $20,000 for the family member that died.

3. COST OF LIVING RIDER

The Cost-of-Living Adjustment (COLA, or COL) rider will increase the death benefit at the rate of inflation, which is based upon the **Consumer Price Index;** if deflation occurs, the benefits ARE NOT reduced. Since inflation devalues money, this rider is extremely important when determining a person's long-term insurances needs.

* Mike is 35 and looking to purchase a final expense policy to cover burial needs. Current funeral costs average between $15,000 and $20,000; however, Mike is expected to live to age 85. The cost of a funeral 50 years from the date will likely increase dramatically due to inflation, and $20,000 in coverage would not be enough. Mike adds the COLA rider onto his policy; after having the policy for 1 year and inflation has been 4%, Mikes new death benefit would be $20,800.

4. RETURN OF PREMIUM (ROP)

One of the most common riders added onto policies is the Return of Premium rider, which performs exactly as it sounds. When this rider is included, if the insured dies, the policyowner will receive a full refund of all premiums paid into the policy; if the policy is surrendered, cancelled, or the insured outlives the term, the policyowner will also receive a premium refund (usually a percentage of premium, depending on how long the policy was in force).

The ROP rider does not actually return the premiums though; the added cost of the rider is used to purchase an **increasing term policy**, which in effect adds another life policy to the original policy; thus, the ROP rider is used to **increase the death benefit,** rather than refunding premiums. This is called a ROP term life policy in most states.

* Youssef purchased a 15-year $100,000 level term policy for a cost of $1,000/year and added the ROP rider at a cost of an extra $500/year, for a total premium of $1,500/year. If Youssef dies five years into the policy, his beneficiary will receive the death benefit of the original life policy, plus the benefit of the ROP increasing term policy; $100,000 + 5 years of premiums = $107,500

```
                      $1,000  premium of 100k term life insurance
                      $500    premium of ROP increasing term rider
                      $1,500  total premium of policy
   Multiplied by      5 years = $7,500 total in ROP increasing term
```

The policy will pay out the $100,000 death benefit + $7,500 of ROP increasing term for a total of $107,500.

PRACTICE QUESTIONS: LIFE PROVISIONS

1. Which of the following best describes the transfer of rights in a policy?
a. Assignment
b. Absolute Assignment
c. Collateral Assignment
d. Partial Assignment

2. T and L are married, with T being the insured, L being the primary beneficiary and K as the contingent. T, L & K are going on vacation during the 4th of July and a fireworks display prematurely explodes killing T immediately. L & K survive the accident, but L dies 15 days later due to the same cause of loss. Who receives the death benefit in this scenario?
a. L's estate
b. T's estate
c. K
d. K's estate

3. Which of the following riders would allow for the death benefit to increase?
a. Waiver of Premium
b. Accelerated Benefit
c. Payor Benefit
d. Return of Premium

4. Which of the following is part of the entire contract?
a. Buyers Guide
b. Policy Illustration
c. Policy Summary
d. Producers Report

5. All of the following are true about the guaranteed insurability rider EXCEPT:
a. It encourages young people to purchase insurance
b. The insured may increase the death benefit every three years
c. The insured may increase the death benefit without proving insurability
d. The insured may increase the death benefit without a higher premium

6. All of the following may be beneficiaries EXCEPT:
a. Insured
b. Policyowner
c. Tertiary
d. Irrevocable

Life, Accident & Health Exam Study Book | TX

7. Which settlement option will conserve the face amount, but pay the insured small amounts of earnings?
a. Fixed amount
b. Fixed Period
c. Life Income
d. Interest Only

8. Which nonforfeiture option provides for the longest period of coverage?
a. Reduced Paid Up
b. Extended Term
c. Cash Surrender Value
d. Childs Term Rider

9. P and Q are married, with P being the policyowner and insured, while Q is the beneficiary. P and Q get divorced; P remarries R and performs an absolute assignment to R but makes no other changes. When P dies, who receives the death benefit?
a. P
b. Q
c. R
d. P's estate

10. In order to use an accelerated benefit rider, the insured could be in which scenario?
a. The hospital for a broken leg
b. Hospice with Kawasaki disease
c. An allergist office with a bee sting
d. The local clinic with pneumonia

Life, Accident & Health Exam Study Book | TX

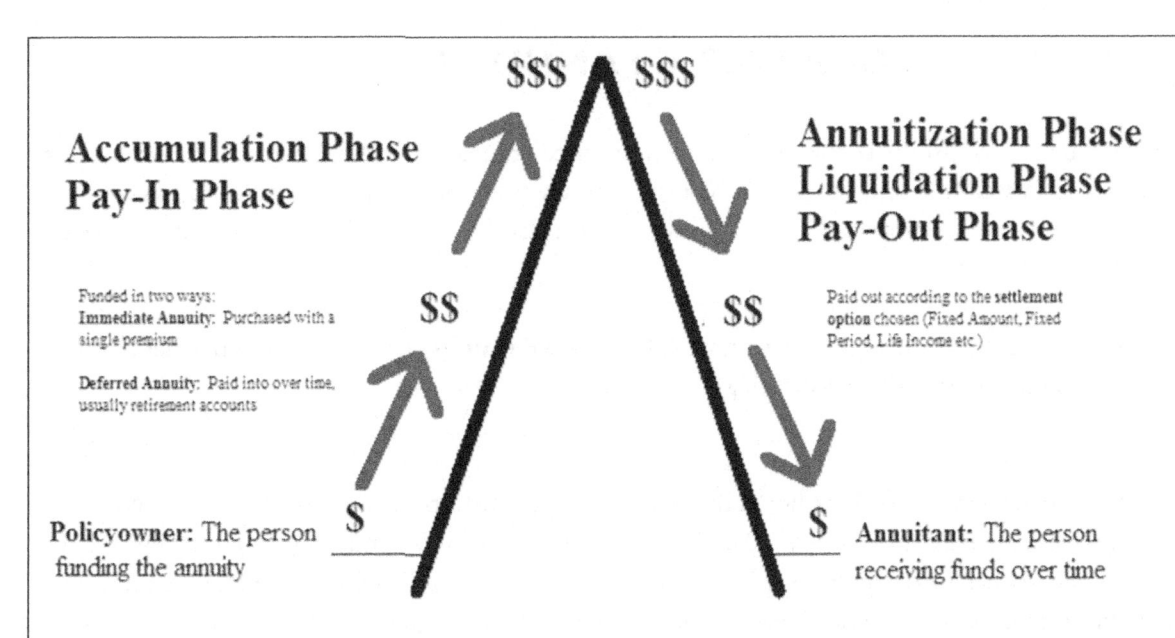

Accumulation Phase / Pay-In Phase

Funded in two ways:
Immediate Annuity: Purchased with a single premium
Deferred Annuity: Paid into over time, usually retirement accounts

Policyowner: The person funding the annuity

Annuitization Phase / Liquidation Phase / Pay-Out Phase

Paid out according to the **settlement option** chosen (Fixed Amount, Fixed Period, Life Income etc.)

Annuitant: The person receiving funds over time

Annuity: An interest earning account funded by a policyowner with premiums(principle), then systematically liquidates those funds to an annuitant over time. Typically used for retirement, education savings, lawsuit settlements and even the lottery. Annuities are sold by life insurance companies, but do not have a death benefit.

Retirement Accounts/Annuities

Variable Annuity:	An annuity invested in the stock market, hopefully protecting against inflation.
Fixed Annuity:	Provides a level fixed interest rate, for safe growth.
Immediate Annuity:	Funded with a single premium, and first installment payment is made within 1 year of opening.
Life Annuity:	Payments will be made for life to an annuitant, has many extra options such as Joint & Survivor.
Refund Annuity:	Returns principle to a beneficiary without interest should the annuitant die early.
401k (CODA):	Funded primarily by an employee with deferred growth.
403b (Tax Sheltered Annuity):	Public School employees and nonprofits
Keogh (Unincorporated):	Sole proprietorships, partnerships and LLCs with a high contribution amount; also known as an HR-10.
Traditional IRA:	Individual retirement account funded with pre-tax dollars and providing tax-deferred growth.
Roth IRA:	IRA funded with AFTER tax dollars, but tax-free growth. Must be open for 5 years.
Simplified Employee Pension (SEP):	Typically, a SEP IRA provides high contribution tax-deferred limits for self-employed individuals.
SIMPLE (SIMPLE 401k, 403b, IRA):	Small employers with less than 100 employees and has a 25% penalty if withdrawn within first 2 years.

CHAPTER 12: ANNUITIES

Annuities are financial products sold through life insurance companies with the purpose of prolonging funds to create a steady income stream. They are typically used for retirement, education savings, lawsuit settlements, lottery jackpots and any other time a person may need a steady income for years or even the rest of their life.

The annuity account may be funded over-time **(Deferred Annuity)** or with a single payment **(Single Premium Immediate Annuity)**.

* Maryanne has saved $500,000 for her retirement through a 401k plan and she's in good health at age 65; she feels she may spend the $500,000 too quickly and not have enough income for her older years. Maryanne decides to purchase a $500,000 annuity, selecting a $3,000/month fixed amount settlement option. Along with her Social Security income of $2,000 per month, Maryanne will have a total of $60,000 income per year without needing to work. Her annuity has prolonged the original $500,000 investment for almost 25 years, because it was earning interest during that time.

In short, an annuity is typically used as a retirement savings account that will earn interest, and upon achieving a certain age (usually 59 ½) the annuity will begin repaying those funds; but instead of receiving the funds all at once, the payments will be made over time.

How do Annuities differ from Life Insurance?
Life insurance is based around death and creation of an estate, with a settlement that will be paid to a beneficiary only upon death; whereas, annuities are based upon life and the liquidation of an estate. Annuities provide for the living and life insurance protects survivors in the event of death. The two may act the same in many regards, but only life insurance has a death benefit, **annuities do not include a death benefit.**

There are some key terms to understand with annuities:

- **Policyowner:** The person who purchased the annuity and makes the premium payments to fund the annuity, the policyowner **does not** have to receive the benefits of the annuity.
- **Annuitant:** The person receiving the benefits from the annuity and whom payments are made to, this person is typically the policyowner but may be a different person entirely.
- **Beneficiary:** Should the policyowner die during the accumulation period or the annuitant die during the annuitization phase, the funds may be available to the beneficiary. The beneficiary will only receive funds in the event of death.

A. ANNUITY PHASES

- **Accumulation & Pay-In phase:** The beginning phase of an annuity when funds are being placed into the account. Annuities may be funded with a single lump sum, or over a long period of years. The terms accumulation phase and pay-in phase are interchangeable, they have the same meaning, but different insurers may use one or the other in terminology.
    - **Immediate Annuity:** An annuity that is purchased with a **single premium,** and will begin paying benefits within **one year** of opening. Not all payments must be paid within the year of opening, but at least one pay-out must begin.
    - **Deferred Annuity:** An annuity paid into over-time, and will begin payments after one year of opening. Most similar to retirement accounts, where they are funded for tens of years, only to pay out at say age 59 ½.

- **Annuitization, Liquidation & Pay-Out phase:** The end phase of an annuity, when funds are being paid out to an annuitant; the way the funds are paid out is dependent upon the settlement option chosen.

* Dana just won the jackpot of her state lottery to the tune of $20,000,000 and is weighing her options on how to take the funds. The $20,000,000 figure is if she receives the funds over fixed 20-year period, paying her $1,000,000 for each installment; she also has the option of receiving a lump-sum payment of $10,000,000 today but no future payments. What Dana has won is a Single Premium, Immediate Annuity from the lottery; even though the fixed period option pays out over-time, she would receive her first check within 1 year of winning, which makes it an Immediate Annuity, not Deferred.

* Kelly, age 29, has a 403b Tax Sheltered Annuity retirement account, for which $100/month is taken out of her check each month. Kelly will not receive funds from her retirement account until age 59 ½; since this is past one year of opening, Kelly has a Deferred Annuity.

* Jahi, age 12. Has been injured during a tonsil surgery by the hospital and will no longer be able to speak; severely impacting her future job prospects. Jahi's family sued the hospital and won a settlement of $5,000,000 to offset her expected future income lost until age 65. The hospital places $2,000,000 into a Single Premium, Deferred, Judicial, Fixed Annuity, with the Fixed Period settlement option. Over the course of time, the $2,000,000 will earn a fixed interest rate, to add up to the total $5,000,0000 judicial court settlement; since Jahi would not have earned income until age 18, the annuity is Deferred until then for its first payment. She would then receive set payments until 65, because that is the current expected retirement age.

B. ANNUITY SETTLEMENT OPTIONS

Settlement options are designated by the **policyowner**, and line out the method of distribution for the annuity funds. These are the exact same as life insurance settlement options, except taxes are based off the **exclusion ratio**. Where the taxes are owed on a ratio of principle to interest, or possibly all of the funds depending on which type of annuity it is.

1. **Lump Sum:** The annuitant receives a one-time check from the insurer for the full amount of the death benefit.
2. **Interest Only:** A temporary option, which will conserve the face amount until a later date, but pay the annuitant small amounts of interest over time.
3. **Fixed Amount:** The annuitant will receive a fixed amount of money each year until funds are exhausted. During this time, the cash value will grow interest, so the money lasts much longer.
4. **Fixed Period:** The annuitant will receive the funds over a period of time. This is commonly used for lottery payments and court settlements.

* Halfway through Mitch's divorce his father dies, leaving him a $100,000 death benefit in a lump sum. Since Mitch is going through a divorce and possibly bankruptcy, he does not want to share the money with his ex. Mitch chooses the interest only option instead of receiving the lump-sum. He receives a small check of $3,000 to account for the interest and a year later when his divorce is finished, he receives the full $100,000 from the insurer for the full death benefit.

* Elisia's husband died leaving her $100,000 but he chose the fixed amount settlement option to cover her mortgage of $10,000 per year. Elisia receives a check in the amount of $10,000 each year and her funds will last much longer than 10 years…actually 23.5 years. This is because the remaining money in the annuity is still earning interest, allowing for the $100,000 lasting much longer than she expected.

* Oscar has a $100,000 business loan for 10 years owed to the bank, when he dies due to a known cancer. Oscar's business partner realizes he only left him with a $60,000 death benefit, which is not enough to cover the loan. Oscar was smart and instead of leaving his business partner the money as a lump sum, he had chosen the fixed-period option. The funds will be paid out over 10 years, which during that time the money is earning interest and will be more than enough to cover the loan.

5. LIFE ANNUITY OPTION

Life Annuity (Life Settlement Option) provides monthly income to the annuitant for life, even if funds are exhausted early. This option is also known as the "life income settlement" option.

- **Pure Life:** Payments are made only to one person
- **Joint Life:** Income will be split amongst two annuitants for life; when one annuitant dies, the payments will cease to all annuitants
- **Joint & Survivorship:** Income provided to two+ annuitants, when one annuitant dies, payments continue on to the survivor either with full benefits or reduced to 66 and 2/3 of the total payment (SEE PICTURE: AT END OF CHAPTER 10 UNDER JOINT & SURVIVORSHIP POLICIES)

    - **Period Certain Option:** The period certain option may be attached to any *life annuity* and would guarantee income for a certain period of time.

* Amy was considering the purchase of a life annuity for the guaranteed $1,500/mo. income for life, but she was afraid if she died early that she may waste the principle amount of the annuity. Amy's agent notified her that she could add the period-certain option of ten years, which would reduce her monthly income from $1,500 to $1,200, but should she perish within the first 10 years; her beneficiary would consider receiving money. Thus, protecting the principle amount from the surrender to the insurer in the event she perished early.

C. ANNUITY REFUND OPTIONS (REFUND ANNUITY)

A refund annuity option **returns** principle without interest to a beneficiary in the event the annuitant dies prior to all funds being distributed. This is a safety-net option to ensure funds are not lost in the event the annuitant dies and will reduce the total amount paid out for the added security.

- **Cash Refund:** Provides for a lump sum refund of principle to a beneficiary should the annuitant die while receiving funds. The beneficiary would not receive any interest earned and this option will reduce the amount of income earned by the annuitant due to the added protection.
- **Installment Refund:** Instead of a lump sum payment to the beneficiary in the event of an annuitant's death, the beneficiary will receive payments over a period of time. This is very similar to the period-certain option added to a life annuity.

- **Variable Annuity:** During the accumulation phase, annuity funds may be invested within the *stock market* and other investment vehicles. Once annuitized, the cash value is turned into **annuity units,** which are shares purchased in the insurance company and provide higher interest rates than just Fixed Annuities.

D. NEGATIVE ASPECTS OF ANNUITIES

Annuities are not suitable for all people, specifically because the annuities are **NOT** liquid investments. Meaning, once the annuitant begins receiving payments, they cannot go back and change their original settlement choice, the annuitant is stuck. Annuities may also have high fees, tax consequences and even **surrender charge** for early withdrawal. The surrender charge is a penalty for cancelling an annuity early, and decreases each year.

If a policyholder dies during the annuity's accumulation phase, the annuity funds may be left to a beneficiary, which is not an issue. However, once the annuity has been annuitized and the annuitant begins receiving payments, should the annuitant die before receiving all of the funds; the insurer will keep the remaining money. It is important to add the **Refund Annuity** option onto an annuity to prevent this from happening and allow the funds to continue on to the annuitant's family. As annuities may have many disadvantages, it is **the producer's** responsibility to determine if the annuity is suitable for each customer.

F. USES OF ANNUITIES

Planning for retirement is the primary use of annuities. A common purpose of purchasing an annuity is to provide future income security as payments do not fluctuate.

Life, Accident & Health Exam Study Book | TX

1. PERSONAL & NON-EMPLOYER ANNUITIES

Most personal annuities are utilized for retirement or education planning, but annuities may be used as Judicial (Court) settlements, or lottery pay-outs, or any time a **structured liquidation of funds** over time is needed. Many game show and special event winnings are annuities, because the company contributes funds which will grow over-time with interest, allowing for a lower upfront payment into the account.

2. EMPLOYER SPONSORED RETIREMENT ACCOUNTS

There are various retirement plans offered by employers for the benefit of employees; the names are typically derived from the title of the IRS code. Such as 401k plans are called 401k, because that is the line where it can be found in IRS Rules. Most employers "match" a certain contribution percentage of an employee's salary; **the employer tax deducts the contribution,** which will grow tax deferred to the employee, upon withdrawal, the **employee will pay ordinary income tax** on the contribution.

- ✓ Any time an employee makes a contribution, the funds become vested immediately; however, employer contributions may have vesting requirements. Vesting means ownership rights, and some employers require a certain number of years until employer contributions are vested to an employee; vesting requirements promote loyalty to a company.

A few large employers offer **defined benefit plans** where employees are guaranteed a set amount of income upon retirement. For example, Social Security is a defined benefit plan, where an annuitant (S.S. is an annuity as well) can expect a specific income amount each year from the retirement plan. Employer based defined benefit plans follow the **50/40 rule** where at least 50 employees or 40% of employees must participate in order for the IRS to treat it as a qualified plan.

a. 401k RETIREMENT PLAN – CODA (Cash or Deferred Arrangement Plan):

A 401k plan is a **voluntary** employer sponsored retirement plan which is primarily funded by an employee; 401ks allow for a $17,500 **pre-tax** contribution in 2014 by an employee, and employers may choose to make extra percentage contributions if they wish. If the employer chooses to match contributions, the contribution will not be included in the employee's gross income, but may be taxable upon distribution past age 59 ½. There are three primary ways a 401k plan may be funded:

- **Pure Salary Reduction:** Funded by an employee on a pre-tax basis from each paycheck; where the employer matches a set percentage or amount each year.
- **Bonus/Profit Sharing:** The employer offers an employee a bonus each year that the employee may elect to be applied into the 401k plan. Profit sharing plans typically include vesting limits of 2, 5 or 7 years until the employee gains access to the funds.
- **Thrift Plan:** Specifically designed for employees of the federal government, working very similar to a pure salary reduction plan.

- ✓ Remember, employer contributions are tax deductible to the employer, but taxable upon withdrawal to the employee.

* Ellen, a television host, has a 401k retirement plan through her employer for which she maxes the $17,500 contribution each year. Her employer opted to utilize the profit-sharing option, and this year the employer contributed an extra $4,000 to her account. The employer was able to tax deduct the $4,000 contribution, but will be taxable to Ellen upon retirement at age 59 ½ when she withdraws the funds.

b. 403b – TAX SHELTERED ANNUITY (TSA)

403b plans are very similar to 401k plans, except 403b plans are specifically for **public school employees** (even janitors) and **nonprofits** such as religious organizations or charities; which are defined by IRS code 501© as tax exempt employers. The employees may still only contribute up to $17,500, and the funds still grow **tax deferred** like a 401k; the only real difference between a 401k and a 403b is the employer's administrative costs. Both a 401k and a 403b are vested immediately for any employee's contributions.

* Julianne has left her for-profit company which provided a 401k as a retirement plan, for a non-profit company offering a 403b. She was amazed to find out that both plans were almost exactly the same, providing for tax deferred growth and immediate vesting; however, her new 403b plan was through a different financial institution providing fewer choices of investment.

c. SIMPLE PLANS (SIMPLE 401k, SIMPLE 403b etc.) – Under 100 employees

A Savings Incentive Match Plan for Employees (SIMPLE) is available to small business employers with less than **100 employees.** As the plan is for small employers, the IRS has incentivized the employer to establish the plan through specific tax credits; but in order to establish the SIMPLE plan, the employer must contribute **3%** of an employee's annual compensation and also offer the plan to all full-time employees earning over **$5,000 in compensation.** SIMPLE plans become **vested immediately** for an employee with the regular 59 ½ 10% penalty, but if the employee chooses to withdraw within **the first two years**, there may be an additional **25% penalty.**

✓25% penalty w/in first 2 years	✓Vested Immediately	✓Tax Deferred Growth	✓Under 100 employees

d. KEOGH (UNINCORPORATED) PLAN – HR-10 – Sole Proprietorships

A Keogh (HR-10) retirement plan may be established by any self-employed **sole proprietorship**, partnership or LLC business who remains **not incorporated** as an S Corp or C corp. The Keogh plan is very similar to a SEP IRA (listed below) in which it allows a high amount of $52,000 to be contributed to the account; however, the HR-10 plan requires much more paperwork each year. The Keogh plan was named after congressman Eugene Keogh in 1968; since then, the plan has been changed multiple times and almost completely phased out by Solo 401k and SEP IRA plans as of 2001. The only benefit an HR-10 currently holds over any other retirement plan is that the Keogh typically allows for $1,000 more than a SEP IRA each year, but some years differ based on inflation.

* In 2012, Karen, a high-income small business owner, wishes to set up a retirement plan for herself but also remain a sole proprietorship. Since Karen wishes to remain a sole proprietorship, she has the option of a SEP IRA or an HR-10; the SEP IRA allows for a 2012 contribution of $50,000 whereas the Keogh (HR-10) allows for $51,000. Karen retains the advice of a tax professional who will file the 110-page IRS document of the Keogh for her; thus, the Keogh would be best suited for Karen, since she can contribute an extra $1,000. If she had planned to setup the account herself, a SEP may have been a better choice.

5. INDIVIDUAL RETIREMENT ACCOUNTS (IRA's)

American citizens who do not qualify for employer sponsored retirement plans may qualify for Individual Retirement Accounts. A person may not qualify for an employer sponsored account due to many factors such as, **unemployed spouses,** part-time employment, not earning enough, or being self-employed. Funds are **immediately 100%** vested upon deposit and there are two variations of IRAs:

a. TRADITIONAL IRA's

Traditional IRAs are funded with **pre-tax dollars** (or tax-deductible dollars) and funds grow **tax deferred.** Since the account was funded with non-taxed dollars, the IRA owner will pay ordinary income taxes only when funds are withdrawn from the IRA, Traditional accounts are best used when a person is expecting their income taxes to be lower in the future, essentially deferring the payment of taxes to a later date; however, withdrawals must begin by age 70½ (more precisely, by April 1 of the calendar year after age 70½ is reached), which limits the length of deferment on taxes. This limitation typically affects higher income earners who may have other sources of retirement income than the traditional IRA.

* Shep at age 45 began funding his traditional retirement account in 1986 when taxes were high, with the understanding taxes will likely be lower in the future. In 1986 when Shep funded his account, he did not pay income taxes on the contributions; and from 1986 to 2013, when the account was earning interest (gains) in the stock market, Shep did not need to pay taxes either. When Shep retires in 2014, taxes are much lower than in 1986, and upon withdrawing from his traditional IRA, he will pay taxes on all of the money. He has however saved quite a bit by delaying the taxation from 1986 to 2014, due to the lower tax rates.

b. ROTH IRA's

Roth IRAs are funded with **after-tax dollars** but grow completely **tax free**; the person funding the Roth account will not take a tax deduction on contributions, but upon reaching retirement age, all contributions and the interest (gains) earned will be tax free. Roth IRAs are preferable when income tax rates are lower and expected to rise in the future. To prevent abuse of Roth IRA's, the accounts must be open for **5 years** to gain access to tax free growth; however, Roth IRA's do NOT need to begin withdrawal at age 70 ½ like Traditional accounts.

* Joe, age 29, realizes in 2014 taxes remain at historical lows compared to the past 100 years and expects them to rise before his retirement age of 59 ½, so he chooses a Roth IRA account. Today he will have to include his contributions on his income taxes, but when he attains age 59 ½ and retires, he will not need to pay taxes upon withdrawal. Even the interest he has earned in the stock market will be completely tax free. Joe has saved a lot on taxes

	TRADITIONAL	**ROTH**
Tax Considerations:	Funded pre-tax or tax deductible and funds grow **tax deferred.**	Funded after-tax and grows **tax free.**
Under 59 ½ 10% Penalty:	Yes	Yes
First Withdrawal must be taken	By April 1st after the persons 70 ½ birthday	No limit, does not need to be withdrawn by 70 ½
Contributions:	$5,500 (6% excess contribution penalty). Over age 50, a catch-up payment of an extra $1,000 may be made for a total of $6,500. Contributions are **immediately vested (owned by the depositor).**	
Loans Allowed:	No loans are allowed	
Early Distributions (before 59 ½) without 10% penalty:	1. $10,000 down payment of a first home 2. Post-Secondary Education expenses (college) for family members and grandchildren 3. Catastrophic medical bills (over 10% agi) 4. Sudden Disability 5. During divorce if assets are to be split by a judge ruling	

c. SEP IRA (Simplified Employee Pension)

A SEP IRA, is a Traditional IRA established by an employer for an employee, where the employer makes all contributions into the account and must contribute the same amount to all employee's retirement accounts. SEP's have a much higher contribution limit than regular Traditional IRA's because the business is making the contributions; in 2014, contributions may be up to 25% of an employees' salary to a maximum of $52,000. SEP's are ideal for high income earning small businesses for either the self-employed or family-owned businesses.

- ✓ Employer Funded
- ✓ Tax Deferred Growth with high limits
- ✓ 59 ½ age requirement 10% penalty
- ✓ Self Employed
- ✓ Small Family Businesses

* Sammy and his wife own a small insurance agency, where they are the only employees. They established SEP IRAs for themselves to save for retirement, but never thought about the consequences if the business expanded. Each year, the insurance agency contributes the maximum $52,000 to their accounts, but when Sammy began adding employees to the business, he realized that all employees must have the same percentage contributed to their SEP IRA's. Sammy would either have to switch retirement plans or keep the business small for the SEP IRA to continue to be feasible.

d. SECTION 1035 EXCHANGES

Insurance, endowment and annuity policies are considered to be property, so the gain or loss on each exchange of the policies would be considered for tax purposes. Under section 1035 of the Internal Revenue Code, there is no taxes in the following situations:

- When a life insurance contract is replaced with another life insurance contract or for an endowment or annuity contract.
- An endowment contract for another endowment contract or for an annuity contract replaced by another annuity.
- An annuity contract replaced for another annuity contract.

✓ An administrator must hold 20% of income if there is not a direct rollover. If after 60 days the participant has not deposited the 80% into a new retirement account, the government keeps the 20% to pay for the taxes. If the participant is under 59 ½, there is also a 10% penalty incurred on the full amount.

The 20% withholding is meant to stop people from saying they are going to do a rollover and then just running with their money and never paying taxes.

* Derrick has a $100,000 in his 401k and wishes to rollover into a Traditional IRA (both are tax-deferred accounts). Derrick isn't very bright, so instead of moving the funds directly from the 401k to IRA using the banks, he decides to withdraw it and deposit it himself. When Derrick goes to withdraw the $100,000, the 401k plan administrator must withhold $20,000 in case he doesn't complete the rollover. If Derrick does not deposit the $80,000 into the IRA within 60 days, the $20,000 is sent to the IRS to cover a portion of the taxes and Derrick will also incur a 10% penalty on the full $100,000 if he is under age 59 ½.

PRACTICE QUESTIONS: ANNUITIES

1. What is the primary difference between a Variable Annuity and a Variable Universal Life policy?
   a. The annuity may have a living cash benefit while life insurance does not
   b. Variable Universal Life seeks higher gains than Variable Annuities
   c. The Variable Annuity is held in a separate account, while Variable Universal Life is held in a general account
   d. Variable Universal Life has a death benefit, while the Variable Annuity does not

2. W is in a conversation with M about retirement savings. M states he has a 401k through his employer and asks W which type of account she has. W is unsure as to her account, but states she'll have to check with HR at her employer, the public school. Which type of account will the HR department most likely say W has?
   a. 401k
   b. HR-10
   c. 403b
   d. SIMPLE plan

3. The type of annuity that returns principle without interest to the annuitant's beneficiary upon death would be considered:
   a. Refund Annuity
   b. Return Annuity
   c. Life Annuity
   d. Individual Retirement Account

4. What are the tax implications of a 403b?
   a. Funded with after tax premiums with tax free gains
   b. Funded with pre-tax premiums with tax deferred gains
   c. Funded with after tax premiums with tax deferred gains
   d. Funded with pre-tax premiums with non-taxable gains

5. When MUST a Traditional IRA begin payments?
   a. At age 59 ½ to avoid a 10% penalty
   b. April 1st after a persons' 59 ½ birthday
   c. April 1st after a persons' 70 ½ birthday
   d. December 31st after a persons' 770 ½ birthday

6. Variable Annuities are held in which type of account and why?
   a. Separate accounts due to differing investment needs
   b. Separate accounts due to fraud regulation
   c. General accounts due to level predictable growth
   d. General accounts due to low risk investments

7. H is leaving his job at ABC corp. for company XYZ. H currently has a $15,000 401k account with ABC and wants to roll it over to XYZ. H tries to perform a direct roll-over but cannot, so he withdraws the $15,000 from 401k to roll it over himself. Should H fail to re-deposit the funds into XYZ's plan, which of the following would he be left with after 60 day if he never deposits the funds?
a. $15,000 minus 10% penalty incurred on only $3,000
b. $15,000 minus 10% penalty on the full $15,000
c. $12,000 minus 10% penalty incurred on only $3,000
d. $12,000 minus 10% penalty on the full $15,000

8. All of the following statements are true about a 1035 exchange EXCEPT:
a. An annuity may be exchanged for another annuity
b. A life contract may be exchanged for an annuity
c. Unlimited amounts of funds may be exchanged
d. An annuity may be exchanged for a life contract

9. All of the following are true about a SIMPLE 401k EXCEPT:
a. All full-time employees earning over $5,000/year must be included
b. A minimum participation rate of 100 employees is mandatory
c. The employer must contribute 3% to each account
d. There is a 25% penalty if withdrawn within the first two years, but is vested immediately

10. Which type of annuity is most likely to be purchased with a single premium?
a. Fixed Annuity
b. Variable Annuity
c. Life Annuity
d. Immediate Annuity

11. Which type of account MAY a loan be taken from?
a. 401k
b. SIMPLE IRA
c. SEP IRA
d. Roth IRA

12. A Modified Endowment Contract (MEC) failed which test?
a. The 7-Pay Test
b. The Endowment Test
c. The 3-Pay Test
d. The IRS Qualified Test

13. Roth IRA accounts have which tax implications?
a. Funded with after-tax dollars with taxable interest gains
b. Funded with pre-tax dollars, with taxable interest gains
c. Funded with after-tax dollars with tax free gains
d. Funded with pre-tax dollars with tax free gains

14. Annuities are sold by which type of company?
a. Savings & Loan Institutions
b. Life Insurers
c. Banks
d. Federal & State governments

15. The exclusion ratio applies to which type of accounts?
a. Endowment Contracts
b. Adjustable Life Insurance
c. Variable Universal Life
d. Annuities

16. Which plan is best for a small entrepreneur who is a sole proprietorship, but wants to contribute a higher amount of gross salary to a retirement plan?
a. HR-10 Unincorporated Keogh
b. Spousal IRA
c. 1035 Exchange
d. Tax Sheltered Annuity

17. The 50/40 rule of defined benefit plans is best described as:
a. 50% of employees or 40 employees
b. 50 employees or 40% of employees
c. A small employer plan for fewer than 100 employees
d. 50% of employees, with 40% participation rate

18. A retirement plan that is funded with excess income of corporation and for the employees benefit is most likely a:
a. Individual Retirement Account either Roth or Traditional
b. Keogh (Unincorporated) HR-10 plan
c. 401k Bonus or Profit Sharing plan
d. 403b Non-Profit Tax Sheltered Annuity plan

19. What are the tax implications of an employer's contribution to a qualified retirement account?
a. Employer may tax deduct but is tax-free to an employee
b. Employer may not tax deduct but is tax-free to an employee
c. Employer may tax deduct but is taxable upon withdrawal to employee (tax deferred)
d. Employer may not tax deduct but is taxable upon withdrawal to employee (tax deferred)

Life, Accident & Health Exam Study Book | TX

Dollars, Numbers & Dates	
90 days	Temporary license valid
6 Months	Temporary license can be re-applied January 1st – July 1st
2 years	Producer license valid until renewal on **birth date**
30 days	Report changes of name or address
30 days	Report felony or any other regulatory or misdemeanor convictions
24 hours	Continuing Education required every two years
3 hours	Ethics Continuing Education
50%	Continuing Education MUST be in classroom
IMMEDIATELY	Insurer (company) must update producer (agent) registry after termination of appointment
$2,500	Violation of FCRA – Fair Credit Reporting Act
$25,000	Maximum fine for violation of Texas Insurance Laws
$50,000	Maximum fine for Fraud per account
10 years	Imprisonment for felony insurance fraud
18 months	Imprisonment for misdemeanor insurance fraud
5 years	Must wait if a license is **DENIED or REVOKED**
June 30th	Insurers must file annual financial report
March 1st	HMO's must file annual report stating numbers of subscribers, profit and loss and reserves
5 years	Commissioner will examine domestic insurers (companies)
60 days	Examiner will prepare final report
30 days	Commissioner will send a copy of report to party examined before filing report
30 days	Party examined may request hearing on the report

CHAPTER 13: STATE REGULATION

A. LICENSING

Insurance is a state regulated product, not federal; therefore, each state has different requirements in order to obtain a license. In this section, we will discuss the different types of licenses and requirements to obtain those licenses. There will be a chart at the end of this chapter explaining the dollars, numbers, dates and different types of licenses to aid in your studies.

1. INSURANCE PRODUCER LICENSE:

Producers only receive **one license number,** with different "lines" of insurance attached to the license number. There are two primary lines of insurance "General Lines – Life Accident & Health" and "General Lines – Property & Casualty"; even if you take both exams and pass both exams, you would still only have one license number, but obtain the ability to sell all lines of insurance.

2. REQUIREMENTS TO OBTAIN A RESIDENT LICENSE:

- Age 18+ and a trustworthy character
- Pass the required exam within the past 12 months
- File the application, with recent fingerprints
- List the past **5 years** of residence and include business experience
- Have a principal office located in Texas
- Pay the required fee of $50 to the Department of Insurance
- Attorneys and Accountants are still required to take the exam if engaged in selling insurance
- No pictures, credit reports or education history needs to be submitted

Certain people are **NOT** required to take the exam to work in insurance:

1. People not soliciting insurance (secretary's & receptionists)
2. Underwriters (CPCU, CLHU)
3. Executive officers of insurance companies
4. Certified Financial Planners (CFP)
5. Funeral Directors
6. Selling Life Insurance Under $25,000

3. RESIDENT INDIVIDUAL PRODUCERS LICENSE:

An individual residing in Texas, who is actively engaged in soliciting (selling) insurance and appointed by an insurer, will receive a resident individual producers license; this is the most common type of license, and is likely the license you are studying for. The license will remain in effect for two years and renew every **two years** on the last day of the month of your **birth date.**

4. LICENSE RENEWAL
In order to renew the license, a few requirements must be met:

- **Continuing Education (CE):**
    - **24** total hours every two years, with **3 hours** in ethics
    - If selling annuities, the producer needs a **4-hour** certification CE course
    - If selling Medicare Supplement or Long-Term Care there is an **8-hour CE course**
    - **Zero** excess hours may roll-over into the next 2-year period
    - Records must be kept in a separate file and maintained for **4 years**
    - Producers licensed for 20 years, you may be exempt from CE requirements

- **Failure to complete Continuing Education**
    - For the first 30 days, a $25 fine is assessed,
    - 31 to 120 days, a $50 fine and the producer must submit a new application
    - After 1 year of failure to complete CE's, a new exam must be taken

Upon moving (even down the street), conviction of a felony, name change, or regulatory action, the producer must notify the commissioner within **30 days** to update records.

5. NON-RESIDENT LICENSE
Upon receiving a resident license in the producer's home state, the producer may apply for a non-resident license to sell insurance in other states. The producer must only file an application and pay a fee to the non-resident state and **no additional exams** or continuing education credits are required. Only Texas continuing education and exam requirements would be required; the non-resident state accepts these on the basis of a **reciprocal agreement.**

* Kai lives in Texas, passed his exam and became a licensed producer in Texas. Kai has some family who would like insurance in Wisconsin, so he will apply for a non-resident license in Wisconsin. All Kai needs to do is fill out an application and pay a fee in Wisconsin. His continuing education will be completed only in Texas, but he will need to renew his Wisconsin license per the Wisconsin Rules. Kai can have as many non-resident licenses as he would like in other states.

To obtain a non-resident license visit http://www.NIPR.com

6. BUSINESS ENTITY AND BANK LICENSING
All insurance agencies must also become licensed with the state in order to transact insurance. Typically, an agency is a company set up as an LLC, S Corp, C Corp or LLP; but there are also partnerships, dbas and sole proprietorships (unincorporated). They must all follow the same rules:

- At least one of the owners or officers must be licensed; other officers do not need to be licensed
- The agency must be appointed by one or more insurers

- Maintain financial responsibility of **$25,000** or more, typically through Errors & Omissions insurance.
- All employees acting as an agent must be licensed as well

7. TEMPORARY LICENSE

The commissioner of insurance may grant a temporary license for a length of **90 days** and may not be renewed; there must be a 6-month waiting period between applications. Temporary licenses do not require an exam, they allow the producer to begin working and collecting commission while they study and pass the state exam.

There are a limited number of temporary licenses a state may issue, and are typically used for three scenarios:

- Death of a spouse who owned an agency
- Disability of a spouse who owned an agency
- Divorce of spouses where the agency was split during settlement

* Porters wife owned an insurance agency that has been collecting commission for 10 years. Porter's wife was involved in a car accident and died suddenly, leaving no licensed owner to the agency. The agency could not collect commission without a licensed owner, so on January 1st Porter applies for a temporary license. His license is good for 90 days, and then expires; if he has not passed the exam by the end of 90 days, he could not re-apply for a temporary license until July 1st, which is six months after his initial application.

B. APPOINTMENT & AGENCY PRACTICES

When a producer represents an insurer, they become appointed with that insurer and now represent the insurer to sell their products. Upon appointment, the insurer must notify the commissioner within **30 days** and upon termination of the appointment, the insurer must notify the commission **immediately**, but has up to 30 days to file the documents. If the termination is due to misconduct (stealing etc.), the producer and commissioner must receive notice in writing within 15 days.

If an agent's appointment is terminated, the policies they sold still remain in force.

1. CONTROLLED BUSINESS

Controlled business is the act of only insuring yourself, your family or your business interests and not offering insurance to the public. It is illegal for a producer to obtain a license, become appointed, or start an insurance agency for the sole purpose of controlled business; in Texas an agent may have 75% controlled business, 25% of all sales must be toward the public. An agent may **lose their license** if they only sell insurance to friends, family or only their own business entities.

2. CHARGING OF FEES

Charging of fees is allowed, as long as they represent a reasonable business expense and may NOT be discriminatory in nature. All fees that are charged must remain the same for all customers, for example charging $3 for postage and mailing is fine, but charging $10 to only people with bad credit is NOT allowed.

3. FIDUCIARY CAPACITY

Producers and insurers act as fiduciaries, which is a money handling, trust capacity to the **insurer and insured**. Customer funds and agency funds must be correctly segregated and not comingled. The producer has until the close of the fifth business day to promptly forward funds to the insurer; unless the funds are deposited into an escrow (trust) account.

An escrow account is a separate bank account used by a producer specifically to hold premiums for an insurance company. The producer may earn interest on funds held in escrow if the insurer specifies, they are allowed to do so in writing.

C. COMMISIONER AND REGULATION

The Commissioner of Insurance heads the Texas Department of Insurance and is **appointed** by the **governor** for a term of **two years**. Prior to becoming the commissioner, he/she must have had at least five years of relevant business experience in accounting, **business or law**; becoming an insurance agent will not qualify you to become the insurance commissioner.

The Commissioner has three primary duties:

1. Regulate insurance agents and insurance companies
2. Create, Enforce and Counsel the governor on all state insurance laws & regulation
3. Educate the public in consumer protection and insurance fraud

Along with those three primary duties, the commissioner performs these other functions

- Manage the day-to-day activities of the Texas Department of Insurance, through hiring and delegating duties to those employees.
- Examines insurance companies once every **five years** and HMO's every **three years** by utilizing an examiner. The insurance commissioner has the right under state law to inspect more often.
- The insurance Commissioner approves rates, forms, policies and marketing materials by insurers and producers.
- During emergency situations, change policy provisions to accommodate public interest; such as increasing the Grace Period to **60 days**, as long as the insurers receive advanced written notification.

1. UNFAIR CLAIMS AND SETTLEMENT PRACTICES.

Unfair Claims Settlement Practices is the act of an insurer altering a claims process for the benefit of the insurer. Claims are supposed to be paid immediately by the insurer without delay, any unnecessary delays or procedures would be illegal and the insurer may be fined or sanctioned for such actions:

Unfair Claims Settlement Practices:
1. Arbitrarily (without cause) denying or delaying a claim without cause
2. Intentionally failing to include a **written letter** accurately describing why a claim was denied or delayed
3. Failing to conduct a proper and timely investigation during a claims process
4. Failing to acknowledge communications with all parties involved and request additional information if needed
5. Making a material misrepresentation to an insured or any other person having an interest in the proceeds payable under such contract or policy on less favorable terms than those provided in, and contemplated by, such contract or policy.
6. Trying to compel an insured to make a decision with the use of a verifiable claim
7. Delaying a physician's report in order to delay the claims process

Insurers are allowed to investigate claims, and even reinvestigate claims, as long as they have substantial and founded cause; however, all reasoning for denial or delaying of claims must be sent in a written letter to the insured.

2. INSURER RECORDS, INSPECTIONS AND REPORTS

Insurance companies must maintain records in a **separate file** for all insureds and must be inspected once every **five years** by the insurance commissioner or his/her accountants, who has 60 days to complete the examination. Along with being inspected the insurers are also required to file an Annual Financial Report on **June 30th** which must contain these provisions:

1. A list of all products sold and rates charged for that year
2. Profit Margins of the year
3. Any complaints filed against the insurer and the method of handling complaints
4. The number of subscribers for the previous year (not names).
5. The insurer is not required to project future subscriber numbers or profit.

HMO's file their annual financial report on **March 1st** and are inspected once every **three years**; this is due to the fact HMOs are regulated by the Department of Health and the Department of Insurance. The insurance commissioner may inspect more often under state laws at their discretion and if the results are contested, hearings must be held within 30 days; otherwise, reports must be completed within 60 days of examination.

3. UNFAIR TRADE PRACTICES

Unfair Trade Practices has to do with the marketing procedures used during the promotion or sale of an insurance product. Unfair Trade Practices may be committed by either the insurer or insurance company.

a. MISREPRESENTATION

An insurer or producer making untrue statements about a policy or other aspect of insurance is considered misrepresentation. Misrepresentations are illegal and may be performed in multiple ways:

- **False Advertising:** Pertains to misleading statements about dividends, policy benefits and coverage lengths; stating dividends are guaranteed would be considered False Advertising.
- **Defamation:** Intending to injure another insurer or agents' reputation by criticizing their financial condition is illegal and is committed through slander (oral), or libelous (written) statements.
- **Intimidation or Coercion:** It is illegal to coerce or intimidate a person into purchasing insurance through fear.
- **Twisting**: Misrepresentation during policy replacement is considered twisting; primarily when an agent persuades a customer to cancel a policy when it is not in their best interest.
- **Inducements:** No rebates or inducements may be given for the purchase of a policy other than the policy itself.
- **Unfair Discrimination:** Race, national origin, creed, sexual preference and other non-factors may not be used to discriminate for rates, fees or benefits.
- **Rebating:** It is illegal to give commission, or a portion of commission, to an unlicensed person. All persons receiving commission or referral fees must have a license; it is extremely common for insurance agents to share in commission, this is allowed because they both have licenses. **Zero rebates may be given** in the state of Texas.
- **Blank Forms:** It is illegal to have a customer sign a blank or incomplete insurance application.

An **insurer is ultimately responsible** for any and all advertisements that reach the general public. Even if an insurer hires an outside marketing firm, the insurer still bears the liability for each advertisement.

4. FRAUD

Fraud is intentional and knowingly deception for the specific purpose of monetary gain. Fraud may be considered a crime of trickery by: stealing, embezzlement, false financial statements, misrepresentation or acting as an imposter in order to cheat a person out of money. Insurance fraud may be committed by producers, insurers and even insureds themselves; but, the most common insurance fraud committed by producers is **comingling of funds.** If the commissioner suspects a person or entity of committing fraud, the commissioner will hand the case over to the attorney general.

* Tom is a producer with ABC Corporation and has been selling policies for years. One day Tom runs into hard financial times and decides to take customers premiums and mix them into his general operating account. Tom has comingled insurer's money with his personal/business money and is guilty of fraud and violating his fiduciary capacity.

5. INSURANCE INFORMATION AND PRIVACY PROTECTION

It is a requirement that a licensee provides an opt-out notice, which must provide a clear and conspicuous notice to each of the licensee's consumers, which accurately explains the right to opt out and states the following:

- That the licensee discloses or reserves the right to disclose nonpublic personal financial information about its consumer to a non-affiliated third party.
- The consumer has the right to opt out of the disclosure.
- A reasonable means by which the consumer may exercise the right to opt out. A consumer may exercise the right to opt out at any time. A consumer's direction to opt out is effective until the insured (client, consumer) revokes it in writing, or if the consumer agrees by electronic means. A licensee must comply with a consumer's opt out direction as soon as reasonably possible after receiving it.

D. PENALTIES AND PROCEDURES

When an agent is suspected of improper business practices, the commissioner of insurance will mail a written **Cease and Desist** order which states the agent must stop selling insurance **immediately.** Upon receiving the order, the agent has **30 days** to request a hearing with the commissioner. The commissioner then has **ten days** to schedule the hearing, unless both parties can agree to a later date.

The penalties for different charges will be listed at the end of the chapter in a chart, but remember the commissioner does not prosecute, if charges are found to be true, they are sent to the Attorney General and held in District court. All penalties may be appealed through District Court, so the **Commissioners decision is not final.**

* Tate has had multiple complaints about giving rebates, so the insurance commissioner sends him a Cease-and-Desist order. Tate receives the order on June 2nd and must stop conducting all insurance business immediately. Tate believes the complaints are unfounded and requests a hearing on July 1st, to which the commissioner must schedule his hearing before July 11th. Should Tate be penalized, he may appeal through the court system.

E. INSURANCE COMMISSIONER LIMITATIONS

The Insurance Commissioners decisions are NOT final, the licensee may appeal at any time. Also, the Commissioner is NOT able to imprison an agent or act as a private prosecutor. She is also NOT able to activate an insurance companies claims reserves, which would be forcing them to pay claims. There is a judicial process for all of the above.

F. CHEMICAL DEPENDENCY

Chemical Dependency is considered the physical and mental dependency on a specific drug, alcohol, or other mind-altering substance

G. MANAGING GENERAL AGENT (MGA)

A managing general agent is just a general agent, which was outlined in Chapter 1: General Insurance. The managing general agent **EARNS COMMISSION**, but may be reimbursed for office expenses by an insurer. This is a type of license a person may obtain, where their primary duties are to recruit insurance agents and train them; then each policy the agent sells, the MGA will earn a small amount of commission on.

H. LEGAL RESERVE AGENT

A legal reserve agent does NOT earn commission; they are paid a salary for their job. Legal Reserve agents are in charge of handling an insurance companies cash reserves. This person does not sell insurance.

I. CERTIFIED FINANCIAL PLANNER (CFP)

A CFP is a person who completed much more in-depth coursework in order to work in financial planning; which encompasses taxes, asset management, insurance, and cash flow projections. A CFP is **not required to take the state test** to sell insurance because they have a more rigorous criteria to meet, which includes a mandatory bachelor's degree. They may also charge **fees** for insurance.

J. CHARTERED LIFE AND HEALTH UNDERWRITERS (CLHU)

A CLHU agent also does NOT need to take the state exam. These people are engaged in insurance, but have completed a 5-year coursework to obtain the designation.

K. FUNERAL DIRECTORS

Funeral Directors are not required to take the state exam to sell insurance if the death benefits remain under $25,000.

L. LIFE INSURANCE COUNSELORS

Life Insurance Counselors are required to take the state exam, but they may **charge a fee** for insurance just like CFPs and LRAs.

- ✓ A Certified Public Accountant (CPA) would still have to take the exam to sell insurance.

Life, Accident & Health Exam Study Book | TX

PRACTICE QUESTIONS: INSURANCE REGULATION

1. Which type of license will you be applying for?
a. Independent Producers License
b. Resident Individual Producers License
c. Non-Resident Individual Producers License
d. Life, Accident & Health Insurance License

2. A person who advises about life insurance for a fee is known as:
a. Life Insurance Advisor
s. Life Insurance Counselor
c. Funeral Pre-Need Director
d. Life Insurance Producer

3. A producer who has had a temporary license for 50 days has how much longer until it expires?
a. 90 days
b. 60 days
c. 50 days
d. 40 days

4. XYZ insurer hired ABC marketing agency to put out television ads. ABC marketing company misrepresented XYZ insurers' products during the commercials. Which party is ultimately responsible for these misrepresentations?
a. XYZ insurer
b. ABC Marketing agency
c. The consumers for believing the ads
d. The commissioner of insurance

5. A producer must receive what percentage of continuing education in classroom?
a. 100%
b. 75%
c. 50%
d. 25%

6. A producer in Texas may have what percentage of controlled business?
a. 100%
b. 75%
c. 50%
d. 10%

Life, Accident & Health Exam Study Book | TX

7. The commissioner must schedule a hearing within how many days after request during a Cease-and-Desist order process?
a. 60 days
b. 30 days
c. 10 days
4. 5 days

8. Which of the following would constitute an illegal rebate?
a. Holding a giveaway for a new television for all insureds
b. Offering to pay an insureds first month premium
c. Raffling off a $100 steak dinner
d. Charging a fee for reasonable business expenses

9. Which of the following is NOT a duty of the insurance commissioner?
a. Advising the governor on all state insurance laws
b. Conducting investigations into agents and insurers
c. Setting financial claims reserve limits for insurers
d. Activating claims reserve limits of insurers

10. How does the commissioner of insurance receive their job, and how long?
a. Appointed by the governor for two years
b. Elected by the people for two years
c. A complicated vetting process and for five years
d. Applying and hoping for the best for one year

11. A producer who states that dividends are guaranteed would be an example of what?
a. Twisting, an Unfair Trade Practice
b. Misrepresentation, an Unfair Trade Practice
c. Failing Good Faith, an Unfair Claims Settlement Practice
d. Misrepresentation, an Unfair Claims Settlement Practice

12. A producer has how long to notify the commissioner upon Moving, Regulatory Action or Felony Conviction?
a. 90 days
b. 60 days
c. 30 days
d. 15 days

13. The definition of chemical dependency would be best described as:
a. The physical and mental dependency on a drug or alcohol
b. The physical dependency on a drug or alcohol
c. The mental dependency on a drug or alcohol
d. There is no such thing as chemical dependency

Life, Accident & Health Exam Study Book | TX

14. Which of the following WOULD need to pass the insurance exam in order to obtain a license?
a. Chartered Life Underwriter (CLU)
b. Chartered Health Underwriter (CHU)
c. Certified Public Accountant (CPA)
d. Certified Financial Planner (CFP)

15. An agent may NOT perform all of the following, EXCEPT:
a. Start an agency for controlled business
b. Sell insurance with a nonresident license
c. Comingle premiums with their general account
d. Tell an insured their policy is guaranteed by the Guaranty Association

16. Insurers file an annual financial report with the commissioner on which date?
a. March 1st
b. June 31st
c. July 1st
d. June 30th

17. All of the following are TRUE about the insurance commissioner EXCEPT:
a. She is a member of the National Association of Insurance Commissioners (NAIC)
b. Her decision is final when a ruling is made
c. She creates procedures for the Department of Insurance
d. She may increase the grace period to 60 days during disasters

18. A producer who misrepresents policy provisions during replacement is guilty of:
a. Churning
b. Twisting
c. Rebating
d. Boycotting

19. An insurer would be guilty of Unfair Claims Settlement practices in which situation?
a. Failing to provide a reason for denial in writing
b. Failing to pay a claim due to fraud
c. Advising an agent his commission is being reduced
d. Paying a claim minus any unpaid premium

20. All of the following are Unfair Trade & Settlement Practices EXCEPT:
a. Intimidation
b. Coercion
c. Arbitrarily denying claims
d. Not guaranteeing dividends

21. Insurers must be inspected every ____ years and HMO's every ____ years:
a. 3 and 5 years
b. 5 and 3 years
c. 1 and 3 years
d. 1 and 5 years

22. A general lines producer must have how many hours of continuing education every two years, and what excess amount may roll over into the next reporting period?
a. 30 and 50%
b. 50 and 30%
c. 50 and 0%
d. 30 and 0%

23. A producer may have their license application declined for which reason?
a. Bad Credit
b. Previous Work History
c. Felony Conviction
d. Physical Fitness

24. Which of the following statements is TRUE if a producers' license is revoked for 5 years?
a. All policies previously sold are cancelled
b. The producer may face other consequences
c. The commissioner posts their picture on a bulletin board
d. The National Association of Insurance Commissioners performs an inquiry

25. A business or bank that becomes licensed as an insurance agency in Texas must have what amount of financial responsibility?
a. $100,000
b. $50,000
c. $40,000
d. $25,000

Life, Accident & Health Exam Study Book | TX

CHAPTER TEST ANSWERS

CHAPTER 1: GENERAL INSURANCE
1.a, 2.c, 3.a, 4.d, 5.c, 6.b, 7.a, 8.c, 9.b, 10.b, 11.a, 12.d, 13.a, 14.c, 15.d, 16.b, 17.a, 18.b, 19.b, 20.c, 21.a, 22.c, 23.b, 24.d

CHAPTER 2: HEALTH BASICS
1.d, 2.c, 3.c, 4.a, 5.b, 6.a, 7.b, 8.a, 9.c, 10.b

CHAPTER 3: DENTAL INSURANCE
1.c, 2.d, 3.a, 4.c, 5.b, 6.a, 7.a, 8.c, 9.b, 10c

CHAPTER 4: HEALTH PROVISIONS
1.b, 2.c, 3.d, 4.d, 5.c, 6.b, 7.c, 8.b, 9.d, 10.a, 11.b

CHAPTER 5: DISABILITY INSURANCE
1.c, 2.b, 3.b, 4.c, 5.a, 6.d, 7.d, 8.a, 9.c, 10.c,

CHAPTER 6: HEALTH PLANS
1.d, 2.a, 3.a, 4.c, 5.a, 6.d, 7.b, 8.d, 9.b, 10.c

CHAPTER 7: GROUP INSURANCE
1.a, 2.d, 3.b, 4.c, 5.a, 6.c, 7.d, 8.c, 9.c, 10.b, 11.a

CHAPTER 8: SOCIAL INSURANCE
1.a, 2.a, 3.b, 4.c, 5.b, 6.d, 7.d, 8.a, 9.b, 10.c

CHAPTER 9: LIFE INSURANCE BASICS
1.d, 2.c, 3.a, 4.c, 5.d, 6.b, 7.d, 8.b, 9.b, 10.c

CHAPTER 10: LIFE INSURANCE ANSWERS
1.d, 2.c, 3.a, 4.a, 5.c, 6.d, 7.d, 8.d, 9.a, 10.c, 11.a, 12.c

CHAPTER 11: LIFE PROVISIONS ANSWERS:
1.a, 2.c, 3.d, 4.c, 5.d, 6.a, 7.d, 8.a, 9.c, 10.b

CHAPTER 12: ANNUITIES ANSWERS:
1.d, 2.c, 3.a, 4.b, 5.c, 6.a, 7.d, 8.d, 9.b, 10.d, 11.a, 12.a, 13.c, 14.b, 15.d, 16.a, 17.a, 18.c, 19.c

CHAPTER 13: INSURANCE REGULATION ANSWERS:
1.b, 2.b, 3.d, 4.a, 5.c, 6.b, 7.c, 8.b, 9.d, 10.a, 11.b, 12.c, 13.a, 14.c, 15.b, 16.d, 17.b, 18.b, 19.a, 20.d, 21.b, 22.d, 23.c, 24.b, 25.d

Life, Accident & Health Exam Study Book | TX

LIFE & HEALTH GLOSSARY

Accelerated Benefits- Life insurance rider that allows a loan to be taken from the death benefit when diagnosed with a terminal illness

Accident- An unforeseen and unexpected incident

Accidental Bodily Injury- When only the injury is unforeseen and unexpected

Accidental Means: - An accident where the cause and injury are both unforeseen and unexpected

Accidental Death and Dismemberment- Supplemental Health insurance that pays a principal amount due to death, loss of 2+ limbs or eyesight. If only one limb is lost, it will pay the capital sum (a percentage of the principal)

Accidental Death (Life Insurance)- Pays extra benefits if the insured dies in an accident

Accumulation Period- The pay-in phase of an annuity, while the insured is paying into the annuity for savings.

Acquired Immunodeficiency Syndrome (AIDS) – An illness caused by HIV, a person can be tested and denied life insurance if they are found to have it.

Activities of Daily Living- Long Term Care insurance - Bathing, Dressing, Showering, Moving, Toileting

Actuary- A mathematician who uses statistics to predict losses utiizing the law of large numbers

Actual Charge- The amount a doctor actually charges Medicare for a service

Adhesion- A take it or leave it contract with no negotiation. If ambiguous, it is read in the favor of the insured.

Adjustable Life- Convertible life insurance that the insured can adjust the death benefit, premiums and length of coverage. It builds cash value when it is in the whole life portion, but it builds slow cash value.

Adjuster- A person who negotiates and settles claims for an insurance company

Admitted (Authorized)– An insurer who has a certificate of authority and can transact business within the state

Adult Day Care- Similar to a childs daycare, but for adults. Also considered Home Health Care in LTC policies

Administrator- A person who manages a financial trust, typically appointed by courts if both parents die

Adverse Selection- High risk (adverse) people will seek (select) insurance more than low risk people.

Agency- An insurance sales office that represents the insurer

Agent- A person who sells, solicits and transacts insurance on behalf of an insurer

Aleatory- A contract of unequal amounts, for e example the insured pays $10/month for $100,000 in coverage

Alien Insurer- An insurer based out of another country, such as France, Mexico, Canada etc

Alzheimer's disease- A disease found in older people where they forget who/where they are

Ancillary- Required portions of surgeries, like Xrays, Lab Work and Anasthesia

Annual Statement- A financial report submitted to the Department of Insurance each year, showing profit, loss, number of claims and number of current insureds

Annuity – Similar to a savings account, except when you withdraw money, it begins paying a set amount each month/year. Publishers Clearing House, Social Security and the Lottery are all annuities.

Life, Accident & Health Exam Study Book | TX

Apparent Authority- The appearance of an agent's authority through Ratebooks, Signs and Training material. To the customer, the agent appears to have the authority to sell insurance.

Applicant- The person (prospect) applying for insurance and offering themselves to the insurance company

Application- Filled out by the agent, in black ink, and can use scratch out/initial to make changes. The agent and the insured both sign the application.

Approved Amount- The amount Medicare Part B will pay for a particular exam/doctor service

Assignment – The transfer of ownership from one policyowner to another (see Viatical)

Attained Age – The current age of the insured; whatever age you are now, is your attained age

Attending Physicians Statement (APS) – A medical report by a doctor about the insured's health status used during underwriting

Avoidance – A method of risk management/handling that removes risk. Such as never driving again.

Basic Hospital Insurance- Health insurance that covers Room and Board in a hospital

Beneficiary – The person who the life insurance policy pays the death benefit. Usually a spouse or children.

Benefit Period- How long a person receives insurance payments for

Binding Receipt– Temporary coverage before a policy is issued, used when medical exams are not required

Birthday Rule- When 2 parents have health insurance on a child, the insurer uses whoever's birthday comes first in the year to determine which parents' insurance to use. (Dec 11th vs. May 22nd...May 22nd is primary)

Blanket Insurance – Health insurance that covers every person in an activity, such as sports teams

Boycott – Unfair Trade Practice where an agent doesn't work with a person unless they buy something else

Buyer's Guide- A pamphlet the Commissioner wrote, that describes the different types of Life Insurance.

Buy-Sell – Insurance used to fund the sale of a company if the owner/officer dies or becomes disabled

Cafeteria Plan – Supplemental Insurance under Section 125....the employee picks which policies they want

Cash Value- A savings account in life insurance policies. Principle + Interest = Cash Value

Certificate of Authority- A document the Commissioner gives to Admitted insurers that allows them to transact business in the state.

Certificate of Insurance- Evidence of coverage given to an employee in group insurance

Claim – A person files to their insurance company for payment after a loss

Coercion – An unfair trade practice similar to intimidation and boycotting

Coinsurance – The sharing in a claim, typically the insurer pays 80%, the insured pays 20% in health policies

Commingling of funds- When an agent mixes customer money with the agent's money against their fiduciary capacity.

Commission- You receive this for selling policies. This is your income.

Commissioner – The director of the Department of Insurance

Comprehensive Policy – Health insurance that covers Accidents, Sickness and preventative care

Life, Accident & Health Exam Study Book | TX

Concealment – Withholding or Omitting information from an application. Hiding information on an application.

Conditional Contract – The insured and the insurer both must meet conditions in order to have a contract

Controlled Business- Only selling insurance to yourself, your business or your family.

Convertible- Exchanging term life for whole life without taking a medical exam.

Consideration – The exchange of monetary value. The insured pays premiums, the insurer promises to pay claims. You pay $100 a month for insurance, they pay $100,000 for your surgery. Consideration means money.

Consolidation Omnibus Budget Reconciliation Act (COBRA) – Allows an employee to continue group health insurance for 18 months after they lost their job.

Consumer Report – A credit report checking the financial status of an applicant. Used for underwriting.

Contributory- Sharing in premiums in group insurance. Employer pays $300/month, employee pays $100/month.

Coordination of Benefits – The provision in health insurance that determines which plan is primary and which plan is excess if you have multiple insurance policies. This prevents insureds from double dipping in claims.

Co-payment – A small payment made to a doctor to prevent nuisance claims. Usually $5-$30 dollars.

Credit Life Insurance- Insurance used when a lender requires a borrower to purchase insurance to cover a loan. If you buy a house, the mortgagee might force you to buy insurance in case you die to pay off the house.

Custodial care – Nonskilled care used to help with activities of daily living. A person who usually comes to your home to help you get dressed, showered and fed. Used in Long Term Care insurance.

Death Benefit – The face amount of life insurance. This is what is paid to a beneficiary when the insured dies.

Decreasing Term – Life insurance where the death benefit goes down over time. Typically used to cover Mortgages or other loans.

Deductible – An amount of money the insured must pay before a claim is paid by the insurer.

Defamation – An unfair trade practice of either libel or slander against an insurers financial condition. Speaking poorly about a competitors insurance company.

Dependent – A child or other person in the care of the insured

Disability – Loss of income due to chronic injury or illness

Domestic Insurer- An insurance company headquartered in the state you're currently in

Dread Disease/Critical Illness– Insurance that covers cancer, diabetes and heart disease.

Earned Premium – If you pay $1000/year for insurance and cancelled halfway, the insurer only earned $500.

Effective Date – When the premium is paid and the policy is issued, the policy will begin.

Elimination Period – A waiting period on each new claim before an insured is paid. Similar to a deductible.

Endodontics – Dental work dealing with root canals and dental pulp

Endorsement – A change to an insurance policy. Updating your mailing address is an endorsement.

Endow – The time when a policy pays out its benefits. Whole life endows at age: 100

Enrollment Period- When a new employee begins their job, they can enroll in benefits. (30 days)

Errors and Omissions (E&O) – Insurance for insurance agents in case we make mistakes. Does not cover lying

Estoppel – If an insurer waives a right, they cannot take the right back.

Excess Charge – The amount the insured is responsible for in Medicare between the Actual charge and the Approved amount.

Exclusions- Things that are not covered by the policy. Elective surgery, suicide (within 2 years) etc.

Explanation of Benefits: A letter sent to the insured stating how much the insurer paid and how much the insured owes on a claim.

Exposure – How prone a person is to loss, their risk level.

Express Authority – Authority given to an agent by an insurer that is in writing.

Face Value – The amount a life policy is worth (death benefit + cash value), listed on the first page of the policy.

Fiduciary- Handling money in a trustworthy capacity. The agent is a fiduciary because we accept payments.

Fixed Annuity – An annuity that provides guaranteed payments and has a guaranteed interest rate

Flexible Spending Account (FSA) – Use it or lose it. A health plan where you set aside dollars at the beginning of the year pre-tax for medical uses. If you don't use it by the end of the year, you lose the money.

Foreign Insurer – An insurer based out of ANOTHER state.

Fraternal Benefit Insurer – Insurance companies that only sell to members of their organization. USAA

Fraud- Willful and Intentional misrepresentation for financial gain.

Free Look – A provision in the policy that allows the insured to return the policy for a full refund from the day the policy is delivered. This allows the insured to determine if a policy is suitable for them in case the agent sold them something they did not need.

Gatekeeper: The primary care physician in an HMO. The insured must obtain a referral from the gatekeeper to see a specialist.

Grace Period – If a person forgets to pay their premium, the policy is still in force for a period of time (31 days usually). If the insured has a claim, they are still covered during the grace period.

Hazard – A risk that increases the chance of loss. A broken step or a pothole in the road are both hazards.

Health Maintenance Organization (HMO) – Health insurance that focuses on preventative care and is considered a prepaid health plan because it pays the doctors on a capitation basis before the insured sees them

Health Reimbursement Accounts (HRA's) – An employer sponsored plan used to save for the deductibles of a Major Medical plan. The employer places the money into the account for the employees use.

Health Savings Accounts (HSA's) – A savings account used for medical expenses that the insured puts money into and receives a tax deduction on the contributions. Typically used for the deductible of Major Medical plans.

Home Health Care: Healthcare done at home, covered by Long Term Care and Medicare Part A. Includes Custodial Care, Adult Day Care and Respite care.

Hospice: Care provided at the end of life for terminally ill people in home or at a hospital. Hospice is covered under Medicare Part A.

Illustration- A quote sheet used in life insurance to show the guaranteed and non-guaranteed portions of the policy. Typically it will show the premiums and cash value but those numbers may change depending on health.

Life, Accident & Health Exam Study Book | TX

Implied Authority – Authority given to an agent by an insurer that is NOT written in a contract, but the agent may assume in order to complete day-to-day activities such as collecting premiums and printing business cards.

Indemnity – To be made financially whole in the event of a claim without profit or loss. This is the founding principle of insurance contracts.

Insurability – Passing a medical exam and all of the insurers requirements. Proving insurability is what you have to do before a policy may be issued.

Insurance – The transfer of risk. The insured (customer) pays premiums so that the insurer keeps money on hand. When a claim arises, instead of the insured paying out of pocket, the insurer will pay the claim.

Insured – The person who has insurance, typically the customer.

Insurer – An insurance company. They enter into contracts with insureds, and the insurer pays the claims.

Insuring clause – The scope of coverage, it shows the perils and exclusions in a policy. This is where the details of the policy are found.

Intermediate Care – Not 24 hour nursing home care, but is still under the supervision of doctors.

Investigative Consumer Report – A more thorough report of the customer under the Fair Credit Reporting Act that checks hobbies, habits and reputation.

Issue Age – The customers age when they first purchased insurance.

Joint Life – One policy insuring two or more people that pays the benefits upon the first persons death.

Juvenile Life – Insurance on minors or children.

Lapse – A policy that cancelled due to nonpayment.

Law of Large Numbers – Actuaries use this "law" to predict claims. The more people included in a statistic, the more likely the prediction will be true. Flip a coin 2 times and it may be heads both times, flip a coin 500 million times and it'll probably be 50/50.

Legal Cash Reserve – Insurers are required to have a certain amount of money saved in order to pay claims. HMOs are required to have $1,500,000 minimum.

Level Premium – Also known as fixed premium, the remains remain the same.

Life Expectancy – Found on a mortality table, it states how long a person SHOULD live by using the law of large numbers.

Limited-Pay Whole Life Insurance – Paying off whole life early. Such as 10 pay, is paid off in 10 years. These policies still endow at age 100, it is just paid off early.

Limited Policies – Supplemental insurance that only covers one or two things. Typically have no exclusions.

Living Benefits Rider – Take a loan from life insurance's death benefit to pay for long-term-care when diagnosed with a terminal illness.

Lloyd's – A surplus lines company that accepts higher risk customers.

Loan – Borrowing money from cash value life insurance. Loans must be paid back with 6-8% interest

Long-Term Care (LTC) – Insurance that covers aging. This type of insurance is sold by private insurance companies and will cover nursing homes and home health care for at least 12 months.

Life, Accident & Health Exam Study Book | TX

Long-Term Disability Insurance – Insurance that provides income in the event a person is disabled. It has to provide income for at least 2 years and typically ends at age 65.

Loss – The reason a claim is filed, the insured has lost some form of money after a peril.

Lump Sum – Receiving all of the benefits at one time

Major Medical Insurance – Health insurance such as an HMO or PPO that has a deductible and coinsurance. It was designed for catastrophic coverage.

Medical Information Bureau (MIB) -- A nonprofit company that shares application information between insurance companies. Used during underwriting of Life and Health insurance to catch lies and fraud on applications.

Medicare – Federal health insurance for people over age 65, or disabled 2+ years, or blind.

Medicare Supplement – Private insurance that covers what Medicare does not, also known as Medigap or SELECT.

Misrepresentation – An intentional lie. If it is Material (significant) and would change whether or not the policy was issued, the insurer can deny a claim and void a policy due to that material misrepresentation.

Mode of Payment – Frequency of premium payment, Annually, Quarterly, Monthly.

Morbidity Table – A table showing at what age people get sick. IE: Most heart attacks occur after age 50.

Mortality Table – A table showing at what age the average person dies.

Multiple Employer Trust (MET) – Two or more small employers who self-insure to provide health insurance for their employees.

Multiple Employer Welfare Association (MEWA): A union plan with 100 or more members

Mutual Companies – Insurers owned by policyholders who participate in the dividends. Mutual companies do not have shares of stock and will never be listed on a stock market.

Nonadmitted (Unauthorized) – An insurer who cannot transact business within the state.

Nonmedical – Life or Health insurance issued without a medical exam

Noncancelable – Disability insurance that the insurer cannot cancel and the insurer cannot raise the premiums.

Nonforfeiture Value – Cash value that cannot be kept by the insurance company. Forfeit means to give up, nonforfeiture means you cannot give up your cash value. It's your money.

Nonrenewal – When the insurer decides not to allow you to continue coverage next year

Nonqualified Plan – Retirement plans that do not qualify for IRS tax deductions.

Nonresident Agent – An agent who lives in another state. This is allowed if the Commissioner approves you.

Notice of Claim – How long you have to notify the insurer when you have a claim.

Oral Surgery – Basic dental coverage such as wisdom teeth extraction

Orthodontics – Major dental coverage that uses braces to align teeth and make them straight.

Out-of-Pocket Costs – The amount the insured pays or health services. Deductibles, copays coinsurance.

Life, Accident & Health Exam Study Book | TX

Paid-Up – Paying off a life insurance policy early.

Paid-Up Additions: A life insurance option that uses dividends to increase the death benefit to keep up with inflation. There is no medical exam to increase because a dividend is used to purchase it.

Partial/Residual Disability – Pays the difference of income if the insured can still work part-time

Participating Policies – Mutual insurance companies that pay dividends to policyholders.

Payment of Claims – A provision that states who gets paid when a claim occurs.

Peril – The cause of loss.

Periodontics – Basic dental care that covers gum disease such as gingivitis.

Personal Contract – A contract between the insured an insurer on a real life person.

Policyholder – The insured.

Policy Loan – Borrowing from life insurance cash value, tax free, but you must pay the loan back with interest.

Policyowner – The person who owns the policy, could be the insured. In group, this is the employer.

Preexisting Condition – An injury or illness the insured had before they applied for insurance.

Preferred Provider Organization (PPO) – Health insurance where the insured may go to any doctor, and the doctors provide discounts to the insurance company. Also known as fee-for-service insurance.

Preferred Risk – A low risk person who receives a discount on premiums for being healthy.

Premium – The money paid to the insurance company for the insurance policy.

Presumptive Disability – Automatically disabled people, such as blind in both eyes or missing 2 limbs or deaf.

Primary Beneficiary – The person who receives the death benefit in life insurance.

Principal Amount – The amount of money you paid into a cash value account. If you put $100 into an annuity/savings account and it earns $10. Only the $100 is the Principal.

Private Insurance – Insurance not through the government. Blue Cross, State Farm, Allstate, etc.

Pro Rata – Sharing. If you paid $100 and cancelled 25% of the way in. The insurer keeps $25, you are paid $75.

Probationary Period – The waiting period when you first get a policy before you actually receive coverage. In group, it's usually a 30, 60 or 90 day probationary period.

Producer – Insurance agent, most likely you.

Proof of Loss – A signed sworn under oath written statement made to the insurer after a claim.

Prosthodontics – Major dental care that creates dentures or dental implants

Provider – A doctor or hospital.

Pure Risk – The type of risk with no chance of financial gain

Qualified Plan – Retirement plans that meet IRS guidelines for pre-tax or tax deductions. 401k, 403b etc.

Rebating – Giving a customer a part of your commission or paying referral fees from your commission.

Reciprocal Exchange – An unincorporated insurer formed with an attorney-in-fact offering liability insurance.

Life, Accident & Health Exam Study Book | TX

Reciprocity – When states allow other agents to obtain a license without an exam because if you're good enough to get licensed in your state, you're good enough to get a nonresident in another state.

Recurrent Disability – Injuries that happen again within 12 months, the insured will not have an elimination period.

Reduction – Lowering the chance of loss, such as working out or eating healthy.

Reinsurance – Insurance for insurance companies to protect them from catastrophic losses. It allows an insurance company to insure more people.

Renewability– A policy continuing on into the next year.

Renewable Term Insurance – Term insurance that continues on next year without a medical exam. Premiums typically go up each time it renews.

Representation – True statements to the best of your knowledge. Applicants (customers) make representations. Sometimes they are wrong, but if they believed it is true, that is a representation.

Respite Care – Temporary relief for caregivers (family members) of long-term-care patients. Similar to a babysitter while the caregiver goes out of town.

Restorative Care – Fillings or crowns in dental insurance

Retention – Similar to a deductible. The amount of money a customer has to keep on hand or pay out of their own pocket when a claim arises.

Rider – Extra coverage added to a life insurance policy, it costs money but it upgrades the policy.

Risk – The uncertainty of loss.

Rollover – Moving money from one retirement account to another. An administrator must keep at least 20% if you do your own rollover.

Settlement Options – How life insurance death benefits are paid: Lump sum, interest only, fixed amount, fixed period, life income.

Short-Rate– A policy that is cancelled by the customer and the insurer charges a penalty.

Short-term Disability– Disability insurance that provides income less than 2 years.

Spendthrift Clause – Paying out death benefits over time instead of a lump sum. This stops creditors from putting a lien against the death benefit proceeds.

Skilled Nursing Care – A nursing home under a doctor's supervision.

Standard Risk –A regular person who is not high risk or low risk.

Stock Companies – Insurance companies owned by stockholders and pay dividends to stockholders.

Straight Life Insurance – Whole life insurance that continues for the persons entire life. It is not paid off early and is the most expensive whole life insurance.

Subrogation – The transfer of rights of recovery. Allows the insurance company to sue on your behalf if a claim arises.

Surrender – Cancelling a policy early. May incur a penalty.

Term Insurance – Temporary life insurance.

Life, Accident & Health Exam Study Book | TX

Terminally Ill – A person who will die within 6 months, typically due to cancer, may end up in hospice.

Twisting – Misrepresentation during policy replacement. Twisting the truth to make term life sound like it is whole life so the customer will buy it.

Underwriting – The insurer is checking over a policy and classifying risks, deciding to approve or deny an applicant. Underwriting is when you check medical information.

Unilateral Contract – The insurer is legally required to follow the laws for all policies.

Universal Life Insurance – Most flexible life insurance that has a target premium and corridor.

Utmost Good Faith – All policies are made in the utmost good faith, each party must trust each other.

Viatical Settlement – Life insurance that is already in force, but is sold to a third party in the event the insured becomes terminally ill.

Waiver -- Giving up a known right in a contract.

Waiver of Cost – Waives the cost of the death benefit in universal life if disabled, and does NOT build cash value.

Waiver of Premium – A rider, if added, allows the insured to NOT pay premiums if they become disabled. The first 6 months the customer must pay premiums, but after 6 months of being disabled, they receive that 6 months premium back and all future premiums are waived. This is an OPTIONAL rider.

Warranty – A literal guaranteed to be true statement. Warranties are NOT made on applications, but they are things such as you guarantee you have a burglar alarm.

Workers Compensation – Insurance that covers employees injured on the job. Workers Compensation is primary if you get hurt on the job.

Made in the USA
Middletown, DE
29 July 2024